BEATING THE CLOTH DRUM

BEATING

— THE —

CLOTH DRUM

THE LETTERS OF
ZEN MASTER HAKUIN

Translated by Norman Waddell

SHAMBHALA
Boston & London
2012

Shambhala Publications, Inc.
Horticultural Hall
300 Massachusetts Avenue
Boston, Massachusetts 02115
www.shambhala.com

9 8 7 6 5 4 3 2

Printed in the United States of America

⊗ This edition is printed on acid-free paper that meets
the American National Standards Institute z39.48 Standard.
♻ Shambhala Publications makes every effort to print on recycled paper.
For more information please visit www.shambhala.com.

Distributed in the United States by Random House, Inc.,
and in Canada by Random House of Canada Ltd

Designed by James D. Skatges

Library of Congress Cataloging-in-Publication Data
Hakuin, 1686–1769.
[Correspondence. English. Selections]
Beating the cloth drum: letters of Zen master Hakuin /
translated by Norman Waddell.—First Edition.
p. cm.
Translated from Japanese.
ISBN 978-1-59030-948-3 (pbk.)
1. Monastic and religious life (Zen Buddhism)—Japan.
2. Buddhism—Japan—Discipline. I. Waddell, Norman, translator,
writer of added commentary. II. Title.
BQ9399.E593E5 2012
294.3'927092—dc23
2011046572

In the capital Lo-yang there was a gigantic drum at the Thunder Gate that produced a sound that could be heard for tens of thousands of leagues around. This gave rise to a saying, "Don't carry a cloth drum past the Thunder Gate." As a drum with a cloth drumhead can produce no sound whatever, the phrase "beating the cloth drum" is used to refer to someone who foolishly attempts something beyond his powers. In commenting on the phrase, Hakuin said, "Does it mean no sound is made? Does it mean doing something foolish? Or performing a worthless act? No, that's not it. Find out what it means by going right to it and engaging it yourself."

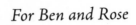
For Ben and Rose

Contents

Introduction

This book is a collection of letters by the seventeenth-century Japanese Zen priest Hakuin Ekaku (1685–1768), who is by any reckoning one of the most influential figures in the long history of the school as well as the history of Zen Buddhism altogether. At the turn of the seventeenth century, when Hakuin set out as a young novice on pilgrimage around Japan, the Zen school was in what he would later describe as "an advanced stage of spiritual stagnation." By the time of his death sixty years later, Hakuin had employed the full force of his formidable personality to almost singlehandedly revitalize the Rinzai school's traditions, reshape its teachings, and produce a group of gifted disciples that enabled the school to survive as a vital force to the present day.

Remarkably, Hakuin carried out this formidable task while serving at a tiny provincial temple far from the centers of power in Kyoto and Edo (present-day Tokyo). By mustering his considerable talents as a teacher, writer, calligrapher, and painter, he created an extraordinary legacy, which includes a remarkable body of writings and paintings that has vastly enriched the Zen tradition. So strong and pervasive has the imprint of Hakuin's distinctive style and teaching been on the Rinzai sect over the last two centuries that it is now commonplace to refer to Rinzai Zen simply as the school of Hakuin.

His chief disciple Tōrei, who knew the real-life Hakuin as well
as anyone, left some observations about Hakuin's character that
agree in many respects with the person who is disclosed through the
letters in these pages:

> An extremely imposing man, he combined the fierce gaze of
> a tiger and the gait and movements of an ox, with a Zen
> activity so sharp and intense that it made him exceedingly
> difficult to approach. Virtually tireless, he brought the
> same degree of care and compassion to whatever he did. In
> settling troubles, in rectifying wrongs, he worked with si-
> lent persuasion, private discipline. His behavior, whether
> moving, standing, sitting, or lying, was such as to be un-
> fathomable to non-Buddhists and demons alike. The man-
> ner in which his teaching activity prospered recalled the
> days of the great Chinese master Ma-tsu. The adversity
> under which he lived and taught was reminiscent of the
> great hardships faced by Zen Master Ta-hui. (Epilogue to
> *The Chronological Biography of Zen Master Hakuin; Hakuin's
> Precious Mirror Cave*, 235)

The idea for this book evolved as I was working on another project, a translation of Hakuin's Zen records, titled *Poison Blossoms
from a Thicket of Thorn*. In selecting the letters for that work, I noticed that in them Hakuin was disclosing a side of his character that
did not come through in his other writings. In jotting down spontaneous thoughts and feelings to send to students and friends, he revealed fascinating glimpses, and often more than glimpses, of
unknown areas of his life and personality.

This revelation led me to a batch of newly discovered letters that
had recently been published in *Zen Master Hakuin's Zen Painting
and Calligraphy*, and then to another group included in the *Complete
Works of Priest Hakuin*, the modern edition of his works. In both
groups of letters, I encountered many passages that enlarged, in sudden and unexpected ways, my understanding of Hakuin's complex

personality. They revealed, for example, the extraordinary efforts he made to get his writings into print, the details of the arduous trips he made in his final decades in order to fulfill his teaching obligations, the friendships he formed with lay followers in his home province as well as with eminent provincial Daimyo, and his quite detailed knowledge of the current Kabuki theatre in Edo. It was clear that these letters deserved a book of their own.

So far, about ninety of Hakuin's letters have been published, the earliest dating from his twenty-ninth year when he was still on the road pursuing his pilgrimage around the country. A few have survived from his forties, giving hints of the great adversity he faced as head priest of Shōin-ji, the temple in the village of Hara where he taught from his thirty-first year until his death at eighty-three. But the majority of his extant letters were composed between his late fifties and midseventies, a period when he was vigorously widening the scope of his teaching activity, and busily inventing new ways of taking his message outside the Zen community. Most of the earlier letters are brief, businesslike dispatches dealing with temple affairs; the later ones, which are generally longer, are often provoked by some perceived laxity, error, or lack of resolve in one of his students, or in the case of Tōrei and other leading disciples, by a need to prod someone to return to the fold. About a half dozen letters (not translated here), including those in the well-known *Oradegama*, are teaching epistles of great length that Hakuin later revised and published as books.

The earliest of the letters shows Hakuin in full possession of the epistolary powers that were evident later, and given what we know of him, I see no reason to presume that he was generally less active with his writing brush in his thirties, forties, and fifties than in his sixties and seventies. It seems likely that the disproportionate number of letters from his later years reflects not just Hakuin's inventiveness at spreading the Dharma, but also his growing fame, since people cherish and collect the detritus of renown. Certainly a considerable number of his letters have been lost. We can also be fairly sure that many are still gathering dust on the shelves of temples and private collections, and that the increasing focus on Hakuin and his work that has recently begun will encourage further discoveries.

Features that are characteristic of Hakuin in other writing genres are abundantly present in the letters, too. Some are given over to the hard-core discourse familiar from his other writings, the Zen master scolding students for showing less than absolute dedication to their training, or exhorting and prodding them to keep up the good work. Few are entirely devoid of homiletic intent. Still, their overall range remains quite varied. Within the body of letters now extant, almost half are quite brief, just a page or less that Hakuin jotted off to accept or refuse invitations to teach, or to express thanks for gifts received or services rendered. Others are addressed to the sick, offering support and encouragement together with detailed recipes for health and long life. Many contain appeals for donations for building or publishing projects, or for assistance in one of his endless schemes for promoting the Zen teaching. Two letters in the present collection show him as a village priest advising lay followers troubled by family feuds and other domestic infirmities, a role that is somewhat at odds with our standard image of him.

Two spiritual autobiographies that Hakuin wrote in his final decade, *The Tale of My Childhood* and *Wild Ivy*, chronicle the first half of his life, taking as their focus his quest for enlightenment, and breaking off at the point in his early thirties when he returned from pilgrimage and took up residence at Shōin-ji. He left no such account of the outwardly less dramatic teaching activity that dominated the second half of his life. For that period, therefore, we are obliged to fall back on the details that can be gleaned from the large body of fragmentary material contained in Hakuin's extensive writings, and use it to flesh out the basic framework of events in the *Chronological Biography*. By far the most important of these sources are the letters and the records contained in *Poison Blossoms from a Thicket of Thorn*. Both provide firsthand accounts that fill in and humanize many unknown areas of Hakuin's later years and his teaching work, often with a directness and spontaneity not even the autobiographies, didactic in purpose and composed for publication, can match.

Still, compared with the first part of Hakuin's life, the record for this period remains sketchy. For example, few letters of any length or substance have survived from the first decades of his incumbency at Shōin-ji, so our knowledge of those years is confined largely to the terse recital of events in the *Chronological Biography*. They show that Hakuin was still dedicated to an austere regimen of daily practice focused primarily on completing his religious quest, though he was teaching a few students, including laymen, who had come to him requesting instruction. This essential priority did not change until Hakuin experienced a decisive enlightenment in his forty-first year. Only after that was he able to turn his attention single-mindedly to the task of teaching others.

Tōrei pointed to the large lecture meeting held at Shōin-ji in Hakuin's fifty-fifth year as a turning point in his career, establishing Hakuin's preeminence as a Zen teacher once and for all. In the aftermath of this meeting, monks began arriving at Shōin-ji from all over the country in numbers that totally overwhelmed its meager capacities. This obliged the new monks to fend pretty much for themselves. They camped in shrines, temples, and other empty buildings throughout the surrounding countryside, and commuted to Shōin-ji for interviews with the master. Before long, the rundown old temple became "a great and vibrant center for Zen practice the likes of which had rarely been seen." (*Chronological Biography*).

A prominent feature of Hakuin's teaching during his sixties and seventies—one of the methods he adopted to make his teaching accessible to a wider public—was a growing use of the printed word, what he called his "verbal *prajna*" (*moji hannya*). He was already in his late fifties when his first book appeared (*Talks Introductory to Lectures on the Record of Hsi-keng*), but it was followed over the next twenty-five years by more than thirty others, including works of great diversity and compelling originality. The many vicissitudes involved in getting these books published, especially the problems

Hakuin encountered in financing them, are a motif that crops up in some form in most of the letters in this selection. This is the central concern of the series of six letters Hakuin wrote his disciple Daishū (Letters 13–18) dealing with the printing of *Poison Blossoms from a Thicket of Thorn*, one of his major works. These letters disclose an aspect of Hakuin's teaching activity that would otherwise have remained an almost complete blank.

Officially, in prefaces and colophons to his books, Hakuin can be found disavowing any intention of publishing his teachings, and belittling them as "totally worthless." He tells stories of how he quashed attempts that students or others had initiated in this line. But the letters show that unofficially, behind the scenes, Hakuin was doing everything in his power to get his teachings into print. The descriptions of pretended indifference are in large part a literary convention, and the great gusto with which he threw himself into his publishing ventures is no doubt yet another manifestation of the tremendous zeal, evident in all phases of his teaching activity, that Hakuin demonstrated in trying to make his message available to the widest possible audience, which certainly included future generations.

Another matter of great importance occupying Hakuin's thoughts during this time, one that increased in urgency with advancing age, was the need to produce a student worthy of receiving his Zen transmission. Hakuin's delight at finding such a man in Tōrei, Hakuin's subsequent frustration when Tōrei rebuffed all attempts to install him at Shōin-ji as Hakuin's successor, Tōrei's escape to Kyoto and continued resistance to Hakuin's relentless prodding and cajoling, and finally, after all that, Tōrei's decision to return some years later and supervise construction of a training temple being built for him in nearby Mishima—these matters are scarcely noted in Hakuin's records, but are set forth in fascinating detail in the Hakuin-Tōrei correspondence (Letters 19–24). Tōrei's behavior during these years becomes much less puzzling when examined, as it is here, in light of the surviving correspondence and other documents that the two men exchanged at the time, and in the chronological order in which the events unfolded.

While involved in these many concerns, the elderly Hakuin also set out each year at least once—and usually two or more times— in response to requests from temples and lay groups to conduct lecture meetings. Most of the sites he visited were located in Suruga Province and neighboring areas fairly close to home. But others involved long and fatiguing journeys through the mountainous provinces of Nagano and Kai, around the Mino-Gifu region (long a heartland of Rinzai Zen), to Edo, on occasion to Kyoto, and once, at sixty-five, all the way to Harima Province in western Honshu. The letters supply details of great interest about these visits that would otherwise be completely unknown.

A good example are the letters written during the long teaching trip of 1758, which not only provide a rather detailed itinerary of Hakuin's movements at the time, but also make us privy to his personal impressions about what he saw and encountered along the way—even his grumblings about the distances and his fatigue, and grousings over perceived shortcomings in his attendant monks. Hakuin traveled by palanquin, a choice that was dictated not only by his advanced age; he complains in more than one letter that his corpulence made it very difficult for him to walk even rather short distances. On one stretch of the way, while he was being carried through a difficult mountainous region of Kiso, Hakuin apparently composed an entire book, *Precious Mirror's Lingering Radiance*.

The question of why, at his advanced age, Hakuin would undertake these arduous journeys is probably best explained by the simple fact that to the very end of his life he showed extreme reluctance to forego any opportunity to spread his Zen message. Now that he was widely recognized as an unrivalled teacher, more requests were coming in.

At some point in his midseventies, the letters suddenly seem to stop; none of the existing letters can be dated to Hakuin's final decade. It could simply be that none has survived, but a more likely reason is probably Hakuin's increasing senility, which the *Chronological Biography* records as "the growing evidence of a general debility brought on by old age and illness." Hakuin signs off many of the later letters, long screeds that must have taken him hours to compose, with words that probably convey the truth of the matter: "It is now very late at night and I continually [have to] rub my bleary old eyes as I write this." The stamina that had allowed Hakuin to continue teaching at such an extraordinary pace and had inspired him to sit up late into the night composing letters exhorting and rebuking individual students was no longer there. Or perhaps he had decided to focus his reserves of energy on direct personal instruction, on publishing, painting Zenga, or brushing calligraphy, activities he continued to engage in up until the end of his life.

Hakuin dated the original letters using only the day and month, never the year, but from information provided in the texts themselves, it is usually possible to discover the year as well, though in some cases only within a span of two to three years. I have arranged the letters in chronological sequence according to these dates. I have given them headings that indicate to whom they were written, and to facilitate cross-referencing, I have numbered them as well.

Brief descriptions of the recipients and their relationship to Hakuin as well as basic background information are given in the headnotes to the individual letters; more extensive explanatory notes and commentary are provided in the afterwords. Exceptions to this are the six letters Hakuin wrote Daishū (Letters 13–18) and the six that make up the correspondence with Tōrei (Letters 19–24); I have embedded both of these within a narrative account that sets forth in some detail the events in which they figure. Several of the Zen technical terms in Section 3 that I thought could use more extensive explanation have been moved to the end notes. The chronology of Hakuin's life at the beginning of the volume is keyed to the letters.

Dates given throughout are as they appear in the letters themselves, according to the lunar calendar in use in Edo Japan. This means, for example, that Hakuin's birth is given as the twenty-fifth day of the twelfth month of 1685, not January 19, 1686, as it would be if converted to the Western calendar. However, I have used the Western method of calculating age, subtracting one year from the ages given in the original texts, which follows the Japanese system of counting a person one year old at birth.

There is still no comprehensive Japanese edition of Hakuin's letters. Fifteen letters, the only ones published during Hakuin's lifetime, are found in *Poison Blossoms from a Thicket of Thorn*; a group of thirty-five in volume six of the *Complete Works of Zen Priest Hakuin* (HOZ) published in 1935; and forty letters in *Hakuin's Zen Painting and Calligraphy* (HZB), some of which had been previously published but some important new discoveries as well. For the present translation, I have used all three of these collections. I have also profited greatly from Yoshizawa Katsuhiro's annotations of seven of the letters, included in *Zen Master Hakuin's Complete Dharma Writings in Japanese* (HHZ), volume fourteen. Sources are indicated immediatedly following each of the letters.

I wish to express my deep gratitude to my friend Nelson Foster for patiently reading early drafts of these letters and offering many valuable suggestions; and to Katsuhiro Yoshizawa for generously allowing me access to the proofs of his upcoming edition of *Poison Blossoms from a Thicket of Thorn*, and for kindly answering my questions on a broad range of other Hakuin-related topics.

A Chronology of Hakuin's Career

1. Religious Doubts, Ordination, Pilgrimage

1685 Born the youngest son of five children into the Nagasawa family of Hara, a village situated beneath Mount Fuji that served as a post station on the main Tōkaidō Road linking the new administrative center in Edo with the capital Kyoto. The Nagasawas were proprietors of the Omodakaya, a post house that stabled and supplied packhorses to travelers. His mother was a devout Nichiren Buddhist.

1695–98 (Age 10–13) Austerities and sutra recitations to allay fears of hell.

1699 (Age 14) Ordained by Tanrei Soden at Shōin-ji next to the family home; receives name "Ekaku," "Wise Crane." Becomes student of Sokudō Fueki at Daishō-ji in nearby Numazu.

1703 (Age 18) Sets out on pilgrimage. Reads of great priest's murder by bandits, doubts efficacy of Zen training; regrets leaving home. Resolves to devote life to secular pastimes, literature, and painting.

1704 (Age 19) Studies literature with Priest Baō. Picks *Spurring Students through the Zen Barrier* at random from temple library, reads "Tzuming Jabs a Gimlet in His Thigh," takes it as sign to resume training.

1705–06 (Age 20–21) Resumes pilgrimage, travels to Matsuyama on the island of Shikoku. Feeling goal now within his grasp, rededicates himself to Zen practice.

1707 (Age 22) Walks homeward along Inland Sea, "working his way deeper into the Mu koan at each step." Nurses Priest Baō while devoting nights to zazen. At Shōin-ji, remains doing zazen while great eruption of Mount Fuji causes catastrophic destruction throughout surrounding areas.

II. Study under Shōju Rōjin and Post-satori Practice

1708–10 (Age 23–25) Enlightenment at Eigan-ji (Echigo). Accompanies monk Sōkaku to Shinano Province, studies with Shōju Rōjin for eight months; another enlightenment. Resumes pilgrimage, bothered by lack of freedom in everyday life. "Zen sickness." Visits Hakuyū in Kyoto, learns meditation that enables him to cure himself.

1711–12 (Age 26–27) Nurses teacher Sokudō, devotes spare moments to zazen and study of Zen records.

1713–14 (Age 28–29) Visits Ōbaku priest Egoku in Kawachi for advice on completing training. Enters Inryō-ji, Sōtō temple in Izumi. Writes letter of remonstration to Watanabe Sukefusa (Letter 1). Visits Kyoto. At Hōfuku-ji in Mino, experiences definite signs of deeper attainment.

1715–16 (Age 30–31) Solitary practice at Mount Iwataki (Mino); at father's request leaves to reside at Shōin-ji.

III. HEAD PRIEST OF SHŌIN-JI; FURTHER POST-SATORI PRACTICE

1717 (Age 32) Installed as priest of Shōin-ji. Death of father. Continues training.

1718 (Age 33) Receives rank of First Monk (Dai-ichiza) from Myōshin-ji, adopts name "Hakuin," becomes Dharma heir of Tōrin Soshō. Lectures on Bodhidharma's *Breaking Through Form* and *Record of Lin-chi*.

1721 (Age 36) Death of Shōju Rōjin.

1726 (Age 41) Decisive enlightenment while reading *Lotus Sutra*: "Long-held doubts and uncertainties suddenly dissolve. . . . Attains enlightening activity of the Buddha-patriarchs without any lack whatever."

IV. FURTHER TEACHING AT SHŌIN-JI

1727–33 (Age 42–48) Post-satori training continues. Gives instruction to small number of lay students. Layman Ishii begins study. Lectures on *Four-Part Collection, Poems of Cold Mountain, Record of Lin-chi, Precious Lessons of the Zen School,* and *Blue Cliff Record.* Declines invitation to lecture on *Vimalakirti Sutra* (Letter 2). Over twenty monks in residence at Shōin-ji.

1734–47 (Age 49–52) Lectures on *Record of Hsu-t'ang, Vimalakirti Sutra, Precious Lessons of the Zen School,* and *Blue Cliff Record.* Letter to Layman Ishii (Letter 3).

1738–40 (Age 53–55) Lectures on *Ta-hui's Letters.* First large lecture meeting, on *Record of Hsu-t'ang;* attended by over four hundred people. "Now recognized as leading Zen teacher in country."

1741–42 (Age 56–57) Lectures on *Blue Cliff Record* (Kai); two hundred in attendance; lectures on *Precious Lessons of the Zen School* at Ryōtan-ji (Letter 4).

1743–44 (Age 58–59) Tōrei begins study with Hakuin. Lectures on *Ta-hui's Arsenal*. *Talks Introductory to Lectures on the Record of Hsi-keng* appears (his first publication). Lectures on *Chuan-lao's Comments for the Diamond Sutra* (Rinsen-an, Suruga). Tōrei presents letter to Hakuin (Letters 25 and 19).

v. Final Decades

1745 (Age 60) Lectures on *Vimilakirti Sutra* (Jitoku-ji, Kai); three hundred participants. Begins promoting recitation of the *Ten Phrase Kannon Sutra for Prolonging Life* (Letter 28).

1746 (Age 61) Lectures on *Lotus Sutra* (Suruga). Tōrei achieves great enlightenment; accepts Hakuin's Dharma transmission (Letter 20). *A Record of Sendai's Comments on the Poems of Cold Mountain* published. Suiō begins study at Shōin-ji. Lectures on *Lotus Sutra* (Kai).

1747–49 (Age 62–64) Yamanashi Heishirō comes to study. "Letter to a Certain Layman" ["The Tale of Heishirō of Ihara Village"] (Letter 7). Lectures on *Record of Hsi-keng, Record of Lin-chi,* and *Blue Cliff Record. Dream Words from a Land of Dreams* published. Presents Tōrei the robe signifying Dharma transmission. *Oradegama* published.

1750 (Age 65) Lectures on *Dream Words from a Land of Dreams* (Tōtōmi) and *Blue Cliff Record* (Kai). Lectures at Ryōkoku-ji in Akashi (Harima) on *Record of Hsi-keng*. Meets Confucian scholar Yanada Zeigan (Letter 13). Yotsugi Masayuki comes from Kyoto to study.

1751 (Age 66) Lectures on *Chuan-lao's Comments on the Diamond Sutra* and *Four-Part Collection* (Bizen). Ike Taiga and Ōhashi-jo receive instruction at Yotsugi Masayuki's Kyoto residence. Lectures on *Blue Cliff Record* (Yōgen-in, Myōshin-ji).

1752–54 (Age 67–69) Tōrei becomes head priest of Muryō-ji (Letter 21). "Letter to Senior Monk Gin" (Letter 8). Lectures on *Blue Cliff Record* (Shōin-ji). Publishes *Cloth Drum Refitted* (Letter 1). Lectures on *Record of Bukkō* (Izu); *The Eye of Men and Gods* (Suruga; three hundred participants); *Poison Words for the Heart* (Kai). Begins awarding "Dragon Staff certificates" to students who pass his One Hand koan (Letter 26).

1755 (Age 70) Lectures on *Vimalakirti Sutra* (Ryōshin-ji, Suruga). Enshrinement ceremony at Kannon-ji in Hara for image of Akiba Gongen donated by Uematsu Suetsuna (Letter 12). "Letter to Murabayashi Koremitsu" ["A Miraculous Cure for Eye Disease"] (Letter 9). "Letter to Yoda Takanaga" (Letter 10). "Letters to Sakai Kantahaku Sensei" (Letters 11–12).

1756 (Age 71) Lectures on *Heroic March Sutra* (Shōin-ji), *Precious Mirror Samadhi* (Tōtōmi), *Poison Words for the Heart* (Suruga), *Tahui's Arsenal* (Kai). Kida Ganshō takes *Poison Blossoms from a Thicket of Thorn* manuscript to Osaka to have it printed. Hakuin tries to force Tōrei to succeed him at Shōin-ji (Letter 21).

1757 (Age 72) Tōrei quits Muryō-ji, goes to Kyoto (Letter 21). Lectures at Kōzen-ji (Shinano), Kenchū-ji, and Nanshō-in (Kai); *Lotus Sutra* (Kōzen-ji, Hida); teaches at Kaizen-ji and Ryōshō-ji (Iida), Enryō-ji (Mikawa). *Idle Talk on a Night Boat* published (Letter 14). "Six Letters to Senior Priest Zenjo" written 1757–58 (Letters 13–18). Deletes Yanada Zeigan's preface from *Poison Blossoms* (Letters 14–15).

1758 (Age 73) Lectures on *Blue Cliff Record* at Rurikō-ji (Mino) in memory of Gudō Kokushi (Letter 16); teaches at Kakurin-ji, Zuiō-ji, Seitai-ji, Bairyū-ji (Mino). Lectures on *Blue Cliff Record* at Sōyū-ji (Takayama). Writes and publishes *Precious Mirror's Lingering*

Radiance (Letter 18). Teaches at Rinsen-ji, Ryōmon-ji, Myōraku-ji (Mino). Lectures on *Treatise on the Precious Storehouse* at Ryōgen-ji (Suzuka). Teaches at Tenshō-ji, Ryūtaku-ji, Hakurin-ji (Owari). Lectures on *Hsu-t'ang's Verse Comments on Old Koans* (Tōtōmi). Purchases Ryūtaku-ji in nearby Mishima.

1759 (Age 74) Lectures on *Blue Cliff Record* (Edo); purchases Shidō-an, Edo hermitage of Shōju Rōjin's teacher Shidō Munan. *Poison Blossoms from a Thicket of Thorn*, and *Supplement* published this year or next. *Accounts of the Miraculous Effects of the Ten Phrase Kannon Sutra for Prolonging Life* published.

1760 (Age 75) Lectures on *Talks Introductory to Lectures on the Record of Hsi-keng* (Ryūtaku-ji). Appoints Tōrei abbot of Ryūtaku-ji. "Letter to Daimyo Matsudaira Sadataka" (Letter 25).

1761 (Age 76) Performs enshrinement ceremony for protective deity Akiba Gongen (Ryūtaku-ji). *Tale of My Childhood* and *Tale of Yūkichi of Takayama*. "Letters to Katayama Shunnan" (Letters 26–27).

1762 (Age 77) Lectures on *Heart Sutra* (Numazu); on *Record of Hsu-t'ang* (Seiryō-ji, Suruga). Hakuin's followers reprint *Spurring Students through the Zen Barrier* and present to him (Letter 28).

1763 (Age 78) Lectures on *Blue Cliff Record* (Numazu). Talks at Ryōun-ji, Igen-ji, Eishō-ji, Gōin-ji, and Senryū-ji (Suruga). Lectures on *Blue Cliff Record* (Kōhō-in, Enashi); on *Record of Sung-yuan* (Jiun-ji, Ejiri). Increasing physical debility.

1764 (Age 79) Lectures on *Record of Daiō*; attended by seven hundred people. Eboku receives rank of First Monk (Dai-ichiza) from Myōshin-ji, adopts names Suiō Genro. Hakuin formally retires from Shōin-ji; Suiō installed as abbot.

1765 (Age 80) Enshrinement of Buddha relics at Ryūtaku-ji. Illness.

1766 (Age 81) Announces will no longer receive students. Travels to Edo to see newly built Shidō-an, stays six months. Lectures at Seiun-ji (Sagami) and Fukuju-in (Mishima). Autobiographical *Wild Ivy* published.

1767 (Age 82) Spring and summer relaxing at Kona hot springs on Izu Peninsula. Lectures on *Poison Blossoms from a Thicket of Thorn* at Ryūtaku-ji.

1768 (Age 83) Lectures on *Supplement* to *Poison Blossoms from a Thicket of Thorn* at Tokuraku-ji (Mishima). Teaches at Daijō-ji (Ihara) and Jōen-ji (Yui). Condition deteriorates. Entrusts Suiō with personal affairs. Dies in sleep at daybreak on the eleventh of the twelfth month.

BEATING THE CLOTH DRUM

I

To Watanabe Sukefusa

LETTER I, 1714

This is Hakuin's earliest surviving letter, written in 1714 when he
was twenty-nine years old and the only one from the years of his
pilgrimage. In it, he scolds a childhood friend named Watanabe
Sukehiko, eldest son of the wealthy Watanabe family of Hara, for
unspecified unfilial acts. Citing cautionary stories, Hakuin warns
his friend of the dire karmic consequences lying in store if he doesn't
mend his ways. The letter owes its survival to its inclusion in
Hakuin's publication *The Cloth Drum Refitted*, subtitled *A Letter to
an Unfilial Son*, which first appeared in his fifties.

I HAD INTENDED to deliver the inscription I wrote with the
Dharma name you requested on it in person on my way home,
but since I wanted your father to see it as soon as possible I decided to send it on ahead.

As I said in my previous letter, I was disturbed to learn you have
recently been indulging in your reprehensible habit of using strong
and unfilial language to your elderly parents. This has caused them
much pain. It is altogether abominable. Never forget that there is
indeed such a thing as heavenly retribution. The wrath of the gods is
very real.

Until this spring I was staying at a place called Shinoda in Izumi Province. In a village nearby named Tsukumi, there lived the son of a very wealthy man named Shinkichirō. He was talented, handsome, had a clever mind, and was dearly loved by all the members of his family, who coddled and protected him as he grew up. Shinkichirō turned eighteen last year, his father having passed away three or four years earlier. Arrangements for his marriage were begun this past winter. An agreement was reached with the bride's family, and the bride was being fitted out with a trousseau and so forth. A minor disagreement of some kind between Shinkichirō and his mother flared suddenly into a serious altercation. Shinkichirō lost control of himself and grabbed his mother by the hair, yanking some strands of it out by the roots. He picked up a sewing needle and jabbed it into her shoulder. His mother fainted away. Members of the household ran in and lifted her up. By sprinkling cold water on her face, they were finally able to revive her.

After the incident, mother and son both acted as though nothing had happened. But later that night, at about eleven o'clock, Shinkichirō suddenly broke into loud screams that shook and convulsed his entire body. "How terrible! Please forgive me! It's all my fault!" he moaned over and over. Violent sweat began pouring down his body, increasing as the night wore on. He fell in and out of consciousness. His screams resounded through the streets, causing a flurry of excitement to pass through the village.

By morning the fever had subsided, and people began coming by to see how he was. "It sounded like you were in terrible agony last night," they said. "Actually," he replied, "I was in some kind of a trance. An old man appeared to me wearing the headdress, white court garments, and black footwear of ancient times. Crowds of monstrous-looking creatures were milling around him, so ghastly I was forced to turn my eyes away. 'This is an emissary from hell. Do exactly as he says,' the creatures commanded. They held what looked like green-colored fans in their hands, and when they moved them, the fans sent out a breeze of unbearable heat. One of the creatures produced an iron nail—it must have been ten inches long—that was heated red-hot and had sparks flying from it. He began pounding the nail into my shoulder with a strange green hammer. The pain was indescribable. I became dizzy and so terrified I thought my breathing had stopped.

"Look," he said baring his shoulder. "It is still hot and extremely painful." There was an ugly, purple scar burn several inches square, blackened at the center. "Oh, how miserable I am! What have I done to deserve this!" he wept sadly. Then he began shouting out delirious cries, begging for medicine and hollering loud prayers. His suffering continued throughout the next night and the following nights as well. The purple scar on his shoulder grew steadily larger and more inflamed, festering and filling with pus, and producing an excruciating heat that became gradually more intense. His tongue became scorched in his mouth. His breath was foul. His hair all fell out. He became so filthy and unsightly no one could bear to look at him.

It was a truly dreadful state of affairs. Being wealthy, the family freely dispensed money for physicians. Practitioners were called in to employ their magic spells and incantations. But none of them was able to diminish the young man's suffering. At this point, with the situation becoming extremely dire, they came to the temple where I was staying to offer prayers and other devotions. The assembly of monks performed secret rites on the afflicted man's behalf throughout the night. When morning came, they brought me some purified rice, saying, "He should sleep easier tonight."

I immediately scotched that assumption. "No, he will probably suffer even more tonight. Despite your prayers, I am afraid he will undergo even worse sweating spells. Prayers and religious rites cannot help people who are suffering retribution for unfilial acts."

After I left the temple, word reached me that the gods and Buddhas had protected him and that his life was no longer in danger. But his eyes had been destroyed, his hearing was gone, and he seemed to have lost his desire to live.

In ancient China, there was a gentleman named Shu-liang who lived at a place called Han-yin with his mother, wife, and son. He was extremely quick-tempered, and would often fly off the handle, venting his spleen on his wife and mother, causing them great distress. No matter how ferocious a tiger is, it does not devour its cubs; it cares for them lovingly, as though they were precious jewels. One day when Shu-liang was away on a trip, his wife accidentally hurt the son, leaving him with a scar. "Woe is me!" she lamented with tears in her eyes. "When my husband returns, there's no telling what he will do. I would be better off flinging myself from a high cliff." *

Shu-liang's mother tried to allay her fear. "He won't harm either of us if we tell him that it was his own mother who accidentally caused the injury," she said. "Just to be on the safe side, however, I should probably go stay with my second son for the time being." She set out immediately.

When Shu-liang returned home and saw his son's face, he cried out, "How in the world did you get that scar?" Taking his son in his arms, he said, "Tell me who did this to you!" The son pointed at his mother. Enraged, Shu-liang threw his wife to the floor and pressed her body down with his knee. "Horrible woman, vengefully scarring my son's face!"

"Wait," she replied, regaining her composure. "Don't be so hasty. It wasn't me. It was your mother. But it was completely unintentional."

"You mean she did this terrible thing and she didn't kill herself?" he replied bitterly. "Harming your own flesh and blood is an unpardonable offense." Half out of his mind, he kept repeating, "I'll avenge my son's injury. I'll avenge my son's injury."

The very next day, Shu-liang visited his brother's home. "I understand our mother is staying here," he said casually. "Please tell her my wife wanted me to come and take her to worship at the shrine." The mother, though suspicious and disinclined to see her son, appeared from her room and fearfully agreed to visit the shrine with him. As they walked along, Shu-liang said, "Our worries are

---

* It was considered extremely unfilial to injure or disfigure the body of one's (male) children. This was especially heinous in the case of an eldest son, who, according to the canons of filial piety, is venerated because of his superior birth, age, and gender.

over, mother. I'm going to show you a secret place where many precious gems have been dug up. I promise you, by tomorrow our family will be rich and prosperous." Coming to a grim-looking place at the base of a mountain, he pointed to a hole in the ground seven or eight feet deep. "Come here and look into it, mother," he said, leading her to the hole. Suddenly, he reached out to grab her and push her over the edge into the hole, but in doing that he lost his footing, slipped, and fell in himself.

"Help me, mother," he pleaded. "Please, take hold of my hand. Pull me out of here. The earth in this hole is sandy and burning hot. I can't bear it any more." His mother, confused and upset, moved this way and that attempting to reach out her hand to him. But by then the intense heat inside the hole was sending up thick billows of black smoke.

Hearing his cries, villagers came running to help. They tried in various ways to rescue him, but flames shooting up from the hole grew to such strength they seemed bent on scorching the very skies. It was impossible for anyone to get near. Shu-liang's terrible screams were heard over half a mile away. After three days and three nights of continual agony, death finally came. When the fires died out and the villagers came and peered into the hole, they found that although the earth and grass inside were untouched by the flames, Shu-liang had been burned so badly that his body resembled a lump of charcoal.

There is also the story of a priest who was passing an old shrine late one night and saw crowds of tall, strange-looking people within the precincts. Their heads were wrapped in yellow silk and they were sweeping and cleaning the approaches to the shrine with sacred branches of the *sakaki* tree. They kept working through the night, muttering words like, "*Ahh!* How disgusting," and "*Oh!* How unclean." Approaching them, the priest said, "Why are you cleaning and purifying this place with such great care?"

"Since you ask," one of them replied, "an unfilial son has defiled this shrine. See over there where he entered through the sacred hedge and walked through the sacred precincts. Now we must dig up every particle of earth that his feet contaminated, down to a depth of seven feet, and dispose of it. But that fellow will soon receive his just reward from the lord of heaven." By the time he had finished speaking, light was appearing in the morning sky, and he and all the other strange beings had vanished. Not long afterward in that same area, a man was struck and killed by a single bolt of lightning.

There is another story about a priest who went to an ancient shrine for an overnight retreat. In the deepening silence he heard the sound of a fleet horse galloping by. Presently, a rider pulled up before the shrine and proclaimed in a harsh voice, "Greetings to the fellow inside the shrine. We have vowed to take you from here. Come out this instant!"

The priest heard a voice from within the shrine proclaim, "A messenger of death has come for an old man about to die. I would ask that his sentence be commuted for this one night."

"Just as you wish," the voice outside replied.

Then the voice inside the shrine laughed and said, "It is true we have a man here tonight who has been unfilial to his parents, but one of the lords of hell has already decreed that he will be killed at dawn by a bolt of lightning. I've been waiting to see him receive this punishment for a long time now. It will do my heart good to see him burned to a crisp. He's well deserved it for more than three years."

As the rider departed, he said, "There are many others just like him that I have to deal with in other areas of the country." That very dawn, a man was struck and killed by a single lightning bolt, just as the deity had foretold.

Stories like these are not uncommon. There is an account, for example, of a man whose hand burned fast to the handle of an ax he raised to strike his father, and who went to his death without ever getting it free. Others tell of a son who raised an ax against his mother but ended up burying it in his own head instead, or a son who tried to feed his mother a soup of worms and was struck by lightning on the spot, his hair going white as a wild boar's, or a wife who suddenly turned into a sow when she offered her blind mother-in-law a rice cake she had smeared with her child's feces. Another woman who promised her mother-in-law some mutton but ate it all herself and gave her a stewed placenta instead, found her head transformed into that of a white mongrel dog. Still others tell of a sword that a man concealed on a mountain road intending to use it on his mother-in-law, which turned into a venomous snake, wrapping itself around his head and crushing his skull, and of a son who piled up large bags of sand planning to crush his parents under them, but ending up flattening himself instead.

I have taken these stories from various different books.* But there are many more. They are truly endless in number.

In contrast to these terrible tales of retribution, there are also accounts of children who thanks to heaven's miraculous intervention were enabled to carry out acts of great filial devotion: the story of a rare medicinal stone suddenly appearing in the garden of a son who needed it to cure an ailing father; of midwinter ice breaking up and fresh carp leaping into the arms of a son whose stepmother had a craving for minced fish; of a poor man whose shovel struck a cauldron filled with gold as he was about to bury his child alive to ensure his mother would be adequately fed; of bamboo shoots emerging in midwinter for a son anxious to feed them to his mother; of a carp-filled fountain gushing up in the garden of a son who wanted to satisfy his mother's yearning for fine water and minced fish.

But even if you don't perform acts of filial devotion like these, of a caliber that elicits heavenly intervention, I devoutly hope you do not commit acts of an unfilial nature that will bring punishment down upon you. A person who ignores or refuses to acknowledge what takes place right under his nose and insists on merely doing as he pleases must be either a stupid man or an evil one.

The people in the half-dozen stories I related, having turned away from reasonable courses of action, convinced themselves that

---

* Although not all of these references can be traced, most of them are found in *Tales of the Twenty-Four Paragons of Filial Virtue* (*Ehr-shih-ssu hsiao*), a popular Confucian text of the Yuan dynasty that was reprinted and widely read in Edo Japan.

their transgressions were minor and that any retribution would be minor as well, and because of that they ended up receiving the severe judgment of heaven, dying very unfortunate deaths, leaving behind them names blackened forever as unfilial sons or daughters, and falling into the interminable suffering and torment of the Burning Hells. That this happened because they did not fear the wrath of the gods and were ignorant of heavenly retribution is a matter each and every person should give the greatest care and consideration.

Last winter when I heard that story of Shinkichirō of Tsukumi village, I immediately thought of you. It bothered me, and I decided to write you, but one thing came up after another and I never got around to sitting down and doing it.

The *Book of Changes* states, "Unless you are habitually good, you do not make a name for yourself; unless you are habitually bad, you do not ruin yourself." In other words, our fortune and misfortune result from the gradual accumulation of small increments of good or evil deeds.

The events I have related may seem dubious to you, incredible and remote. But what about Kyūza of Nakasato village, or Sajibei of Sawada village? Those incidents both took place in your own neighborhood. When young Sajibei clubbed his mother with an ax handle, he immediately took leave of his senses. Now over seventy years old, he lives miserably in the Grove of the Deva Guardians in Sawada, weeping his final years away.

Good deeds, no matter how many you perform, need no repentance. But evil deeds, even minor ones, are a cause of endless regret and heartache. According to what is written in the sutras, even if a person erects a pagoda twenty *yojanas* in height, adorns it with the seven precious gems , and enshrines Buddha relics in it, so that every arhat in the world comes to revere it, the arising in his mind of even a single angry thought becomes a fire that will at once turn into a great, all-consuming conflagration. The fires of wrath and anger consume entire forests of merit and virtue.

Until now, your mother could not devote herself to good works because from the time you were born she lavished her every moment on you, caring for you and seeing that you were provided with everything necessary for your upbringing. If she did find time to enter the family altar room, the sutras and *dharanis* she recited were always dedicated to your good health and long life, without a thought for her own karmic future, and heedless of her own physical exhaustion. Now, having retired in recent years from her former busy life, she has time to spend quietly on Buddhist devotions— but you come around, hatching your malicious schemes to frustrate and upset her, spreading silly rumors at the year-end cleaning, thinking up ways to anger her at the busy year-end season. What a bitterly cruel thing to do.

How heartwarming it is to see ordinary sons and daughters attending to their duty to their parents with benevolent smiles on their faces, sparing no expense to provide for their needs and amusement: "You must use a palanquin when you visit the shrine." "Why don't you take your friend so-and-so with you when you attend that Buddhist service?"

But never forget, that no matter how long-lived your parents are, they cannot remain forever in this illusory world of dreams. Accounts have been transmitted throughout the past of brave samurai whose minds were filled with thoughts of filial devotion, of virtuous priests of deep attainment whose love and compassion for their parents was a constant concern. Still, perhaps you think it strange my saying these things to you. "Ekaku is quick to grab his brush and write letters of this kind to people. But what about him? Hasn't he left his father, who is well into his eighties, to go wandering off to the far-flung corners of the country, never so much as sending him a letter?"

However, a person who leaves his home to take the vows of a Buddhist monk has, in doing so, renounced his former self completely. He sets out in search of a good master who can help him achieve his goal, engaging in arduous practice day and night, precisely because he is concerned with obtaining a favorable rebirth for his parents into the endless future. He is performing the greatest kind of filial piety.

It is said that on receiving a just remonstrance, you should not consider the person who delivers it. In ages past, the Great Yu was always pleased to hear wise words of advice, valuing them even if they came from shopkeepers, hunters, or fishermen.* His only regret was that he had not heard them sooner.

If you should feel that the words I have written here are reasonable, then take this letter and preserve it in a safe place. If you mend your ways, regretting your misdeeds and fearing their consequences, then this letter, inadequate as it is, will be an auspicious jewel of great worth—although even a jewel of incalculable price cannot dispel the delusion in a person's mind. No one can predict when another person with your bad habits will appear; it may even be your own son. If you preserve this letter and show it to him, it may influence him to cease his evil ways, even to do good deeds as well.

If, on the other hand, you decide that what I have said is unreasonable nonsense, just toss the letter into the fire. From now on, everything will inevitably depend on your mind alone.

THE FIRST [FOURTH] YEAR OF SHŌTOKU (1714),
AT THE INRYŌ-JI TEMPLE AT SHINODA IN IZUMI PROVINCE.
HHZ, 12:39–396

Hakuin was still a young monk when he composed this letter, nearing the end of a decade-long pilgrimage and well into the post-satori phase of his practice, having achieved several satori experiences earlier in his twenties. He was staying at Inryō-ji, a Sōtō temple in Izumi Province south of Osaka, and was writing in response to a letter from Watanabe Sukefusa's father Heizaemon, who was the proprietor of an important *honjin* inn at the Hara post station (the kind reserved for the use of Daimyo and others of high rank), informing him of his son's unfilial behavior.

---

* A legendary sage ruler of ancient China. According to *Mencius*, when ministers came to him with good advice, Yu always received it with deep gratitude.

It is interesting to note Hakuin's deep concern with filial devotion at this early stage of his career, a theme that continues to have a significant, though subordinate, role in his mature Zen teaching. It is most conspicuous in some of the calligraphic works he distributed, which are discussed below. Another example of the consistency of Hakuin's views is his willingness to take up the village priest's function of moral correction, a purpose he fulfills through his attempts to resolve family discords in other letters in this volume. Also to be noted is that Hakuin does not offer Sukefusa a specific Zen solution to his problem, as he no doubt would have later on.

At some point, either when Hakuin wrote the letter itself or soon afterward, he transcribed it in manuscript form, added a short preface, and titled it *The Cloth Drum: A Letter to an Unfilial Son.* Years later this brief letter became the basis for *The Cloth Drum Refitted [with a New Drumhead],* a series of accounts of retribution for unfilial behavior that appeared as a single volume in 1747. It was greatly enlarged and reissued in 1753 in a five-volume edition. This edition opens with the letter to Watanabe Sukefusa, which takes up less than a third of volume one, and is followed by twenty-two more stories of karmic cause and effect. Hakuin returned to this genre in later collections such as *Accounts of the Miraculous Effects of the Ten Phrase Kannon Sutra for Prolonging Life.* Whereas *Accounts of the Miraculous Effects* describes wondrous escapes from disaster and death thanks to recitation of the *Ten Phrase Kannon Sutra,* all but one of the stories in *The Cloth Drum Refitted* are of the retributive type and recount instead the terrible punishments meted out to unfilial sons and daughters.

In the preface Hakuin wrote for *The Cloth Drum Refitted,* he alludes briefly to his friendship with Watanabe Sukefusa, then explains the circumstances that led him to send Watanabe the remonstrance. After stating that unfilial behavior invariably arises from an addiction to wine and women, presumably the vices his friend had succumbed to, Hakuin goes on to say:

> Obsession with these seductions is a serious disease, and it is one that neither the wise nor the foolish can escape. A

wise person blinded by delusion is like a tiger that falls into a well and yet has sufficient strength to claw its way out without losing its skin. When a foolish man is similarly blinded, he is like a tired, skinny old fox that falls in but perishes miserably at the bottom of the well because he lacks the strength to clamber out. Even a person who is just tolerably clever will, once he has fallen victim to these seductions and begins behaving in an unfilial manner, heed the warnings of his elders and the advice of the good and virtuous, immediately change his ways and become a kind and considerate son to his parents. Receiving heaven's favor and the gods' hidden assistance, he will be blessed with great happiness and long life. When he dies, he will leave a sterling reputation for wisdom and goodness behind him.

Not so a foolish man, for once he engages in unfilial behavior he neither fears the warnings of his elders nor heeds the advice of good, upright people. He defies the sun, he opposes the moon, and in the end he receives the punishment of heaven and the dire verdict of the gods. In this state, self-redemption is no longer possible.

The difference between the two men does not exist from the start. It arises only because the former heeds to the warnings, and the latter does not.

[As this next paragraph seems addressed to Watanabe Sukefusa, it must have been written when Hakuin composed the original letter. Did Hakuin leave it in unintentionally when he reworked the preface for inclusion in the published edition of *The Cloth Drum Refitted* forty years later?]

You yourself have recently fallen prey to delusions of a similar kind. Your relations look on with wrinkled brows, your friends with foreheads furrowed. You have come right up against a firmly locked barrier that you will find extremely difficult to pass through.

Forty years ago, my childhood friend Watanabe Sukefusa contracted a serious illness of this nature, throwing his parents into a state of constant distress. I was staying at a temple in Shinoda, Izumi Province, at the time, so I sent Sukefusa a long letter. It made a strong impression on him. He immediately changed his ways and became a devoted son.

Now, on happy and auspicious occasions, Sukefusa puts on a clean robe, clears his desk, takes out the letter, and slowly and carefully rereads it, treasuring it as a precious jewel. After I returned home from my pilgrimage in my early thirties and took up residence in Shōin-ji, a strong friendship formed between us. We became closer than brothers. He kept the letter inside a fabric slipcase on which I had inscribed the characters *nuno-tsutsumi* (the "cloth drum") [something that is utterly useless].

One day during a conversation he said, "You know, at first the words 'cloth drum' seemed strange to me. But now, after having read and reread the letter with great care, I have come to understand what a welcome and valuable work it is." Seeing the joy beam from his face as he spoke, I was filled with joy as well.

Today his son cherishes the letter as a family treasure. Recently, on the occasion of an annual festival, some elderly laymen who frequent my temple borrowed the letter and brought it to my temple. They asked me to copy it out and write some prefatory remarks. I complied with their wishes, and have taken the opportunity to add much new material as well.

What joy it is to imagine readers of this work taking out the letter from time to time as Watanabe did, and then proceeding to perform kind and wonderful deeds for their parents. Perhaps they may even succeed in hearing the secret rhythms of the cloth drum. However, if any of them finds the ideas set forth here absurd or unreasonable, they should return it forthwith to me!

In the spring of 1746, shortly before writing this preface, Hakuin had acted on the advice he had given thirty-three years earlier about recycling the letter. Learning that one Murabayashi Tokusaburō, the son of a friend and a student in Edo, whom the father had praised as an "extremely sincere, mild-mannered, and obedient young man, loved by one and all," was in fact given to wild drinking sprees and other generally reprehensible behavior, Hakuin retrieved the letter, made some necessary revisions, and sent it to the young man (also see Letter 9). As this occurred only months before Hakuin prepared *The Cloth Drum Refitted* for publication, it seems reasonable to conjecture that revamping the letter for Tokusaburō stimulated Hakuin to write and publish this almost entirely new work in which he could declare the hazards of unfilial behavior to a much wider audience.

The cardinal Chinese virtue of filiality, applicable to all interactions with one's elders, but especially to a son's dealings with his parents, grandparents, and family, assumed great importance in Edo-period Japan with its formal government sanction of Confucian ethics. Many Confucians, including some with great political influence, regarded monasticism as abhorrent on the grounds that it contravened the basic operating principles of filial behavior by keeping young men from producing heirs to continue the parental line. Buddhists in China, and later in Japan, responded to such charges with some success, arguing the deep filiality of the monk's career, in which "leaving home" for the priesthood, through the redemptive power of awakening, is reconciled with Confucian filial responsibilities.

Sharing these premises, Hakuin launched vehement attacks on what he considered the mistaken understanding purveyed by such architects of Confucian orthodoxy as Hayashi Razan (see pp. 123–127). Hakuin's ideas on the subject may be summed up fairly well in the calligraphic works he prepared and distributed in large numbers to people. These works consisted of one large character, *filiality* or *parent*, followed by the inscription, "There is no more valuable act of filiality than to save one's father and mother from the sad fate of an unfortunate rebirth in the next life"—exactly the sentiments Hakuin had expressed to Sukefusa as a young monk.

2

To Zen Monks Kin and Koku

LETTER 2, 1729

This letter, in which Hakuin declines an invitation to lecture on the *Vimalakirti Sutra*, can be dated from internal evidence to 1729. As one of very few letters that can be dated confidently to Hakuin's forties, it gives us a rare glimpse of Shōin-ji during the early years of Hakuin's residency. Neither Kin or Koku, nor the name of the temple issuing the invitation to Hakuin, have been identified, although the temple was no doubt located close by, probably in Suruga Province.

Note that Hakuin initially refers to the *Vimalakirti Sutra* as the *Beyond Comprehension Sutra*, using one of the *Vimalakirti Sutra*'s chapter titles.

MY HUMBLEST APPRECIATION for the letter Brother Rai recently delivered to me containing your request to conduct a lecture meeting on the *Beyond Comprehension Sutra*, together with the list of expected participants. While I seriously doubt you can rely on a shuffling jackass to perform like a thoroughbred stallion, or hope for an old crow to start caroling like a celestial phoenix, I am nonetheless sincerely grateful that you even remembered this boorish rustic and thought it worthwhile to make a sincere effort to assist in his upbringing. I have no doubt that you were inspired by a deep aspiration to promote the teaching of the Dharma.

I, alas, am not a superior man. I have neither wisdom nor virtue. I am sure you have heard about the adversities we've been experiencing at Shōin-ji. After my first eight years here as head priest, and a great deal of trouble, we finally succeeded in striking a vein of water and reviving the dried-up old well. Now four years and a great deal of additional hardship later, we have managed to finish re-thatching the leaky roofs. I still do not have a student able to aid me in running the affairs of the temple, and there are no parishioners to turn to for financial help.

More to the point, even after scrutinizing my heart from corner to corner, I am unable to come up with a single notion that I could communicate to participants at such a lecture meeting, much less hold forth on the *Vimilakirti Sutra*'s wonderful teaching of nonduality. In view of this, and after repeated and agonizing self-examination, I am afraid I have no choice but to decline the high honor you have sought to bestow upon me. Even as I write this, my eyes are wet with tears and my body drenched in a thick, shame-induced sweat. Certainly there is no lack of veteran priests in your own area, any one of whom I am sure would be capable of carrying out the task you propose.

Asking your forgiveness in this matter, I am, yours truly, [Hakuin]

HOZ, 2:109

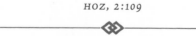

In his autobiographies, Hakuin describes his small, impoverished temple as being in an "indescribable state of disrepair" when he was installed as abbot in 1717. Judging from occasional references in his books and letters to the privations of life at Shōin-ji, there does not seem to have been much improvement in living conditions for some time afterward. Hakuin's primary focus in the first decade of his incumbency was his own post-satori practice, although the records mention a small number of students, mostly villagers from Hara, who were coming to him for instruction at this time.

Hakuin's teaching career did not really begin, however, until an autumn night in 1726, a little over two years prior to this letter. While reading the *Lotus Sutra*, he suddenly achieved the decisive enlightenment that brought his religious quest to an end, and with it the knowledge, "beyond any doubt," that he was "ready to teach others with the perfect, untrammeled freedom of the Bodhisattvas."

In view of how vigorously Hakuin dedicated himself to such teaching activity during his sixties and seventies—in one two-year period, for example, he visited and taught at twenty-five different temples—it is interesting to find him here at the age of forty-three, at the start of his teaching career, showing such reluctance to accept a teaching assignment. Evidently, Hakuin did not lecture at the request of another temple until eight years after this. His text was the *Blue Cliff Record*.

3

To Layman Ishii

LETTER 3, 1734

This letter, dating from Hakuin's forty-ninth year, is addressed to his friend and student Ishii Gentoku (1671–1751), a physician who resided in Hina village, six miles west of the Hara post station. Fifteen years Hakuin's senior, Ishii began practicing at Shōin-ji in 1728, eight years after Hakuin was installed as abbot, a little over a year after Hakuin's decisive enlightenment at the age of forty-one.

The closeness of the relationship that formed between the two men is evident in Hakuin's letters to Ishii, as well as from the fact that Hakuin at times secluded himself in Ishii's retirement retreat for periods of rest and writing (*Chronological Biography*, 1731). A number of miscellaneous pieces inscribed to Layman Ishii that are included in *Poison Blossoms from a Thicket of Thorn* confirm that he was considerably advanced in his Zen study, a point further substantiated by the difficulty of the teaching Hakuin addresses to him in this letter.

MY ATTENDANT BOKU, while on a trip to his native place, stopped by the residence of Layman Ishii and claiming to be indisposed threw himself at the Layman's feet and implored him for his help. He took possession of the Layman's private chambers and for ten days devoted himself diligently to *zazen*.*

I recently overheard several of Boku's comrades discussing him. "Boku hit on a truly splendid plan," they decided. "He is sure to return with a much deeper attainment." I wasn't so sure. "Boku," I said to myself. "This is not a good idea. Being a kind and deeply compassionate man, when the Layman sees how troubled you are, he is sure to be greatly concerned and want to help you. But whatever help you receive now, even though you may gain something from it, it is going to stick to your bones and cling to your hide, and will prevent you from experiencing the intense joy that should accompany the sudden entrance into satori. You will remain a humble little stable boy the rest of your life, your wisdom never completely clear, your attainment never truly alive and vital.† A most regrettable outcome!"

Yesterday, the evening of the twelfth, Boku returned to Shōin-ji. I sat waiting for him with a black snake in my sleeve.‡ By and by, an unkempt and disheveled Boku entered the temple gates. His face looked unchanged, no different from when he had left.

"What words did the Layman have for you?" I asked.

"He didn't utter a single word to help me," Boku said, tears raining down his face.

Unable to keep from bursting into laughter, I cried out, "How wonderful! If you had come back here with even a grain of Zen understanding, I would have snatched your robe and begging bowl from you, given you thirty blows with my staff, and chased you out the gate. You had a very close shave! You might have

---

* The word *chambers* (*hōjō*), normally the quarters of a head priest, also alludes to the room where the great Layman Vimalakirti taught. An annotation states that the room may have been Ishii's teahouse.

† *Chijō kōhai*, the second of three kinds of "leakage" posited by Tung-shan Liang-chieh, in which the student, while trying to rid himself of delusory thoughts, still remains within the realm of dualism (*The Eye of Men and Gods*, ch. 3).

‡ That is, a *shippei*, or black-lacquered bamboo stick.

ended up achieving nothing for your efforts but to involve the Layman in your personal troubles. I had no idea he would be so rigorous in dealing with you!

"Boku, the great and essential matter is like partaking of a peach. You mustn't be hasty. You have to wait patiently until the fruit is fully ripe. Then, when the soft, pink fruit is cut in two, the kernel falls out of itself, and the flesh, with its wonderful configurations, can be enjoyed in all its marvelous fragrance and delicious flavor. How marvelous and edifying it is to witness this taking place!

"Watch the way a mother hen warms an egg. When she has warmed the egg sufficiently so that the conditions are ripe for hatching, instead of pecking the egg, she waits, she holds back until she hears faint pecking sounds inside the shell. She gives the shell a single peck, and the baby chick emerges. It is truly heartwarming to watch her forthrightly attending to her task, cocking her head this way and that, up and down, as she restrains herself from pecking. Yet if she did not hold back, if she pecked the shell too early, she would have ruined everything, producing a sight too terrible to behold.

"Or consider the case of a pregnant woman. Although her time has not yet arrived, she and her husband have taken every possible precaution and secured in advance the services of a physician. Now, a physician of only middling talents, eager to achieve results and hasten the delivery, may decide to force the birth prematurely or to attempt a perilous breech delivery, gravely imperiling the lives of both mother and child.

"Or take the example of a man who comes down with the ague, and suffers periodic bouts of convulsive shivering. If the physician attempts to cure the man quickly after he has suffered only one or two paroxysms, the infection will remain in his system, only to recur later in more virulent form. Hence the saying, 'A mediocre physician neither helps nor harms. A poor physician harms without helping. It is wisest not to send for either.'

"One day when I was in Mino Province, I observed a cicada

casting its skin in the shade. It managed to get its head free, and then its hands and feet emerged one after the other. Only its left wing remained inside, adhering to the old skin. It didn't look as though the cicada would ever get that wing unstuck. Watching it struggling to free itself, I was moved by feelings of pity to assist it with my fingernail. 'Excellent,' I thought. 'Now you are free to go on your way.' But the wing I had touched remained shut and would not open. The cicada never was able to fly the way it should have. Watching it, I felt ashamed of myself, regretting deeply what I had done.

"When you consider it, present-day Zen teachers act in much the same way in guiding their students. I've seen and heard how they take young people of exceptional talent—those destined to become the very pillars and ridgepoles of our school—and with their extremely ill-advised and inopportune methods, end up turning them into something half-baked and unachieved. This is the primary reason for the decline of our Zen school, why the Zen groves are withering away.

"Now and again, you come across superior seekers of genuine ability who are devoting themselves to hidden application and secret practice. As they continue steadily forward, accumulating merit until their efforts achieve a purity that infuses them with strength, their emotions gradually cease to arise altogether. They find themselves at an impasse, unable to move forward despite the most strenuous application. It is as though they are trapped inside an invincible enclosure of diamond-like strength, or are sitting in a bottle of purest crystal—unable to move forward, unable to retreat, they become dunces, utter blockheads.

"Suddenly the moment arrives when they become one with their questing mind. Mind and koan both disappear. Breathing itself seems to cease. This, although they are not aware of it, is the moment when the tortoise shell cracks and fissures, when the Luan-bird emerges from its egg. They are experiencing the auspicious signs that appear when a person is about to attain the Buddha Way.

"What a shame if at such a critical moment someone who is supposed to be their good friend and teacher succumbs to tender emotions, indulges them in grandmotherly kindness, and serves them up various intellectual explanations that knock them back into the old familiar nest of conceptual understanding, that drag them down into the cavernous old den of darkness and delusion. That, however, is not the end of the damage they do them, for they then produce a phony winter-melon seal, impress it on a piece of paper, and award it to them:* 'You are like this,' they say. 'I am like this, too. Preserve and protect it with care.' The trouble is, the roots binding the students to life are still not severed. The gardens of the patriarchs still lie beyond their farthest horizons. Any teacher who does this, though he may love his student dearly, causes him irreparable harm. For their part, the students start dancing around, rolling their heads this way and that way, wagging their tails joyfully, eagerly lapping away at the fox slobber doled out to them, completely unaware it is a virulent poison they consume.† They waste their entire lives stuck in a half-drunken, half-sober state of delusion. Not even the hand of a Buddha can cure them.

"A foolish man long ago heard that if you put a leech out under the sun in very hot weather, it would transform into a dragonfly and soar into the sky. One summer day, he decided to put it to the test. Wading into a marsh, he poked around until he found a particularly large old leech. Throwing it on the hot ground, he watched very carefully as the worm squirmed and writhed in agony. Suddenly, it flipped over on its back, split in two, and transformed into a ugly creature with a hundred legs like a centipede. It scowled furiously at him, snapping its fangs in anger. Ahh! This creature that was supposed to soar freely through the

---

* A false makeshift seal carved from melon rind.

† [Wild] fox slobber (*koen*, or *yako-enda*) is generally poison, used by Hakuin with a positive connotation for the "turning words" used by Zen teachers. For a recipe for making it, see *Hakuin's Precious Mirror Cave* (244).

skies had turned into a repulsive worm that could only crawl miserably over the ground. A truly terrifying turn of events!

"There was a servant in ancient China who worked in the kitchen of a temple in the far western regions of the country. The temple was filled with monks engaged in the rigors of training. All the time the servant wasn't engaged in his main job preparing meals for the brotherhood, he spent doing zazen. One day, he suddenly entered a profound *samadhi*, and since he showed no sign of coming out of it, the head priest of the temple directed the senior monk in charge of the training hall to keep an eye on him. When the servant finally got up from his zazen cushion three days later, he had penetrated the heart and marrow of the Dharma, and had attained an ability to clearly see the karma of his previous lives. He went to the head priest and began setting forth the realization he had attained, but before he had finished, the head priest suddenly put his hands over his ears. 'Stop! Stop!' he said. 'The rest is something I have yet to experience. If you explain it to me, I'm afraid it might obstruct my own entrance into enlightenment.'

"How invaluable that story is! There was nothing halfhearted about ancients' practice of the Way; it was difficult and demanding in the extreme. One of them said, 'It is like passing through a region infested with venomous insects. You must pass through with all possible haste. Not stop to accept even a single drop of water from someone you meet.' The great master Yun-men said, 'While you are engaged in practice, if anyone comes up and tries to teach you Zen, I want you to take a dipper of warm shit and empty it over his head.'*

"That is why to outstanding students who are engaged in negotiating the hidden depths I say, 'I would rather you sink into the sea of birth-and-death and remain there until the skin on

---

* Hakuin loosely paraphrases a statement in the *Comprehensive Records of Yun-men* (*Yun-men kuang-lu*). An early Chinese commentary on this apprises us of the fact that warm excrement produced during the summer months has an especially foul smell.

your body is covered all over with festering sores, than for you ever to look to others for your strength.'"

Before I had even finished speaking, Boku performed two prostrations. "Master," he said, "thank you for the great compassion you have shown in giving me this teaching. Although I cannot hope to comprehend it all, I do not doubt it in the least. I do have a few questions about it, however.

"In the past when teachers engaged their students, there was no room for any hesitation—they dealt with them as if they had a naked sword blade raised over their heads. They were like the giant golden-winged Garuda, monarch of the feathered kingdom, cleaving through the whale-backed seas and deftly seizing live dragons beneath the waves. Zen monks are like red-finned carp when the peach trees are in blossom, butting their way upstream into the tremendous current, braving the perilous forked lightning of the Dragon Gate.* They enter realization at the utterance of a single word. They attain cessation at the sound of a single shout. If those who call themselves teachers all behave like dead otters[2] and those who call themselves students all behave like dumb sheep,[3] the halls of Zen throughout the land, training grounds where Buddhas are singled out, will be rendered utterly useless—they'll be no better than coffins for the dead—and the assertions of the perverse silent-illumination Zen teachers with their box-shrub Zen will carry the day.[4] If that happens, the supreme teaching of the Buddha-mind school will plunge to earth forever, and its true and rigorous traditions will disappear from the ancestral groves."

I gave a sigh, and said, "Boku, come over here. I want you to listen to what I say. In studying Zen, it is necessary to pierce completely through when you penetrate to the source. It is the same

---

* The Dragon Gate is a three-tiered waterfall cut through the mountains of Lung-men to open up a passage for the Yellow River. It was said that on the third day of the third month, when peach trees are in flower, carp that succeeded in scaling this waterfall turned into dragons.

with all the workings of heaven and earth. The wonderful trans-
formation of springtime does not take place without the winter's
severity, the intense cold that makes the hundred plants and
grasses fade and shrivel, the bamboo split and shatter. But with
the advent of spring, the ten thousand buds and blossoms emerge,
rivaling one another with their charms and beauties. Hence the
saying, 'To make something grow and develop, you must cut it
back. To make something flourish, you must check its progress.'

"Long ago, when the First Patriarch Bodhidharma was living
in seclusion doing zazen at Shao-shih, he had a student named
Hui-k'o. Hui-k'o possessed outstanding talent and learning, and
a dauntless and heroic spirit. For three years he continued to refine his attainment while serving as Bodhidharma's attendant.
Untold hardship and suffering were his constant companions.

"Today's students practice the Way clothed in warm garments and get plenty to eat, and they are as soft and weak as the
eldest son of a wealthy family. Could any of them venture to stand
stalwart and resolute in a courtyard on a bitterly cold night like
Hui-k'o? Buried up to the waist in icy snow like a stack of fire-
wood? Suffering of this intensity cannot be endured unless one is
made of stone or metal, or has wooden legs like a statue. The
marrow-chilling cold of the northern Wei winter constantly penetrated the thin cotton robe he wore, but he stood resolutely and
silently through that adversity until dawn, never relaxing his efforts for a second, or weeping a single tear. Bodhidharma never
offered him the slightest help whatsoever. Finally, Hui-k'o took a
knife and cut off his left arm.[*] Hsi-sou Shou-t'an was perfectly
justified in holding Hui-k'o up as a model for all Zen monks
throughout the world.

"When the Sixth Patriarch Hui-neng raised the Dharma
standard at Ts'ao-hsi, the priest Nan-yueh came to study with
him. Hui-neng asked, 'What is this that thus comes?' Nan-yueh
stood in a daze, unable to respond. Hui-neng did not utter a

---

[*] *Compendium of the Five Lamps*, ch. 1. Also Case 41 in the *Gateless Barrier*.

single word to relieve his confusion, and it was not until Nan-yueh had practiced arduously for eight more years that the patriarch finally offered him a turning word.* Ahh! This good teacher, a person who had accumulated great merit over eighty rebirths,† now, when the time was ripe, used his marvelous means with incomparable skill to bring about Nan-yueh's liberation. Why didn't he employ them at the start, just lead Nan-yueh to the immense joy of liberation? The incandescent fire to forge fine Pin-chou steel is not obtained by stoking the furnace with kindling. The oranges of Chiang-nan do not assume their delicious sweetness until they have endured bitter frosts. Any honest farmer would be ashamed to cook unripened grain for his meals, would he not?

"Students who have not yet penetrated the source should not be troubled if their entrance into enlightenment is slow in coming; they should be troubled only if their practice fails to attain a state of genuine purity. Students who have already penetrated to attainment should not be troubled if people fail to revere them; they should be concerned only about the difficulty of making their attainment complete.

"Long ago, when Lin-chi practiced for three years at Huang-po's temple, he received words of sanction from Huang-po's disciple Chen Tsun-su: 'Someone whose practice is this pure and genuine is certain to become a great shade tree for the beings of the world.'‡ Lin-chi was by that time widely versed in the sutras and commentaries, and he had exhaustively investigated the pre-

---

* *Compendium of the Five Lamps*, ch. 3.

† Based on lines in a verse by Yuan-wu K'o-ch'in: "I venerate the Sixth Patriarch, an authentic old Buddha who manifested himself in the human world as a good teacher for eighty lifetimes in order to help others" (cited in Tōrei's *Snake Legs for Kaien-fu-setsu*, 21v).

‡ The head monk in Huang-po's assembly at this time is not identified in the standard accounts of this episode in *Record of Lin-chi* and *Records of the Lamp*. He is given as Chen Tsun-su (Mu-chou Tao-tsung, n.d.) in some other accounts. In none of the versions does he utter such words directly to Lin-chi.

cepts as well. Today's students lack this extensive knowledge of the scriptures or precepts. Because of that, they confound their own feelings, perceptions, and understanding for absolute truth, go around shooting off their mouths and retailing their half-baked ideas to others, and end up making a total waste of their lives.

"Observe the manner in which a clear-eyed teacher like Chen Tsun-su was able unequivocally to affirm Lin-chi: 'Your practice is pure and genuine!' That purity and that genuineness of practice are extremely difficult to attain, even if a student devotes an entire lifetime to Zen training. However, once you attain it, you are, without any doubt, a tiger that has sprouted wings.* You should never doubt that you yourself have such a capacity.

"Yet Lin-chi went three times to ask Huang-po about the cardinal meaning of the Buddha Dharma. Each time he received painful blows from Huang-po's stick, and withdrew in tears. But he was still not liberated, so he set out to see Master Ta-yu. Huang-po did not offer him the least bit of help. After experiencing a significant understanding at Ta-yu's, Lin-chi returned to Huang-po and reported what Ta-yu had told him. Huang-po said, 'If that blabbermouth dares show his face around here, he'll get thirty blows from this stick of mine!'†

---

* A winged tiger would be even more formidable.

† In the *Record of Lin-chi* account (also *Blue Cliff Record*, Case 11), the head monk in Huang-po's assembly tells Lin-chi to ask Huang-po about the essential meaning of the Buddha Dharma. He goes to Huang-po three times, each time receiving blows, and he decides to leave the temple. The head monk tells Huang-po, "That young fellow who's been coming to you [Lin-chi] is a real Dharma vessel. If he comes and tells you he's going to leave, please use your expedient means in dealing with him. I'm sure that if he can continue to bore his way through, he will become a great tree that will provide cool shade to all the world." Huang-po suggests to Lin-chi that he might visit Ta-yu. At Ta-yu's temple, Lin-chi explained why he had left Huang-po, adding that he wasn't sure whether he was at fault or not. Ta-yu said, "Huang-po spared no effort. He treated you with utmost tenderness and grandmotherly kindness. Why do you talk about fault and no fault?" Lin-chi suddenly experienced enlightenment, and said, "There's not much to Huang-po's Dharma." Lin-chi returned to Huang-po and related what had happened at Ta-yu's place. Huang-po said, "I'd like to get hold of that fellow and give him a good dose of my stick!"

"An authentic Zen teacher like Huang-po is like a solitary peak towering forbiddingly into the sky. Today, you could comb the entire earth and not come up with a single person like him.

"The great teacher Hsuan-sha practiced arduously at Hsueh-feng's mountain hermitage, forgetting both food and sleep, but was unable to achieve a breakthrough of any kind. He left the temple with tears in his eyes, yet Hsueh-feng did not utter a single word to help him. At this point, you can be sure that one of today's teachers would have burdened him with a copious load of warm shit. As it turned out, when Hsuan-sha reached the foot of the mountain, he tripped and fell, and experienced a sudden realization.*

"It is like a melon grower harvesting his crop. He waits until their fragrance and flavor are at their peak before he goes into the melon patch. When he does, he has no need to carry a knife with him, only a bamboo basket. As the melons are fully ripe, the roots and tendrils and stems don't have to be cut; they have fallen away of themselves, leaving the fruit lying there on the ground. All he has to do is to go and pick them up.

"Don't you see? Hsuan-sha's enlightenment had fully matured just like those melons. It was a stinking fruit whose smell has wafted through the centuries. It has taken the lives of countless pilgrims who partook of it. Yet if Hsuan-sha's teacher Hsueh-feng had taken out his knife at the critical moment and stepped in and cut the stem, Hsuan-sha's Zen would never have been transmitted to future generations.

"Hsiang-yen trained at his teacher Kuei-shan's temple for many years without attaining even a glimpse of realization. Making up his mind to leave, he went to inform Kuei-shan with tears

---

* "One day Hsuan-sha took up a traveling pouch and left his temple to complete his training by visiting others teachers around the country. On the way down the mountain, he struck his toe hard on a rock. Blood appeared, but amid the intense pain he had an abrupt self-realization. 'This body does not exist. Where is the pain coming from?' he said, and promptly returned to Hsueh-feng" (*Essentials of Successive Records of the Lamp*, ch. 23).

in his eyes. Kuei-shan was completely unsympathetic. He didn't even look at him. Hsiang-yen traveled around, and then took up residence in a solitary hermitage. One day as he was sweeping, his broom threw a fragment of tile against a bamboo trunk. When the sound it made reached his ears, all the barriers suddenly fell away. He bathed and put on a clean robe. Facing in the direction of the Kuei-shan's temple, he offered some incense, performed three prostrations, and said, 'It is not my late teacher's religious virtue I revere. I revere the fact that he never once explained everything to me.'*

"A story is told about a monk who visited a Zen teacher and begged insistently for the principles of Zen. The teacher never paid him the least attention. The monk bided his time, waiting for a chance. Then one day he suddenly grabbed the master and hurried him to a secluded spot at the rear of the temple. He seated the master on the ground, spread out his prostration cloth before him, and performed three bows. 'I appeal to your great mercy and compassion,' he said. 'Please teach me the principles of Zen. Guide me to sudden enlightenment.' The master ignored him, enraging the monk, who flew into a fit of passion, sprang to his feet and, eyes red with anger, broke off a large branch from a nearby tree. Brandishing it, he stood in front of the master glaring scornfully at him. 'Priest!' he cried. 'If you don't tell me what you know, I am going to club you to death, cast your body down the cliff, and leave this place for good.' 'If you want to beat me to death, go ahead,' replied the master. 'I'm not going to teach you any Zen.' What a pity. This monk was obviously gifted with special capacity and spiritual strength. He had what it takes to penetrate the truth and perish into the great death. But notice what great caution and infinite care these ancient teachers exercised when leading students to self-awakening.

"Zen Master Tao-wu responded to a monk with the words, 'I won't say living. I won't say dead.' 'Why is that?' asked the monk.

---

* This generally follows the account in *Compendium of the Five Lamps*, ch. 9.

'I won't say. I won't say,' replied Tao-wu.* Tao-wu did not refuse to speak because he was reluctant to teach the monk. He was trying to protect him. Anything he had tried to teach him would only have harmed him. In fact, there is no way a teacher can teach the Buddha-patriarchs' marvelous, untransmittable Dharma to others. If a priest tells you he has liberated students by teaching them the Dharma, you can be sure of two things: he has not penetrated the source, and he is not a genuine Zen teacher. But for you what is essential is not whether he is genuine or not. What is essential is to pledge that you will never have anything to do with false teachers like him. Zen practice must be true and authentic, and it must be practiced under a true and authentic teacher. Could you call Zen sages like Bodhidharma, Hui-neng, Huang-po, Hsueh-feng, and Tao-wu dead otters? Would you characterize venerable teachers like Hui-k'o, Nan-yueh, Lin-chi, Hsuan-sha, and Hsiang-yen as dumb sheep?

"The exchanges that took place when teachers and students faced each other in the past did not necessarily dispense with words, but when the students asked questions, they were generally for the purpose of seeking instruction, receiving appraisal of an opinion, probing the other's insight, resolving a troubling problem, or making a personal assertion.† They were nothing like the half-baked encounters carried out by the pseudo-Zennists of

---

* Tao-wu Yuan-chih (769–835) and his student Chien-yuan went to pay their respects to someone who had passed away. Chien-yuan rapped on the coffin and said, "Living or dead?" Tao-wu replied, "I won't say living. I won't say dead." "Why won't you say?" asked Chien-yuan. "I won't say," replied Tao-wu. On their way back to the temple, Chien-yuan said, "If you don't say it right this minute, I'm going to hit you." "Hit me if you like," said Tao-wu. "I won't say living, I won't say dead." Chien-yuan hit him. When they were back at the temple, Tao-wu told Chien-yuan that the temple supervisor would give him a beating if he found out what he had done, and suggested that he go away for a while. Chien-yuan left and studied under Master Shih-shuang, attaining a realization upon hearing him repeat the words, "I won't say, I won't say" (*Records of the Lamp*, ch. 15. Also *Blue Cliff Record*, Case 55).

† These are some of the eighteen types of questions Zen students are said to ask their teachers. This is a formulation by Fen-yang (947–1024) in *The Eye of Men and Gods*.

today, with teachers who can't tell the difference between fine and coarse, between rock and precious jade, wading in from the outset, doing what they can to free up the cicada's wings,* spewing out great quantities of the worst imaginable filth and lacquering their students' faces with the stuff."

Boku said, "But there are students who reach satori by studying the words and teachings of the Buddha-patriarchs, and there are students who achieve great and final cessation by following a teacher's advice. By comparing them to inhabitants of Uttarakuru, people addicted to worldly wisdom and skillful words, to lump them with the dried buds and dead seeds of the Two Vehicles—wouldn't that mean they have no hope of ever attaining the Buddha's Dharma?† Surely there should be some expedient means within the Dharma that could be used to help them?"

I sighed and replied, "The ocean of true reality is boundless and profoundly deep. The Buddha Way is immeasurably vast. Some priests do nothing but seek fame and success until their dying day, never showing the slightest interest in the path of Zen or the Buddha's Dharma. Others become enthralled in literary pursuits or become addicted to sake or women, oblivious of the hell fires flaming up under their very noses. Some, relying on insignificant bits of knowledge they pick up, shamelessly try to deny the law of cause and effect, though woefully lacking any grasp of its working. Some find ways to attract large numbers of people to their temples, believing to the end of their days that this is proof

----

* *Free up the cicada's wings.* Although a similar expression is used in the *Book of Latter Han* to describe a lord showing great partiality to a favorite, here it refers to the statement made earlier about a teacher ruining a student's chances by stepping in to help the student prematurely.

† Two of eight difficult places or situations (*hachinan*) in which it is difficult for people to encounter a Buddha, hear him preach the Dharma, and attain liberation: *Uttarakuru*, the continent to the north of Mount Sumeru, because inhabitants enjoy lives of interminable pleasure; and being enthralled in the *worldly wisdom and skillful words* (*sechibensō*) of secular life. *Dried buds and dead seeds* (*shōge haishu*) is a term of reproach directed at followers of the Two Vehicles, who are said to have no possibility for attaining complete enlightenment.

of a successful teaching career. Now it is true that compared to fellows of that stamp, students who reach satori thanks to teachings they hear, or arrive at cessation thanks to advice they receive from a teacher, are indeed wonderful occurrences—as rare as lotus flowers blossoming amid a raging fire. They owe the attainment they achieve to the large store of karmic merit they accumulated in previous existences. Attainment such as theirs is not easy to achieve, it is not insignificant, and it must be valued and deeply respected.

"But for all that, there is still no getting around the fact that genuine practicers of Zen must once achieve *kenshō* (see their true nature), and bring the one great matter of their life to final cessation. Satori and final cessation are one thing, they are not two. But differences inevitably appear in the profundity of the satori and the strength or power that results from it. Let me try to describe this to you by explaining how progress toward final cessation, and lack of progress as well, appears in four types of students following their initial kenshō.

"First you have the students who, after engaging in genuine Zen practice for a long time until principles and wisdom are gradually exhausted, emotions and views eliminated, techniques and verbal resources used up, wither into a perfect and unflappable serenity, their bodies and minds completely dispassionate. Suddenly, satori comes. They are liberated. Like the phoenix that soars up from its golden cage. Like the crane that breaks free of its pen. Releasing their hands from the cliffside, they die the great death and are reborn into life anew. These are students who have thoroughly penetrated, who have bored through all forms and penetrated all sounds and can see their self-nature as clearly as if it was in the palm of their hand. After painstakingly working their way through the final barrier koans set up by the patriarchal teachers, their minds, in one single vigorous effort, abruptly transform. Such students are possessed of deep discernment and innate ability that enables them to enter liberation at a single blow from the iron hammer. They are foremost among all the outstanding seeds and buds of our school. The only thing they lack is the personal confirmation of a genuine teacher.

"Next there are students who move forward in their koan practice until they gain strength that is almost mature. Thanks to a word or phrase of the Buddha-patriarchs or perhaps some advice from a good friend, they suddenly achieve kenshō, breakthrough into satori. Let us call them "initial penetrators." Their penetration is complete in some areas, but not in others. They have a sure grasp of Dharma utterances of the *hosshin* type, words such as 'White waves rise on the mountain peak. Red dust dances at the bottom of a well.'* But when they come up against the vital matter of the more advanced koans, they are as the deaf and dumb. As long as they are sitting quietly doing zazen, the principle of true reality is perfectly clear and the true form of things immediately manifested. But the minute they return into the everyday world and begin dealing with some worrisome matter or other, this clarity disappears. It withers away amid the constant disparity between the meditative and active aspects of their life, their inner wisdom and their ordinary activity.

"There are also students who spend much time and effort tenaciously engaged in hidden practice and secret activity until, one day, owing to the guidance of a teacher, they finally are able to reach a state of firm belief. We can call them the believers. They understand without any doubt about essential principles such as the self-nature being apart from birth-and-death and the true body transcending past and present. However, the great and es-

---

* In the system of koan study that developed in later Hakuin Zen, *hosshin* or Dharmakaya koans are used in the beginning stages of practice (see *Zen Dust*, 46–50). The lines Hakuin quotes here are not found in the *Poems of Han-shan* (*Han-shan shih*). They are attributed to Han-shan in *Compendium of the Five Lamps* (ch. 15, chapter on Tung-shan Mu-ts'ung): "The master ascended the teaching seat and said, 'Han-shan said that "Red dust dances at the bottom of the well. / White waves rise on the mountain peaks. / The stone woman gives birth to a stone child. / Fur on the tortoise grows longer by the day." If you want to know the Bodhi-mind, all you have to do is to behold these sights.'" The lines are included in a Japanese edition of the work published during Hakuin's lifetime.

sential matter of the Zen school is beyond them. They can't see it even dimly in their dreams. They are not only powerless to save others, they are unable to bring their own liberation to completion either.

"It was for students of the second and third type, who are engaged in the practice that one of the ancients described as gradual practice followed by sudden realization, that the step-by-step process set forth in the *Ten Oxherding Pictures* and the precious norms laid out in the Five Ranks were devised.* If they continue to practice assiduously, it is possible for them to advance into the ranks of those who have fully penetrated.

"Finally, there are students who come to believe in a teaching they hear, accepting it as true even though it has no more substance than a shadow, and cling fast to it until the day they die. These are the hoodwinked. They have been bamboozled by words, yet continue to follow them scrupulously. They have not penetrated the wondrous and perfect self-nature that exists within their own minds, nor do they understand that the true reality of all forms in the external world is no-form. They follow arbitrarily the movements of their own minds and perceptions, confounding them for manifestations of truth, picking up various plausible notions that they begin spouting to everyone they meet: 'It's like a precious mirror that reflects unerringly a Chinese or a foreigner in all their perfections and imperfections when they come before it. It's like a *mani* gem set out on a tray reflecting all shapes and all colors without a single trace remaining behind. Your own mind is like that intrinsically. There is no need to refine it. No need to attain it through practice.' Having no doubt that they themselves belong to the ranks of the genuine priests who have achieved final cessation, if they hear of someone engaging in

---

* The *Ten Ox-herding Pictures* are a series of illustrations, accompanied by verses, showing the Zen student's progress to final enlightenment. The *Five Ranks*, comprising five modes of the particular and universal, are a teaching device formulated by Tung-shan of the Sōto tradition.

secret training and hidden practice, they fall about clutching their bellies in paroxysms of laughter.*

"*Ahh!* They are plausible, all too plausible. The trouble is, having not yet broken free of that indestructible adamantine cage, they wander ever deeper into a forest of thorn, acknowledging a thief as their own son. It is because of this that the great master Ch'ang-sha said, 'The reason practicers fail to attain the Way is because they confound the ordinary working of their minds for truth. Although *that* has been the source of birth and death from the beginning of time, the fools insist on calling it their "original self."' They are like Temple Supervisor Tse before he visited master Fa-yen, like Chen Tien-hsiung before his encounter with Huang-lung.⁵

"We might compare the ones who have fully penetrated this matter to a prince of royal blood, an heir apparent to the throne. Born of aristocratic stock, with intrinsic nobility that has no need of the benefits others must obtain through practice, he is universally acclaimed in all lands, and brings peace and prosperity to the world. The initial penetrators (those who have attained a partial realization) and the believers (those who have achieved a firm conviction) are like the Chinese emperors Liu Hsiu and Su Tsung,† who strove to establish their authority, but being surrounded on all sides by rebellious tribes who refused them tribute, could never afford to neglect thoughts of armament and defense. Those I termed the 'hoodwinked' resemble rebels like Wang Mang and An Lu-shan,‡ both of whom proclaimed themselves emperor but were unable to maintain their grip on wealth and power.

---

* *Records of the Lamp*, ch. 10.

† Liu Hsiu (first century) was a descendant of Western Han royalty who defeated the usurper Wang Mang and established the Eastern Han dynasty. Emperor Su Tsung (eighth century) regained the throne that his father had occupied before being been driven from power.

‡ Wang Mang (c. 45 BC–23 AD), a powerful official of the Western Han dynasty, and rebellious T'ang general An Lu-shan (c. 703–757) both attempted to usurp the throne and declare themselves emperor.

"As the priest Nan-t'ang declared, 'You must see your self-nature as clearly as if you are looking at it in the palm of your hand, so that each and every thing becomes perfectly and unmistakably your own wondrously profound field of Dharma truth.'* It is a matter demanding the greatest care. For this reason, the Zen school declares: 'Clarifying your self but not the things before your eyes gets you only half, and clarifying the things before your eyes but not your self gets you only half as well. You must know that if you press on, the time will come when it will all be yours.'† It also says, 'If students of the Way want to confirm whether they have truly entered realization, they must examine their mind thoroughly both in the activities of everyday life and amid the tranquillity of zazen: In the realm of active life is the mind different from the way it is during meditation? Do they hesitate or have any trouble in penetrating the various meanings of the words of the Buddha-patriarchs? Someone who has thoroughly grasped the marrow of the Buddha-patriarchs could not possibly fail to understand their words and sayings.'‡

"Therefore to patricians engaged in boring into the secret depths, I say: 'Those of you who have already achieved kenshō should place yourselves in the hands of a genuine teacher, and follow and seek occasional advice from seasoned monks with deep experience as you continue the day-to-day refining of your attainment, concentrating yourself single-mindedly on exhausting the secret mysteries and penetrating completely through the bottom-

---

* Nan-t'ang is Ta-sui Yuan-ching (1065–1135), an heir of Fa-yen Wen-i. The quotation appears in *The Eye of Men and Gods*, ch. 1. Hakuin, who liked to quote it, included it in *Redolence from the Cold Forest*, a selection of quotations from Zen texts he made for students that was first published in 1769 by Tōrei.

† In *Detailed Study of the Fundamental Principles of the Five Houses of Zen* (*Goke sanshō yōro mon*) Tōrei explains the Zen terms "gains you half" (literally, "raises it up halfway") and "gaining it all" as follows: "'Raising it totally up' refers to grasping the treasury of the Buddha's true Dharma eye and making it one's own activity. 'Raising it partially up' refers to not having yet achieved this total attainment; to having achieved only half, or only one tenth" (HOZ, 7:157–58).

‡ No source has been found for this quotation; it may have been written by Hakuin.

less source. Those who have not yet achieved kenshō should be grappling with one of those meaningless koans. You might concentrate on Lin-chi's "person who is standing right here listening to me preach."* Bore into him at all times, whether you are in a quiet place doing zazen or actively engaged in the activities of everyday life. Grasp the person who is engaged in this nonstop seeking. Where is he? What is the mind that at this very moment seeks him? Entering ever deeper into these matters, when mind has ceased to function, when words and phrases have been exhausted, attack it from the sides, attack it from the front and from the rear, keep gnawing away at it, gnawing, gnawing, until there is no place left to gnaw.'

"You may feel as though you are clinging perilously to a steel barrier towering before you, as though you are gagging on a soup of wood shavings, as though you are grasping at clouds of green smoke, or probing a sea of red mist. When all your skills have been used up, all your verbal resources and reason utterly exhausted, if you do not falter or attempt to understand and just keep boring steadily inward, you will experience the profound joy of knowing for yourself whether the water is cold or warm. The practice of Zen requires you to just press forward with continuous, unwavering effort. If you only exert yourself every other day, like a person experiencing a periodic malarial fit, you will never reach enlightenment, not even with the passage of endless *kalpas*.

"There is a sea beach only several hundred paces from my native village of Hara. Suppose someone is troubled because he doesn't know the taste of seawater, and decides to sample some. He sets out down to the beach, but stops and comes backs before he has gone even a hundred steps. He starts out again, this time returning after taking only ten steps. He will never know the

---

* "If you cease your mind from its constant strivings, you are no different from the Buddhas and patriarchs. You want to grasp the Buddhas and patriarchs, but you yourself, the person listening to my teaching at this moment, are the Buddha-patriarch" (see *Record of Lin-chi*, 23).

taste of seawater that way, will he? Yet if he keeps going straight ahead and he doesn't turn back, even if he lives far inland in a landlocked province such as Shinano, Kai, Hida, or Mino, he will eventually reach the ocean. By dipping his finger in the ocean and licking it, he will know instantly the taste of seawater the world over, because it has the same taste everywhere, in India, in China, in the southern or northern seas.

"It is the same for Dharma patricians exploring the secret depths. Proceeding straight ahead, pushing steadily forward, they bore into their minds with unbroken effort, never slackening or regressing. When the breakthrough suddenly arrives, they penetrate their own nature, the nature of others, the nature of sentient beings, the nature of evil passions and enlightenment, the nature of the Buddha-nature, the nature of the gods, the Bodhisattva-nature, the nature of sentient and nonsentient beings, the craving-ghost nature, the contentious spirit nature, the beast nature—they are all of them grasped in a single instant of thought. The great matter of their religious quest is completely and utterly resolved, and there is nothing left for them to do. They are freed from birth and death. What a thrilling moment it is!

"But a matter of particularly bowel-wrenching intensity still remains, and that is the very heart of the matter that has been personally transmitted from one Zen patriarch to another and carefully maintained without alteration or diminution to the present day. Even students who have broken free of the adamantine cage and negotiated their way through the thicket of razor-edged briars, unless they also encounter a genuine teacher along the way and receive his personal instruction, they will be unable to grasp this matter even in their dreams. Why is that? Because from the very beginning, the sage teachers have been like celestial dragons grasping the precious night-shining gem tightly in their claws, not allowing turtles, sea urchins, fish, or other inhabitants of the deep to observe it. They are like venerable dragons, masters of the clouds and rain, whose essential role is totally beyond the ken of frogs and earthworms and other denizens of the waters. I speak of Zen masters like Nan-ch'uan, Ch'ang-sha, Huang-po, Su-shan, Tz'u-ming, Shao-shih, Chen-ching, Hsi-keng, Daiō, and Wu-hsueh [Mugaku Sogen]."

Now, I don't want you to think I've been spinning out these stories to impress you with my insights and learning. I heard them thirty years ago from my teacher Shōju Rōjin. He was always lamenting the fading of the Zen transmission. It now hung, he said, by a few thin strands. These concerns of his became deeply engrained in my bones and marrow. They have been forever etched in my liver and bowels. But being afraid that if I spoke out I would have trouble making people believe what I said, I have for a long time kept my silence. I have constantly regretted that you, Mr. Ishii, and the two or three laymen who study here with you, were never able to meet Master Shōju. For that reason I have taken up my brush and rashly scribbled down all these verbal complexities on paper. Having finished, I find my entire back streaming with profuse sweat, partly in shame, partly in gratitude. My only request is that after reading this letter, you will pass it on to the fire god with instructions to consign it to his eternal storehouse. *Ha. Ha.*

HOZ, 2:166–79

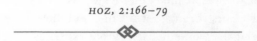

Although a handful of friends and fellow villagers had been studying at Shōin-ji during the first decade of Hakuin's incumbency, Ishii was one of the earliest of the lay students from outside Hara village, another indication that the unsung young Zen teacher's reputation had spread to other parts of the province, and probably beyond as well.

Ishii became an important patron of the impoverished temple, and later helped fund a number of Hakuin's building and publishing projects. Most of the half-dozen or so other letters that Hakuin wrote Ishii are expressions of gratitude for donations and gifts received, or services rendered. In one letter, Hakuin thanks Ishii for a large supply of cut tobacco that Ishii had sent to fuel Hakuin's well-known pipe habit. A long verse Hakuin sent Ishii, one of the most remarkable pieces in the *Poison Blossoms* collection, is an expression of thanks for two large boulders Ishii had donated to the Shōin-ji gardens. The verse is filled with vivid images describing the progress of the unwieldy objects as they are rafted down from the foothills of Mount Fuji, landed on the coast near Hara village, then manhandled overland to Shōin-ji, making us feel the excitement and impatience Hakuin experienced as he awaited their arrival (a translation is found in *The Religious Art of Zen Master Hakuin*, 129–30).

Although remarks of a personal nature are scattered throughout this letter, reminding the reader that it is indeed a letter, it is for the most part a series of discourses that Hakuin apparently composed to express his gratitude to Ishii for having taken care of one of his monks, an attendant named Boku, who had fallen ill. Hakuin presents these as a word-for-word account of the instructions he gave Boku upon the attendant's return from Ishii's residence, although the message they contain seems intended primarily for the recipient of the letter, Layman Ishii himself.

In content and style, the letter is an early example of the expositions of koan Zen—so-called Dharma words—that Hakuin sent to individual students throughout his life, and more or less indistinguishable from the works he later wrote expressly for publication. He criticizes contemporary Zen teachers who, by giving in to feelings of pity and offering untimely advice to struggling students, end up preventing them from carrying their practice through to completion, ruining their chance of ever reaching the release of final enlightenment. Hakuin contrasts this with the method used by himself, as well as the great Zen figures of the past, of refusing to give any such help until the critical moment is reached and the student is ready to benefit from a teacher's timely intervention. The classic image is that of a mother hen pecking an egg at the exact same time the baby chick is pecking from within the shell to make its way out. Hakuin also stresses the importance of the post-satori training that begins after the original kenshō or satori is attained.

This letter is perhaps the earliest written enunciation of these themes, preceding by almost a decade their initial appearance in print, in *Talks Introductory to Lectures on the Record of Hsi-keng* (1743). Several passages in the present letter appear almost verbatim in the printed version of the *Talks*, and since the preface to that work states that Hakuin stayed at Ishii's private retreat for over a month while he was drafting the *Talks*, it is not difficult to imagine Ishii urging his friend to include portions of this letter in the *Talks* so they might be shared with others.

Attendant Boku's unspecified complaint may have been purely physical in nature, but it may also have been practice related, perhaps even a touch of the "Zen sickness" that had troubled Hakuin during his early years of training. The identity of this attendant monk is uncertain. The most logical candidate, Suiō Genro (1717–89), Hakuin's successor at Shōin-ji, who as a young monk used the name [E]Boku, has to be rejected, since Suiō's study at Shōin-ji did not begin until 1746, twelve years after this letter was written. The Hakuin specialist Rikugawa Taiun identified Boku as "a monk from western Japan who fell ill while training at Shōin-ji and subsequently left the temple" (*Detailed Biography of Priest Hakuin*, p. 252), but offered no details. An anonymous annotator inscribed another hypothesis in a copy of *Poison Blossoms from a Thicket of Thorn*: "Attendant Boku is not an actual person. The master seems to be using the name in an allegorical sense for a story on the oxherding theme" [*Boku* translates literally as "herder"]. Again, it would be entirely in character for Hakuin, well-known for his yarn spinning, to create a fictitious character of this sort, but we have no way of confirming this supposition.

Despite its length this letter was never printed as an independent work, but it was included in the section entitled *Sho* (Letters) in *Poison Blossoms from a Thicket of Thorn*.

NOTES TO CHAPTER 3

1. The following story appears in *Records of the Lamp*: "Asked by a monk, 'How should a monk comport himself throughout the twenty-four hours?' Ts'ao-shan replied, 'As if passing through a region filled with poisonous insects (*ku*), not letting a single drop of water pass his lips.'" Understanding of this dialogue requires an explanation of the meanings attached to the word *ku* (translated "poisonous insects"). In *Tso-chuan* (*Tso's Narrative*), the oldest of the Chinese narrative histories, we read: "Chao-meng asked, 'What is the meaning of the word *ku*?' The physician answered, 'It refers to anything that causes excess, agitation, delusion, or trouble. The ideograph *ku* represents a jar filled with insects. The grub that insinuates its way into grain stock is also a destructive *ku* insect. In the *Book of Changes*, women who seduce men and the wind that topples trees in the mountains are also described as *ku*.'" The word also occurs in the records of the Sung master Hsu-t'ang: "There was a custom in the Fu-chien District prevalent since the T'ang dynasty of throwing various insects such as venomous snakes, lizards, and spiders together, waiting until only one of them remained alive, and then mixing its venom and blood into a potion to ward off evil spirits or to kill people by casting a magic spell on them" (*Dictionary of Zen Sayings*, 121). In the Yuan dynasty medical treatise *I-fang tai ch'eng lun*: "It is said that people living in the mountain fastnesses of Min-kuang put three kinds of poisonous insects into a container and bury it in the ground on the fifth day of the fifth month. They allow the insects to devour each other until only one remains, called a *ku*. They extract the poison from this insect, and when they want to harm someone, they put it into their food or drink."

2. *Dead otter* (*shi-katsudatsu*) Zen, according to a glossary of Zen terms dating from shortly after Hakuin's time, refers to quietist practices employed in the Sōtō school's silent illumination Zen. The Sung master Ta-hui speaks of "bands of miscreant shavepates who have not yet opened their own eyes, but who nonetheless strive to lead others into a state of quietistic stagnation in the realm of the blind otters" (*Ta-hui's*

Letters, third Letter to Cheng Shih-lang). In his work *Kōrōju*, the Tokugawa scholar-priest Mujaku Dōchū concludes that the term does not refer to an otter (he suggests instead a red-haired, wolflike animal): "Although I have been unable to discover precisely what this creature is, it is said to 'play possum,' pretending to be dead to draw people near so it can seize and devour them."

The term appears in a number of Hakuin's own works; the following are three examples.

1. "You often find students who lack the determination to place themselves under a teacher and study the Great Way and have no true understanding of the perfection of the self-nature within them, pointlessly trying to empty minds that are caught up in birth-and-death, and ending up like incense burners lying forgotten in the back of an old mausoleum; and if later they do decide they want to attain the Way, they spend all their time in silent sitting. Such people are dead otters this year, they're dead otters next year, and fifteen years later, with white hair and yellow teeth, bad eyes and failing ears, they're still dead otters. Should one of them later acquire students and the students followed their teacher's instructions obediently, accepting silent sitting as ultimate and devoting themselves to practicing it, then if five of them get together and practiced, you would have five dead otters; if there were eight, you would have eight dead otters. Not only would they never be able to benefit others, but they would never be able to save themselves either. No matter how many years they spent sitting silently like this in weed-infested nooks and corners, they would always remain incapable of breaking out of the dark cavern of their old views" (*A Record of Sendai's Comments on the Poems of Cold Mountain*, ch. 1, 61–62).

2. "Not even Buddhas and patriarchs can cure misunderstanding as gross as this. Every day these people seek out places of peace and quiet, but they're dead otters today, they'll be dead otters tomorrow, they'll be dead otters even after endless kalpas have passed. Utterly useless to themselves or to anyone else. The Buddha compared people like this to mangy foxes. Angulimala despised them as people with the intelligence of earthworms. Vimalakirti placed them among the blasted buds and rotten seeds. They are the ones Ch'ang-sha said were unable to leap from the tip of a hundred-foot pole, the ones Lin-chi said lived at the bottom of a deep black pit" (*Oradegama; Zen Master Hakuin*, 115).

3. "These people will tell you that there is no Buddha to seek and there is no Way to practice other than dwelling in a state of no-self, no-thought, and no-mind and doing nothing, good or bad. They themselves

doze their lives away doing zazen, their minds devoid of wisdom or understanding. This is a state that from long in the past has been described as a deep dark pit, or as the realm of dead otters" (HHZ, 6:254–56).

3. *Dumb sheep Zen* is said to refer to monks who are unable to tell good from bad and without sense enough to correct their mistakes. Hakuin generally applies the term to "do-nothing" Zennists, that is to say, those who do not actively seek kenshō through koan study.

4. *Box-shrub Zen.* The growth of the box tree or shrub (*tsuge no ki*) is so slow that it was said to sometimes cease growing altogether, and to even shrink in size during intercalary years. Ta-hui uses the term to describe students who not only cease making headway in their practice, but by attaching to satori actually regress (*Ta-hui's General Talks*, ch. 2). *Carry the day* roughly paraphrases the expression "bare the left arm," referring to a gesture that is made to show one has been won over and will support another's cause. "Marquis Chou Po, before setting out to subjugate the Lu family, issued an order to his army, saying, 'Those who are for the Lu family bare their right arms, those for the Liu family bare their left arms!' They all bared their left arms, and he was able to launch an attack and gain the upper hand" (*Records of the Grand Historian*, 280).

5. A monk named Hsuan-tse was temple steward in the brotherhood of Zen Master Fa-yen Wen-i. The master said, "How long have you been here with me?" "It's been three years now," he replied. "As a member of the younger generation that is responsible for carrying on the transmission, why haven't you ever asked me about the Dharma?" "To tell the truth," Tse replied, "I already entered the Dharma realm of peace and comfort when I was studying with Zen Master Ch'ing-feng." "By what words did you attain that realm?" Fa-yen asked. Tse replied, "I once asked Ch'ing-feng, 'What is the self of a Buddhist monk?' He answered, 'Ping-ting t'ung-tzu [the fire god] comes for fire.'" "Those are fine words," said Fa-yen. "But you probably didn't understand them." Tse said, "I understand them to mean that since Ping-ting is a fire deity, looking for fire with fire would be like looking for the self with the self." "Just as I thought," said Fa-yen. "You didn't understand. If that were the extent of the Buddha Dharma, the transmission could not have lasted down to the present day." Indignant, Hsuan-tse left the monastery, but on his way down the mountain he reflected, "The master is known

throughout the land as a great teacher. He has over five hundred disciples. There must be some merit to his words." Returning penitently to the monastery, he performed his bows before Fa-yen, and asked, "What is the self of a Buddhist monk?" "Ping-ting t'ung-tzu comes for fire," the master replied. At the words, Hsuan-tse attained great enlightenment (*Records of the Lamp*, ch. 17).

Chen Tien-hsiun is Ts'ui-yen K'o-chen (n.d.), a Dharma heir of Tz'u-ming (Shih-shuang Ch'u-yuan, 986–1039) who acquired the nickname "Breast-beater Chen" because on attaining enlightenment he elatedly began pummeling his chest. "As a student living on intimate terms with Tz'u-ming, Chen grew convinced of his superior talents. But while accompanying Chen on a summer practice retreat, Tz'u-ming's senior disciple Attendant Shan (later Huang-lung Hui-nan [1002–69]), soon discerned that Chen's realization was incomplete. One day when they were walking in the mountain, Shan picked up a pebble, put it on top of a large boulder, and said, "If you can come up with a good turning word for this, I will believe that you truly understand Master Tz'u-ming." Chen, glancing left and right, seemed about to make a reply, when Shan gave a loud shout. "You still haven't even overcome mental discrimination! You're hesitant and unresolved! How can you ever hope to know Tz'u-ming's inner meaning?" Chen was thoroughly ashamed, realizing the truth of Shan's words. He immediately returned and resumed his practice with Tz'u-ming, and was finally able to achieve complete enlightenment (*Compendium of the Five Lamps*, ch. 12).

4

To the Priest of Ryōtan-ji

This letter from Hakuin's mid-fifties shows him accepting an invitation from a temple in neighboring Tōtōmi Province to lecture on a Chinese Zen text, *Precious Lessons of the Zen School*. He was in the middle of his second decade of teaching at Shōin-ji, having two years before completed a highly successful meeting that had established his reputation as one of the foremost Zen teachers in the country, and had also attracted a large assembly of trainees to the temple. Hakuin now seems more willing to accept requests from other temples to conduct lecture meetings.

It was a convention to address letters of this type to the attendant rather than to the head priest himself. Hakuin also mentions that this is the third time he has received a letter from the attendant, alluding to a famous episode from the Three Kingdoms period of Chinese history when the warlord Liu Pei paid three visits in person to the wise scholar Chu-ko Liang to solicit his aid in establishing his reign. The "three visits" became proverbial for the sincerity one should evince when seeking someone's help.

[HAKUIN] EKAKU makes nine bows and with the greatest respect sends this to the attendant of the Head Priest of Ryōtan-ji.

Jikō Anjū has come and delivered another letter. I read it while we were having a cup of tea, and was glad to learn that you are in good health. You should not worry about me. I am doing fine, still spending much of my time in the garden checking to see how my eggplants are coming along.

It is the third letter you have written and the third time your emissary has made a trip all this way to deliver it to me. I have been extremely negligent in failing to respond to your requests, but the reason I have not answered is because I find the responsibility involved in accepting such an invitation so intimidating. I know only too well how dim my prospects are for carrying it out. A hedge-parson such as myself is totally unfit for such a momentous task. It's like trying to make an earthworm roar like a dragon, or make a jackass perform tricks like a fine riding horse.

Much closer to home in your own Tōtōmi Province, there are any number of excellent priests, all of them formidable dragons of the Zen seas. What could a shrimp like me accomplish at such a meeting? I break into a nervous sweat just thinking about it. And we are talking about Ryōtan-ji (Dragon-Pool Temple), one of the most celebrated temples in all of Tōtōmi and Mikawa. Even gods and demons tremble in fear when they hear of the dragons lurking in that poisonous pool. The prospect is so terrifying it sets my knees to shaking. In any case, that is the reason I have delayed so long in sending you my answer. Accept my most profuse apologies.

Some time ago Daitō Oshō made the long trip here to Shōin-ji with Senior Monk Zentsū to convey the sentiments of the temple priests in your area, including the abbot of Seiken-ji. They presented their case skillfully, with admirable powers of persuasion. They informed me of your feelings on the matter and of the enthusiastic support shown by other members of the monastic and lay community. It seems everyone is very eager for the talks to be held.

Please understand the reason for my obstinacy. Why, I haven't a single person around to give the kind of advice and assistance I would need to carry out such an assignment. If a priest of my inexperience were to agree to your request and attempt the task you have set, I would only make myself a general laughingstock for not realizing the limits of my ability. On the other hand, were I to give in to my personal feelings, refuse the invitation, and retreat into my carapace, I would no doubt always be reproached for turning my back on the desires and expectations of all those who supported the idea. Thus confused in mind and decrepit in body, this indolent old monk now finds himself forced into a very tight corner.

Things being so, in autumn (the seventh month), after the summer retreat, I will set out from here for Tōtōmi with a large contingent of my assembly. On arrival at Ryōtan-ji I will pay my respects to you, and then do what I can to respond in my own very small way to the love and devotion you have shown for the Dharma in promoting this event. The monks who accompany me will do their share, too—hulling rice, drawing water, gathering fuel, and so forth. As for the rest, I can only entrust it to your sympathetic hands.

We have been having a truly scorching summer, so please take good care of your health.

HZB, 168–69

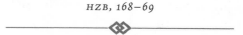

Ryōtan-ji was a large and important Rinzai temple located at Iinoya village in Tōtōmi Province (now incorporated into the city of Hamamatsu in present-day Shizuoka Prefecture). It would have been about an eighty-mile trip west from Shōin-ji in Hara village, traveling along the Tōkaidō Road. The Ryōtan-ji abbot at the time was Dokusō Hōun (n.d.), about whom little is known. Senior Monk Zentsū (Zentsū Shuso) is probably the person later known as Kanjū Etsū (1699–1777), a Ryōtan-ji monk who had gone to Shōin-ji to study with Hakuin. He later succeeded Dokusō at Ryōtan-ji.

Nothing is known of either Jikō Anjū (Master of Jikō Hermitage) or Daitō Oshō (Priest Daitō). Seiken-ji was a large Myōshin-ji temple in Okitsu on the coast west of Hara; Shōin-ji was a small branch temple under its jurisdiction.

The *Chronological Biography* entry for 1742 refers to this meeting without adding much to what is already known: "During the summer the master acceded to a request from Ryōtan-ji and went to Tōtōmi Province to lecture on *Precious Lessons of the Zen School.*"

But we learn from Tōrei's draft manuscript of the *Chronological Biography* that the meeting was actually held in autumn to commemorate the 650th anniversary of the temple's founding, and that "a hundred monks accompanied Hakuin on the journey to Tōtōmi to take part in the meeting." *Precious Lessons of the Zen School* is a late twelfth-century work Hakuin frequently used as a text for lectures. It is made up of words, instructions, and episodes of eminent Chinese Zen priests.

This letter was first published in 2009 in *Hakuin's Zen Painting and Calligraphy.*

5

To Attendant Kō

LETTER 5, C. 1743–47

In this letter, Hakuin urges a monk named Kō, a young man who had recently served as his personal attendant, to return to Shōin-ji so Hakuin can help him bring his training to a successful conclusion. This letter is no doubt typical of the correspondence Hakuin kept up with senior students around the country, some of whom left at the completion of their training, and some of whom were obliged by circumstances to cut short their training and return to their home temples.

Typically, Hakuin would offer these students words of encouragement, and keep them up-to-date on the latest doings at Shōin-ji. But Hakuin's primary concern, seen throughout the letters, seems to have been keeping tabs on his students' progress. He often issued warnings to those who had achieved an initial kenshō, cautioning them to be aware of the dangers of lapsing into the "do-nothing" passivity of "silent illumination Zen," which would occur if they did not continue to devote themselves to their koan practice.

THE NEW PRIEST at Daikei-ji dropped your two letters off when he passed through here. I read them through several times. I was glad to learn you are in good health and earnestly engaged in your practice. Life here at Shōin-ji is poor and simple as always, but not one of my veteran monks has left for other parts. There are now nearly seventy men in the assembly. Monks Chū, Yaku, Gū, Goku, Sha, Rin, and Ro, Chō and Tō, are still here. Mon and Shō are intermittently in attendance, and Ryū and Soku continue to bore steadily forward.* Everyone is resolutely bent on refining and polishing their attainment. They endure the bitter cold and other privations without complaint, never slackening their efforts at all.

At the beginning of spring, seven or eight seasoned monks of superior ability arrived. We accepted them into the brotherhood. Everyone gathered together and engaged in "pure talk" about the Way. I found that they were splendid religious seekers, of the greatest ability, sincere and generous, humble and compassionate, possessed of strength, courage, and wisdom. For a doddery old monk like me, it was a joy that would be hard to match. You were the only one missing. When you finish your lectures on the *Fu-chiao p'ien* (*A Treatise to Assist the Teachings*),† be sure that you bend your steps back here and lend some help to your decrepit old teacher.

I never could understand why you had to run off by yourself to a remote province thousands of leagues from here. Never tying up with a single good companion or teacher. Never acquiring the slightest spiritual benefit from it whatsoever. Just wasting your time—your most precious asset—and for what? People tell me, "He just shifts from one beautiful spot to another." "He's well settled, has plenty of food and good lodgings." "He's looking for a place where he can live out the rest of his days." "He goes and performs devotions at temples and shrines." If that is indeed the

---

* The only monks in this list about whom anything of significance is known are Chū: Bunchū (n.d.); Yaku: Gen'yaku (n.d); Tō: Reigen Etō (1721–85); and Ryū: Ishin Eryū (1720–69).

† This is a work by the Rinzai teacher Fo-jih Ch'i-sung (1007–72) criticizing the anti-Buddhist thought of Han Yu and others, and attempting to show the harmony of Confucian and Buddhist teachings.

ent of your religious aspiration, you are a truly doubtful monk. They also say that what you really want is to spend three, five, maybe seven years ensconced quietly in some solitary retreat where you can devote yourself freely to nurturing and maturing your attainment. If that is your intention, it is equally misguided. For someone in your present situation, now is the time to make certain that the seedling is nurtured and brought fully into flower. Why would you want to cling mulishly to this "withered sitting" style of Zen, hunkered dubiously down in some hinterland, turning your mind to ash, extinguishing thoughts and feelings, blinding your wisdom, blundering your life away? Time, you will find, passes by at great speed. And you go on ludicrously wasting your time, like a young girl sewing up piles of diapers and buying mortars and pestles and other kitchen equipment before she's even found a husband. What a terrible, shameful waste!

It's said you should seek friends who are superior to yourself. The outstanding seekers of the past were determined from the moment they took up their traveling staffs and set out on pilgrimage to locate a teacher of superior attainment, someone who would be able to help them bring their training to completion. Once that teacher was found, they invariably remained with him to receive the benefit of his personal influence.

Today's students are not like that. Lacking the clear eye of wisdom, they linger about worshipping the dust of worthless, toothless old bonzes, they dawdle aimlessly over here, poke blindly around over there, roaming this way and then that way, not stopping for a moment. They are ridiculous. In the past, Bodhidharma, a man possessed of profound innate wisdom, stayed with his teacher for forty years. Wise priests like the Ferryman Monk and Yang-ch'i stayed and served their teachers Yueh-shan and Tz'u-ming up until the day they passed away. Only then did they leave and engage in solitary retreats by themselves. The same was true of Ma-tsu's eighty Dharma heirs, and of superior priests like the "three Buddhas"—Fo-kuo, Fo-chien, and Fo-yen—who studied under Wu-tsu Fa-yen. They all stayed with their teacher until they had completed their training.

The priest Chueh-fan Hui-hung left his teacher Chen-ching too soon, thinking to himself, "I've made off with Chen-ching's precious green rug." Ta-hui later rebuked him for those words. "Chueh-fan attained something," he wrote, "but there was also something he didn't attain."* Tou-shuai Ts'ung-yueh also left Chen-ching too soon, thinking, "I've smashed to dust the secret jewel Chen-ching received from his teacher Huang-lung." Only later, when Senior Monk Ch'ing-su took him to task for those words, did he finally understand that the temple hall also had an inner sanctum. "It must be," he realized, "that I am still unaware that I have contracted an illness from my teachers. Why is that? Because as I try to work for the sake of others, I find I am unable to pour forth everything I have inside me."†

Genuine patricians of the secret depths, in order to be able to undertake the teaching of the true Dharma, enter the training hall, mingle with the brotherhood, sit silently at the rear of the hall, work on koans they haven't yet passed, engage in practice sessions with their comrades, and in this way gradually accumulate Dharma assets and mature into great Dharma vessels. They are

---

* Chueh-fan Hui-hung (1071–1128). The comments by Ta-hui Tsung-kao are quoted in the *Record of Hsu-t'ang* (ch. 4): "Chueh-fan had a satori while he was with Chen-ching (K'o-wen), but soon after that, circumstances arose that obliged him to leave. He left his teacher much too soon, and because of that, although he attained something, there was also something he did not attain." In Zen records *precious green rug* appears as a metaphor for one's most treasured possession. It is based on a story in the *Annals of the Chin State* (*Chin-shu*, ch. 80): When thieves entered the study where a scholar was sleeping and were about to make off with all his belongings, he called out from a corner of the dark room, "Burglars, please do not take the green rug. It is an old and precious family heirloom." The burglars were so startled that they bolted out the door and were seen no more.

† Tou-shuai Ts'ung-yueh (1044–91). Hakuin relates the story on which this is based in *Talks Introductory to Lectures on the Record of Hsi-keng* (*Essential Teachings of Zen Master Hakuin*, 95–96).

then able to uplift the great teaching, raise the Dharma torch, and lead others to liberation, sustaining the life-thread of wisdom and requiting the enormous debt they owe the Buddhas and patriarchs. Such is the ancient, time-honored reality of the groves of Zen.

Think about it. You will have plenty of time later to hide yourself in the boondocks and investigate the matter of your self, but only limited time remains to me in which to sit in these broken-down old chambers, laughing and chatting with my monks. I just wait, counting the days and nights off on my fingers, until you return. After I leave on my final pilgrimage, you will be free to go anywhere you want, hide yourself from the world, if that is what you desire. It won't be too late then.

On the other hand, if you want to forget your fundamental purpose, turn your back on your old teacher's wishes, and follow in the footsteps of failures like Shan-hsien of Hsueh-t'ou or Sheng-chueh of Tung-shan,* even if you bury yourself in some mountain fastness, deserted moorland, or empty valley, or hide away inside a cave and remain there for three, five, or even ten years refining and maturing your attainment, you still will never attain even the ability to teach a poor sort of dunce.

Recently word reached me that the Kyoto priest who ordained you has been seriously ill for some time now and may die at any moment. This is another matter of great importance that you cannot ignore.

When this letter reaches you, don't waste any more time. Hang up your traveling staff that keeps taking you farther and farther away from here. I look forward with keen anticipation to seeing you again. I have entrusted the rest of what I want to say to the Daikei-ji priest, who will transmit it in person to you.

My best wishes, [Hakuin]

HOZ, 2:185–87

---

* Anecdotes about these two priests in *Ta-hui's Arsenal* have them leaving their teachers after an initial realization and failing to complete their training.

Attendant Kō is identified in an annotation inscribed in a copy of *Poison Blossoms from a Thicket of Thorn* as Daikyū Ebō (1715–74), one of Hakuin's most important Dharma heirs.* Like Tōrei and many other of Hakuin's leading students, Daikyū came to Hakuin after first studying with Kogetsu Zenzai. Kogetsu, who was about ten years older than Hakuin, was a highly regarded Rinzai teacher in Hyūga Province on the southern island of Kyushu.

Daikyū entered the priesthood at the age of five. At fifteen he was made an attendant of Zōkai Etan at Tōfuku-ji in Kyoto, and when Zōkai died the following year Daikyū moved to Hōfuku-ji in Bitchū Province (modern-day Okayama Prefecture), an important temple in the Tōfuku-ji branch of Rinzai Zen. At twenty-two he traveled to Hyūga in Kyushu (Miyazaki Prefecture) to study with Kogetsu, then set out several years later (exactly when is unclear) on a pilgrimage to eastern Japan that led him to Hakuin at Shōin-ji. (For an anecdote describing their first meeting, see *Hakuin's Precious Mirror Cave*, xxiv–xxv).

Although in Hakuin's *Chronological Biography* there is a reference to Daikyū as Hakuin's attendant as early as 1739, according to the account in *Biographies of Zen Priests of Modern Times* Daikyū first arrived at Shōin-ji in 1742. This account also has Daikyū being appointed an attendant, achieving a decisive enlightenment the next year (which was confirmed by Hakuin), and then leaving Hakuin not long after the enlightenment to return to Hōfuku-ji.

Since the letter addresses Daikyū as "Attendant Kō" (a title Hakuin could have used until 1755 when Daikyū was installed as abbot at Hōfuku-ji) and was sent when Daikyū was no longer at Shōin-ji, we may tentatively suppose that following confirmation of his satori, Daikyū left the temple to engage in further practice on his own. This was the course Tōrei and Suiō adopted as well, also in the face of Hakuin's opposition. If so, the writing of this letter can be

---

* According to the entry for Daikyū in *Biographies of Zen Priests of Modern Times*, he was born in Iwakura village north of Kyoto and ordained by a priest named Jikuden Den'ō (n.d.) at Shōfuku-an in the neighboring village of Kino.

narrowed down to between 1743 (or 1739) when Daikyū was appointed Hakuin's attendant and achieved his enlightenment, and 1747, which is the year that the monk named Tō (later Reigen Etō), who is mentioned in the letter as studying at Shōin-ji, is known to have returned to his home temple. Hakuin's comments about Daikyū having been away for a long time seems to suggest a date closer to 1747.

In any event, despite the fears Hakuin expresses in the letter, Daikyū seems to have fulfilled his promise and developed into a powerful teacher. In his spiritual autobiography, *Wild Ivy*, Hakuin describes attending a large lecture meeting that Daikyū conducted at the great Tōfuku-ji in Kyoto (p. 67). According to *The Annals of Tōfuku-ji* eight hundred and thirteen priests and monks, among whom were Tōrei and other students of Hakuin, participated in the meeting. Through meetings such as this one at Tōfuku-ji, Daikyū is credited with having introduced Hakuin-style Zen to the large Gozan monasteries in the capital.

Modern Rinzai historians have ranked Daikyū along with Tōrei and Suiō as one of Hakuin's three chief disciples. Suiō, who succeeded Hakuin at Shōin-ji, is reported to have said, "Among the students that came under old Hakuin's hammer, Tōrei alone was able to enter his chambers and make off with all his Dharma assets; and only Daikyū penetrated deeply to his Dharma source" (*Chronological Biography*, p. 32). After Daikyū's death, he was awarded the Zen master title "Daihi Myōgyō Zenshi."

6

To the Rōshi at Ryōsen-ji

LETTER 6, C. 1746–56

Although unnamed, the recipient of this brief letter, titled in the Japanese edition, "To the Former Rōshi at Ryōsen-ji for the gift of a stone water buffalo," is the Zen priest Rokuin Etsū (1685–1756). Born the same year as Hakuin, Rokuin accompanied him on some of his early travels. When Rokuin completed his pilgrimage, he spent some time studying at Shōin-ji, then returned to his home temple Ryōsen-ji in Shimizu, a village just east of Numazu, about eight miles from Hakuin's temple, where he eventually succeeded his teacher as head priest.

It is not known when Rokuin retired from his position as head priest at Ryōsen-ji, but presumably it was toward the end of his life. Since Rokuin died in 1756, Hakuin's letter no doubt dates from his sixties, and probably his mid- to late sixties.

A STONE OX has made his appearance at Shōin-ji. A big water buffalo, flapping his tail and pushing himself forward till he's right under my nose. He won't be wandering off into the winds and mists anymore, entering other people's fields, hankering after their fragrant grasses. He's become a gentle and obedient beast.

Apply the whip to him, he won't budge. Call out to him, his head won't turn. His horns, though small, are still pushing their way upward, and his nostrils proclaim a proud, high spirit that reaches into the heavens. He is perfectly straight and true, utterly distinct, his thick rotundity completely open and unbared. Even the most experienced herdsman could find nowhere to apply his whip; the most skilled butcher nowhere to insert his knife. A water buffalo that would shock Nan-ch'uan into silence, that would set Kuei-shan's teeth rattling in panic fear.

Rumor has it that he bolted from one of the temple's patrons who lives at the foot of the mountain. Chinese characters can be discerned on his lower left flank. What could they be? No one's going to put a cord through this buffalo's nose. I'll see him every day, a calm majestic presence, so distantly aloof, such a perfectly round presence. He will live out the rest of his days performing his marvelous activities in the Zen forest with his solitary dignity and noble bearing unchanged.

Nothing could compare with this wonderful gift. It transcends all measures of secular or sacred. I do not know how to thank you. I find myself dancing joyfully about, humming one of those songs the young village oxherders sing.

I have much more to say, but for now . . . [Hakuin]

HOZ, 2:188

The ox, white ox, and water buffalo appear frequently in Zen literature as a symbol of the ultimate principle or Buddhahood itself. Although the famous *Ten Oxherding Pictures* is the example that first comes to mind (and this letter contains several allusions to that work), in the *Classified Anthology of the Zen Forest*, more koans are listed for the ox or water buffalo (including some stone oxen) than for any other animal.

Hakuin's letter mentions Nan-ch'uan and Kuei-shan, T'ang dynasty Zen priests who appear in a number of well-known koans on the ox theme, some of which will be given below. It also alludes to stories involving other priests, such as the following address that Zen Master Ta-an (Ch'ang-ch'ing Ta-an, 793–883) gave his assembly: "I lived with my teacher Kuei-shan over thirty years, eating his food, passing his excrement—but I didn't study his Zen. All my time was spent looking after an ox. Whenever he left the path and got into the tall grass, I would pull him back. If I caught him trampling peoples' rice fields, I would flog him with my whip to make him stop. For a long time he continued like this. It was a pitiful existence for him, always being ordered about. But now, he has transformed into the White Ox on the Open Ground [*Lotus Sutra*] and is utterly unbared beneath my very nose all day long. He doesn't budge an inch, even if I try to chase him off" (*Records of the Lamp*, ch. 9).

Other allusions: "Chao-chou asked Nan-ch'uan, 'When a person has grasped the Way, where should he go?' 'He should become a water buffalo at the layman's place down the hill,' replied Nan-ch'uan" (*Compendium of the Five Lamps*, ch. 4).

"Kuei-shan addressed the assembly. 'When my hundred years are up, I'm going to go to that layman's place down the mountain and be reborn as a water buffalo. I'll have five Chinese characters on my left flank. They'll say, "Monk So-and-so from the Mount Kuei Temple." When it happens, though you might call me Monk So-and-so from Mount Kuei, I'd still be a water buffalo; though you call me a water buffalo, I'd still be Monk So-and-so from Mount Kuei. So what are you going to call me?' Yang-shan stepped forward, performed a bow, and walked off" (*Compendium of the Five Lamps*, ch. 9).

Rokuin's choice of gift may also be connected with Hakuin's well-known affinity with the Shinto deity Tenjin (the deified form of the statesman and poet Sugawara Michizane enshrined in the Kitano Tenmangu in Kyoto), whose messenger animal is the ox. He is popularly known as Ushi Tenjin, the Ox deity, and stone effigies of the ox are found in many Tenjin shrines.

Hakuin's worship of Tenjin began in early childhood. To calm the fears that arose after hearing a preacher describe the terrible punishments that awaited sinners who fell into hell, his mother told him to worship Tenjin (there was a small Tenjin Shrine next to the family home), who would, it was said, help anyone who sought his assistance. She also informed Hakuin of his close connection with the deity: Hakuin was born on the twenty-fifth day of the twelfth month in the second year of the Jōkyō era (1685), at the first crow of the cock, the year, month, day, and hour all falling under the horological sign of the ox. To overcome his fears, young Hakuin was soon repeating the deity's name and performing religious austerities. In the autobiographies Hakuin wrote in the final decade of his life, he looked back to these experiences as the beginning of the religious quest that led him to Zen and, eventually, to enlightenment.

Details of Hakuin's involvement with the Tenjin cult are found in *Religious Art of Zen Master Hakuin* (204–07).

7

To a Certain Layman

LETTER 7, 1748

This letter was written in response to an unidentified lay student's request for some "Dharma words," instructions to encourage him in his practice. In the letter, Hakuin tells for the first time the famous story of Yamanashi Heishirō and the satori he attained after only two nights of intense zazen practice. Hakuin evidently decided to make a concerted effort to make Heishirō's experience widely known to his Zen students. Versions later appeared in his *Chronological Biography* (see translation below), in a long verse inscription he wrote at Heishirō's request on a portrait of the priest Takusui Chōmo that was included in *Poison Blossoms from a Thicket of Thorn*, and in secondary works such as *Stories from a Thicket of Thorn and Briar*, a nineteenth-century collection of anecdotes about leading students in Hakuin's line.

"The Tale of Heishirō of Ihara Village," to use the title given to the letter in modern editions of Hakuin's works, became a staple text in later Hakuin Zen, used to illustrate the tremendous resolve required to achieve the breakthrough into satori known as *kenshō*. To generations of Rinzai Zen students, this letter is perhaps best known as the "Instructions to the Assembly during the Rōhatsu Training Period" (*Rōhatsu jishū*), a version of the story that is traditionally recited on the fifth night of the intensive, week-long practice session held from the first day of the twelfth month.

Hakuin's letter evidently dates from 1748, the same year that Heishirō visited him. It includes details not found in any of the later versions, most notably the unique record of the dialogue that took place when Heishirō went to receive verification of his satori from Hakuin.

Yamanashi Heishirō (1707–63), otherwise known as Harushige, also known by his lay Buddhist name Ryōtetsu, "Complete Penetration," was a wealthy sake brewer from Ihara, a village to the west of Hara. He and his neighbor Shibata Gonzaemon (n.d.), at the time Ihara's wealthiest citizens, resided in large houses on opposite sides of a small stream that flowed down the village's main street. As seriously dedicated lay Zen students and members of the Shōin-ji congregation, they provided donations on more than one occasion to help fund Hakuin's publishing and building projects.

Although unmentioned in the letter, Heishirō's conversion to religious life, which led to the satori described below, was apparently precipitated by the sudden death of his eldest son and heir. We also know from a letter Hakuin wrote a few years later that after Heishirō's satori, he became a regular member of the Shōin-ji lay community, and his two young daughters became devoted to zazen practice as well (see Letter 8).

Hakuin seems to have regarded Heishirō as one of his most accomplished lay students. He once compared him to Shih-kun, a famous figure of T'ang Zen who lived as a hunter until an encounter with Zen Master Ma-tsu turned him to the priesthood. In the inscription for the portrait of Takusui mentioned above, Heishirō is praised as "a practicer whose equal has rarely been seen in the annals of Zen," which, even allowing for Hakuin's penchant for exaggeration, is an impressive expression of esteem.

Heishirō befriended many of Hakuin's students as well, including most of his leading disciples. The painter Ike Taiga is known to have stayed at the Yamanashi residence in Suruga on trips to the eastern provinces, and a document exists describing a sojourn Heishirō made to Taiga's home in Kyoto. A large collection of paintings, calligraphy, and other records attesting to these associations, including works and letters by Hakuin that would have revealed further details of their relationship, which had been preserved in the Yamanashi residence, which were destroyed in the bombing raids that devastated Suruga Province in final years of World War II.

You have often asked me to write you some Dharma words, something that would inspire you to greater effort in your practice. Since you have no doubt already seen manuscripts of mine that are circulating these days among my followers, there isn't any point sending you one of them. As I was trying to decide what would be appropriate, I remembered a truly exceptional story. I am going to write it out and send it to you. It is entirely true, nothing has been added or left out, so you can read it without doubting its accuracy in the least. Use it to spur yourself to a similar level of heroic effort.

In the autumn of last year, I was asked to give lectures on the *Record of Lin-chi* at Matsuoka village. Every day people came from all around to attend, in some cases traveling distances in excess of thirteen *ri* (almost thirty-two miles), from areas as far north as Kai Province. Among them was a party from Ihara village five or six *ri* west of here, who seemed to listen with a special earnestness. They gathered for sessions of zazen when the meeting ended, and devoted themselves to their practice with great diligence. Some of the men later came and asked me to write some words to encourage them.

Associated with this group of strongly motivated students from Ihara was a man named Yamanashi Hei-something-or-other. He is one of Ihara's wealthiest citizens, and rumors people were circulating about him had occasionally reached my ears. It seems, however, that Yamanashi refused to accompany his fellow villagers to the practice meeting in Matsuoka despite their repeated urgings. Having no use whatever for zazen, he would invariably find an excuse to slip out of the room whenever discussions began to turn in a religious direction. The other villagers came to regard him as something of a lost cause, and left him pretty much to himself.

On the twenty-fourth or fifth of last month, I believe it was, a man showed up at my temple. Standing beside him was this Yamanashi Hei.

"I brought this fellow to you because he says he wants to receive your guidance," the man said. "I would appreciate it if you would grant him an interview."

Since it was evidently a matter of some importance to the man, I came out and spoke to him. "Well, well, I see we have a rare visitor indeed. Let's not waste any time. Hurry up and tell me what it is you want."

Yamanashi was strong and manly in appearance. He performed his bows, and speaking with great care and propriety, said, "I know it is presumptuous of me to come here like this, asking for an interview as if I were a proper Zen student. But I have experienced a realization, and I don't know anyone else who can evaluate it. I was held up because the river was running high, but as soon as the crossing ban was lifted, I came directly here to see you.

"My story begins last autumn when you were in Matsuoka village conducting that Dharma assembly. After the meeting ended, seven or eight students from Ihara got together and began practicing zazen. They continued diligently day and night with a dedication that filled everyone with admiration and respect. As you can see, I am an idle and thoroughly indolent fellow. Not only had I never done zazen, the very thought of undertaking religious practice had never even entered my head. I must confess that I regarded such pastimes as a rather silly waste of time. Anyway, with my dim grasp of things, these are the thoughts that went through my mind:

"'To achieve a great matter such as kenshō, students of even superior capacity have to train for ten or twenty years. They must perform many austerities, such as inflicting burns on their head, arms, fingers, and other parts of their body.* And even then, don't they often fail to achieve their goal? Not to mention someone of my shiftless habits. If I rashly tried to engage in such practice, I would only make myself an object of contempt, a target of village gossip. How mortifying that would be. I shouldn't start something I know I won't be able to finish. At the same time, I probably won't be content just to sit back and watch my life pass idly by. Beginning today, I am going to try to accumulate virtue in secret. It will be an enduring legacy for my children.† It might, perhaps, even be a kind of satori, one in keeping with my capacity and station in life.'

"Having decided on a course of action, I started to perform good acts of various kinds. As unobtrusively as possible, so as not to appear presumptuous or condescending, I made it a point to perform at least one or two good deeds every day. On occasion, I performed as many as fifteen or twenty deeds to benefit others.‡ Meantime, my fellow villagers were practicing zazen and working on koans and urging me to join them. But such things seemed pointless to me, so whenever they began talking about such matters, I just waited for an opportunity and then made myself scarce.

"It seems to me that the awakening of religious aspiration

---

* "In Buddhist monasteries, persons who do not have self-inflicted burns are not considered to be genuine home-leavers and followers of the Bodhisattva path" (*Admonitions for Buddhists*, ch. 4). The infliction of ritual burns and other forms of self-mutilation was much less common in Japanese than in Chinese Buddhism.

† These are from family precepts traditionally ascribed to the Chinese scholar Ssuma Kuang: "If you accumulate money for your heirs, they will only fritter it away. If you build a library of books for them, they will never read them. Far better to secretly increase your virtue and create a lasting legacy for your descendents." Hakuin was fond of quoting them in his writings and often used them as a text for his calligraphy as well.

‡ According to the inscription Hakuin wrote on the portrait of the priest Takusui mentioned above, Heishirō's good deeds included using his wealth to "care for the elderly and infirm and relieve the suffering of the needy."

must wait until karmic conditions are fully mature. In my case, this happened only a few days ago, the night of the twenty-first, when I visited someone to discuss some business or other. I found him standing on his veranda propped on one leg and leaning against a wooden pillar. His left hand was under his chin, and in his right he was holding a book of Buddhist writings—the "Dharma words" of someone-or-other. He was bent intently over the book reading it aloud, as though it was of the greatest importance. He stopped occasionally to clear his throat, and at times tears would begin flowing down his cheeks, making him lose his place in the text.

"As I watched him, I became thoroughly disgusted. I figured that he belonged to the practice group and was boning up for one of those zazen sessions where they sit dozing away with sour looks on their faces like someone had stuck lumps of butterbur miso in their mouths.* I wondered how he could waste his time reading what was undoubtedly one of those worthless screeds about cause and effect. On the other hand, he looked like just the kind of person to enlist in my program of good works. I thought if I could point out weaknesses in one or two of the arguments in the passages he was reading, I would be doing him a good turn, by winning him over to my way of thinking and getting him to perform virtuous acts of his own.

"I sidled up to him with a smile on my face and sat down on the edge of the veranda. I closed my eyes, folded my arms, and listened carefully to his mumblings, poised to stop him the first time I heard something that seemed dubious or false. He was intoning a passage that went:

> Achieving the great matter of kenshō can take two or three years to achieve; in some cases, up to twenty, thirty, or even forty years. Some practice an entire lifetime with-

---

* *Butterbur sprouts* (*fuki-no-tō*), an edible wild plant that appears in early spring, have a decidedly bitter taste, even when mixed, as they sometimes are, with miso paste.

out ever reaching satori. Students must muster all their strength, and with eyes open wide and jaw firmly set, ask themselves, "Right at this moment, where is the nature of seeing, hearing, and perceiving? Is it blue or yellow, is it red or white? Is it within or without? Is it somewhere in between?" As they concentrate on these questions, deeply determined one way or another to find the answers, delusory thoughts will crowd into their minds. But that should not deter them in the least. They must push ever deeper, battle these thoughts as though they were in a fight to the death, struggling alone against a horde of ten thousand. If they continue in this way, the time will come when their entire bodies stream with sweat. It will seem as though they have tumbled into a bottomless, pitch-black abyss, as though mind and body and the life-breath itself have disappeared. At that moment, the great matter of human life will finally be decided, as though they have just wakened from a long dream.

Nor should it take a long time to achieve such an attainment. As the *Awakening of Faith in the Mahayana* says, "For sentient beings who pursue practice with courage and vigor, attainment of Buddhahood can take place in a single moment of thought. Lax and indolent sentient beings cannot hope to attain Buddhahood, even though they continue to practice for many kalpas."[*]

People who do zazen when they happen to think of it for two or three sticks of incense, and people who sit nightly at set times for three or four sticks of incense,[†] both fall into the category of "lax and indolent sentient beings." Although their efforts might strike an outsider

---

[*] The source of the saying is unknown. Although *Records of the Mirror Source* (ch. 17) attributes it to the *Awakening of Faith in the Mahayana* (*Daijōkishin-ron*), it is not found in that work.

[†] A stick of incense burns for approximately forty minutes.

as being highly praiseworthy (they are concentrating on their training with admirable and unfaltering diligence), the unfortunate truth of the matter is that their roots to life remain unsevered, and even if they continue what they are doing till the end of time, they will never be able to attain kenshō, never be capable of saving even themselves, much less others.

"Hearing this, I thought to myself, 'How remarkable. If a person can achieve some measure of kenshō from only a few days of strenuous effort, what is preventing me from giving it a try? If I did acquire some strength from doing it, why, when I went back to performing virtuous acts, I'd be a winged tiger.* If people have reached kenshō after only a single day of zazen, if I can continue doing it for an entire week, I don't see how I can fail. In any case, inasmuch as I've resolved to do it, I have no choice but to see it through to completion.'

"Returning home, I waited impatiently for evening to come. Then I sequestered myself inside a room, set down a cushion, assumed the full-lotus position, and began quietly doing zazen. Contending thoughts one after another were soon crowding their way into my mind. It was like the great battle at Yashima, or the insurrections of the Nine States period.† But steeling myself to the struggle I confronted the thoughts, battling them like a solitary knight surrounded by an enemy host. I gave a loud shout to drive them back, hoping they would disperse. I was like a man who is thrown back after climbing halfway up a precipitous, ten-thousand-foot cliff, but who returns again and again with redoubled effort, each time struggling ever higher, and each time repulsed as he nears the summit. At each attempt, when all my

---

* That is, even more formidable.

† *Yashima*, on the island of Shikoku, was the site of a famous battle (1184) between the Taira and Minamoto clans. The *Nine States* are the states that contended for power during the Warring States period of ancient China.

strength had been exhausted, I would emit low, involuntary moans, *Koh! Koh!* crying out in pain like a sick calf, my eyes bulging out and my jaw clenched so tightly I was sure my teeth would shatter.

"Then, like the snapping of a tightly stretched thread, all the roots that had been binding me to life suddenly severed. The great earth became an utter blackness; I didn't know whether I was alive or dead. My breathing ceased, and for several hours I remained in a senseless, lifeless state. When the first signs of dawn appeared, I felt a faint aching in my thumbs. My senses began to return, and as they did the pain in my thumbs became intolerable. My hands had been joined in the meditation mudra,* and I had been pushing the thumbs against each other with great intensity. When I tried working them free, I found that I was unable to move my arms or legs. My cheeks were soaked with tears. I was unable to blink my eyes, which stared starkly from their sockets and seemed totally paralyzed.

"But my mind was perfectly clear, and I felt a freshness and purity I had never experienced before. It was as though a heavy cloud bank had suddenly lifted to reveal a brilliant sunrise. Yet I had attained nothing, had grasped nothing. Was this satori? Or was it still an illusion? I had nothing at all to express to others. Yet my mind was filled with a great, unexplainable, and unutterable joy.

"When morning came I left the solitude of the room, but when I encountered members of my family, not a word came from my lips and I was still staring out in a pop-eyed trance. They were astonished and concerned at my bizarre behavior. My only response when asked how I felt was that same catatonic stare. A friend came over and invited me outside for a game of kickball, but when I followed him out to where the other players were waiting, I didn't bow or extend any greeting to them at all. I just

---

* In the *meditation mudra* (Skt.: *Dhyāna mudrā*; J.: *jōin*), which is used during zazen, the two hands are placed on the lap, right hand on the left with palms facing upward, fingers extended with thumb tips touching, forming a triangle.

sat down, remaining motionless and staring straight ahead like
an absolute fool. I'm sure they thought I'd suddenly taken leave of
my senses. But I thought to myself, 'I won't stop until I attain the
fundamental power of kenshō, even if I die in the attempt.'

"When dusk came I returned to the same room and once
again assumed the zazen posture. As still and motionless as a
Buddhist statue, teeth clenched and eyes open wide, I resumed
the struggle against delusory thoughts. I remember thinking that
if someone held up a lamp and gazed at my form in the half-light,
he would surely mistake me for a violent yaksha demon. I struggled forward single-mindedly, steadily concentrating my efforts,
and soon entered the deep state of samadhi I had experienced the
previous night. All sign of breathing ceased as I entered the utter
tranquillity of the great death, completely free of past or present.
My body and mind had fallen away.

"Although only the briefest moment seemed to have passed, I
noticed the sky outside was growing light. Emerging from the
depths of samadhi, I rose up and looked around. 'Heaven and
earth are one of my fingers.' 'The ten thousand things are a single
horse.' The world and I were one. 'There was not so much as a tile
over my head, a speck of earth under my feet.'* How could there
be any Zen or Buddha Dharma apart from this? All at once I
found myself howling out great peals of laughter.

I was overjoyed, and all I could think of was setting out for
Shōin-ji so I could have an interview with you and explain what
had happened. I don't have a single phrase of any kind to set before you. Only on my way here, when my palanquin reached the
summit of Satta Pass and I saw the immense expanse of ocean
spreading out below me,† I understood for the first time the true

---

* The first of Heishirō's utterances is from *Chuang Tzu*, "Discussion on Making All
Things Equal." The second appears among the sayings of Zen Master Chia-shan
Shan-hui (*Records of the Lamp*, ch. 15). Both are expressions of the speaker's oneness
with the universe.

† *Satta Pass* is located on a difficult stretch of the Tōkaidō Road in Tōtōmi Province
between Yui and Okitsu. It is the subject of a famous woodblock print by Hiroshige.

meaning of the words, 'Plants, trees, and the land itself all attain Buddhahood.'* Please master, I beg you to examine and evaluate the experience I have had."

I asked him, "At this moment, where is Buddha?"

His gaze went to the pillars on the veranda, then to the steps leading into the garden. I clapped my hands. "When two hands meet, a sound is produced," I said. "Can you hear the sound of one hand?" I held up one hand before him.

"I hear it loud and clear," he replied.

"What proof can you give?"

He hesitated a moment. "When it is heard," I said, "it must be perfectly clear. You only hear part of it."

He covered his ears with his hands.

"You don't have it yet," I said.

He got up and bolted from the room. After taking four or five steps, he returned. "I hear it," he said.

"What do you hear?"

He explained. Everything he said was right on the mark.

"Sometimes a fine rain falls for days on end," I said. "How can you stop it so that not a single drop falls?"

"I stopped it before my mother gave birth to me," he said.

"Anybody can say that," I replied. He struck the tatami with his hand. After exhaling two or three breaths, I said, "Zen adepts like you show up from time to time, but when I examine them, I always find something missing."

He performed his bows and left the room, but returned a while later and said, "I've put a stop to all the fine rain falling in all lands and countries in the ten directions—every last drop."

"How did you manage that?" I asked.

---

* No scriptural source has been found for these words in the *Ekō-mon*, the *Verse on Transferring Merit* that is recited at Buddhist ceremonies after sutra chanting and so on, which expresses the reciter's intention to transfer all the merit accruing from his practice to others, so the others may also attain Buddhahood. The full text is: "When a Buddha attains the Way, he looks out and surveys the entire Dharma universe; / Plants, trees, and the country itself all attain Buddhahood."

When he had set forth his realization, I broke into a wide grin. Heishirō was beside himself with joy. He ran off to the Zen nun Eshō's hermitage and explained to her what had happened.*

"You musn't be satisfied with that small attainment," she said. "I'm an old woman. I can't even get up unless someone lends me a hand. Could you help me up without using a hand?"

Heishirō was thrown completely for a loss. "Don't be impatient for results," said Eshō. "That's why I told you not to be content with this minor attainment."

Hei returned sheepishly to my temple. Eshō came by soon afterward to discuss what had happened. The two of us had a good laugh as we celebrated Hei's kenshō.

Hei unexpectedly entered the room. "You really juggled me back there," he said to Eshō. "I'd like you to ask me that question once more."

"Layman, please help this old nun up without using a hand," she said.

He proceeded to give a response that astounded Eshō.†

I assigned him "Chao-chou's Seven-Pound Jacket."‡ "This is a very difficult koan," I told him. "It has been transmitted from one Zen patriarch to another for many generations. I want you to investigate it very carefully. Don't underestimate it."

He performed three bows and left.

That is the story of Yamanashi Heishirō of Ihara village and a kenshō that was attained in just two nights of practice. You won't

---

* Eshō-ni (d. 1764) entered religious life at Seiken-ji in Okitsu following the death of her husband, an official at the Ejiri post station. She achieved realization while studying under Hakuin, and was also close friends with Tōrei (*Stories from a Thicket of Thorn and Briar*, 103).

† The original description is more picturesque: "Her tongue popped out of her mouth."

‡ A jacket made of hemp from the Ch'ing-chou region in Shantung Province. "Asked by a monk, 'All things are reduced to oneness. What is the oneness reduced to?' Chao-chou replied, 'When I was in Ch'ing-chou, I had a coat that weighed seven pounds'" (*Blue Cliff Record*, Case 45).

find anything like it in the Zen records—not in the *Records of the Lamp* or in the *Compendium of the Five Lamps*. And it took place in the fifth month of this very year, on the night of the twenty-first.

There is no getting around it: for achieving the initial entrance into satori, nothing can excel a direct and expeditious assault fired by intense, vigorous, urgent desire. People who engage in practice a little bit at a time when the thought occurs to them will not achieve kenshō even if they continue doing it for thirty or forty years. As time passes, their efforts physically exhaust them, drain them of the necessary spirit and strength they need to subdue the illusory, passion-ridden thoughts that crowd into their minds. In the end, they are reduced to fingering rosaries and tearfully reciting Nembutsu, a pastime that brings them no more relief than one of those ready-made toothache medicines sold in the streets.

Unless you push forward with urgency and vigor, so that two or three times you reach the point where your breath ceases and you can't tell if you are alive or dead, you cannot achieve a decisive satori.

And once the spontaneous cry *Ka!* does burst from your lips and you are filled with the strength that comes with kenshō,[*] you must then strive to maintain a state of constant right-mindedness,[†] not only during zazen but in all the activities of your everyday life as well.

Next, you must grasp with perfect clarity sayings such as "The stone lantern jumps up and runs into the pillar," "The Buddha Hall dashes out the front gate,"[‡] "In crossing a bridge, the

---

[*] The involuntary cry said to be emitted at the moment of satori; it is also used to refer to satori itself.

[†] The seventh item in the Eightfold Noble Path, in which the mind remains focused on the pursuit of the Way, free from illusory thought.

[‡] These two expressions seem to be Hakuin's own. A similar phrase, "Riding the Buddha Hall out the temple gate," appears in his *Comments on the Blue Cliff Record*, where it is explained as "expressing the great change that takes place when perfect freedom is attained."

bridge flows, the water doesn't,"* "Facing south and viewing the Polar Star in the northern sky." You must see them as unmistakably as if they were lying in the palm of your hand. After that you must press forward into what are known as the "fangs and claws of the Dharma cave," the "divine amulets that rob you of your life"—koans such as "Su-shan's Memorial Tower," "Nan-ch'uan's Flowering Hedge," "Yen-kuan's Rhinoceros-horn Fan," "Ts'ui-yen's Eyebrows," and "Ch'ien-feng's Three Kinds of Illness." Until you have passed through all of these and have experienced in the process a feeling of immense joy, as though you had suddenly encountered your wife and children in a strange land far from home, you cannot say that your study of Zen is over.

People who learned of Heishirō's experience suddenly began practicing with ten times more mettle than before. Hence, I have written this out and am sending it to you in the belief that it surpasses any Dharma words I could think up myself. I have undoubtedly made many mistakes in transcribing it, writing down the wrong characters and so forth, so I would ask that you not show it to others.

Yours sincerely, [Hakuin]

HOZ, 6:77–88; HHZ, 14:85–107

We know from the version of the Heishirō story given below that the book of Buddhist writings mentioned above was *The Dharma Words of Zen Priest Takusui*, a work made up of twenty-eight talks, comments, and exhortations by the Rinzai priest Takusui Chōmo of Daijū-ji in Edo. It was published in 1740, the year of Takusui's death, and eight years prior to this letter.

To give a better idea of how Hakuin's narrative was transformed

---

* From a well-known verse of the Chinese lay teacher Fu Ta-shih: "Empty-handed, yet holding a mattock; / Walking, yet riding a water buffalo, / A man crossing a bridge, / the bridge flows, not the water." In his *Comments on the Blue Cliff Record*, Hakuin comments on these lines: "This is the freedom you gain when you attain kenshō."

in later versions of Heishirō's story, here is the account from Hakuin's *Chronological Biography* (1748, age 63. See *Hakuin's Precious Mirror Cave*, 214–15). Since the letter was virtually unknown until it was published in 1935 in the *Complete Works of Zen Priest Hakuin*, this version became the source of most of the later retellings.

In spring Yamanashi Harushige came to study with the master. From the village of Ihara in Suruga Province, Harushige (also known as Heishirō) was by nature avaricious, was a confirmed womanizer, and had few redeeming qualities. One day as he was paying a visit to his family temple, the retired abbot said to him, "Yamanashi, you should donate a stone image of Fudō Myōō. It would bring benefit to people and inspire Zen practicers with a spirit of courage and fearlessness."

Harushige, agreeable to the idea, commissioned a stonemason to carve a statue of the deity, which he then had enshrined beside a waterfall at Mount Yoshiwara. One fine warm day, he took his children to visit the spot. There wasn't a cloud in the sky and the bright green leaves sparkled in the sunshine. The children wandered off gathering flowers, leaving Harushige alone at the edge of the waterfall. As he sat watching the foam forming on the surface of the pool, he was suddenly struck by the impermanence of the world and the transience of human life. He watched as some of the bubbles vanished under the falling water even as they formed, while others floated a foot or two before disappearing, and some remained and moved over the water for fifty yards or more. Human life is just like that, mused Harushige.

Harushige had experienced the Buddhist truth that all is suffering, and that all suffering originates from human ignorance. He rose, his body trembling uncontrollably with fear, and returned home alone. On arriving, he saw an old man sitting at the back of the house reading *The Dharma*

Words of Zen Priest Takusui. Glancing at the book, Harushige's eyes came to rest on a passage that said: "A true practicer of the Way makes enlightenment alone his standard. A brave and courageous practicer can sometimes realize enlightenment in several days or weeks. Such is the meaning of the Buddhist saying about the brave and fearless reaching attainment in a single thought-instant, but the lax and indolent taking three kalpas."

Harushige plucked up his courage. "I'm certainly capable of making it through a week or two of zazen," he assured himself.

He entered the bath quarters of his house and seated himself in the zazen posture. His resolve was steadfast, but before long his mind was conjuring up thoughts and discriminations in endless variety. Soon his arms and legs were aching, and he became troubled within by a relentless uneasiness. By midnight he was finally able to forget his body and mind. At first light, both his eyeballs seemed suddenly to burst from their sockets and fall to the floor. Soon after that, he felt searing pain in the tips of his fingers. But he just clenched his teeth tightly, determined to sit his way through, and gradually things seemed to return to normal. He rose and looked around him, but unable to perceive any noticeable change from the previous day, he left the room and started his daily routine. At the day's end he returned to the bath quarters and resumed his practice, sitting as resolutely the second night as he had the first. He soon entered a deep state of samadhi and remained that way through the night. He sat through a third night in the same manner. At dawn on the morning of the third day, upon returning to his work, he noticed that a change had taken place. Now everything he saw and heard and experienced seemed totally different. He went to the priest of a small nearby temple and told him what had happened. The priest was unable to help him, but advised him to visit the master.

Harushige hired a palanquin and set out for Shōin-ji. When they reached the summit of Satta Pass, a shining stretch of ocean came into view far below. The moment he saw it, Harushige suddenly grasped the true aspect of things in their individual suchness, and realized for the first time the meaning of the Buddha's words, "Plants and trees and the land itself all attain Buddhahood."

On reaching Shōin-ji, he described to the master what had happened. The master confirmed his realization. Harushige further deepened and refined his understanding while continuing his study under Priest Kan'e Anjū.

One day Harushige encountered a nun named Eshō. "I'm an old woman," she said. "Would you please help me up without using your hands?" Harushige didn't know what to reply. "You said you practice Zen," she said, scolding him. "Is that the best you can do?" He grasped her meaning the following day, and she acknowledged it. Harushige studied with several other priests after that, and passed a number of the koan barriers.

Knowing that this long letter, like many similar ones he wrote, would be circulated among the lay community, Hakuin no doubt attempted to produce a stirring narrative that would stimulate them to greater effort in their own practice. He may on that account have embellished parts of Heishirō's story. It was of course the incredibly short period of time it took Heishirō to achieve his breakthrough that made Hakuin want to tell people about it. Still, it is necessary to add, somewhat anti-climactically, that, despite the assurances Hakuin gives to the contrary, more than a few readers, Hakuin's admirers included, have questioned whether the breakthrough took place in the improbable way he relates it here, with Heishirō attaining a profound satori in just a few nights in his first attempt at zazen.

8

To Senior Monk Gin

LETTER 8, C. 1752

Senior Monk Gin (Gin Shuso) came to study with Hakuin from the Bantō-in subtemple at the Myōshin-ji headquarters temple in Kyoto. Later known as Shizu Sōgin (n.d.), he was appointed head priest at Bantō-in in 1760. His name does not appear in Hakuin's *Chronological Biography*, and there is nothing anywhere else in Hakuin's writings to throw further light on their relationship.

Gin received the letter in Kyoto, probably in 1752, the year after Hakuin had made a three-month visit to the capital, during which he conducted several lecture meetings, including one on the *Blue Cliff Record* at the Myōshin-ji subtemple Yōgen-in that was attended by abbesses of the imperial convents Hōkyō-ji and Kōshō-in, both daughters of the former emperor Nakamikado (1702–37). As one of the few monks from Myōshin-ji in Hakuin's assembly, Gin probably had some part in the arrangements for this meeting.

I WAS GLAD to learn that you had arrived safely in Kyoto. I will soon be fully recovered from my indisposition, so you need not worry about my teaching duties tiring me.

The parcel I promised you should have been sent right away, but circumstances arose that led me to wait a bit. One of my regular lay students here at Shōin-ji, Yamanashi Heishirō from

Ihara village, has two young daughters who also have a keen interest in Zen and are dedicated to zazen practice. This spring, the elder one heard that people in Hina village had presented a painting of a Kongō Stupa to abbesses of two imperial convents in Kyoto, and was suddenly inspired to do something similar herself. She pledged to embroider an image of the Life-Prolonging Kannon to offer them. Preparing herself through a regimen of abstinence and religious practice, she produced an image that reveals her great goodness and purity of heart. The younger sister, after undertaking the same regimen, made an image of her own. Their father Heishirō was astonished when he saw the results of their work.

It was impossible for me to ignore these small tokens of respect they made for the abbesses. Although embroidered by simple, insignificant young girls, they represent the Life-Prolonging Kannon, a Bodhisattva of miraculous virtues. I would like to ask you to serve as a go-between and see that the gifts are delivered to the imperial convents. Their father made this request to me with such earnestness that I was unable to refuse him. I have placed them in a box and am sending them to you together with my sincerest apologies for troubling you.

I had also been meaning to send a letter to the courtier Reizei Muneie and request that he write a preface or colophon for my book of Zen records, but as Senior Monk Jo will be traveling to Kyoto in the spring, it seemed better to wait and have him make the request personally. I will tell you all about it in a following letter. Please keep the head priest at your temple duly informed of these arrangements.

All the best, Hakuin.

HOZ, 6:479–80

◆

Recent evidence shows that Hakuin visited Kyoto more frequently than was previously thought, beginning as early as his years of pilgrimage, which has caused some rethinking of the notion that he had purposely avoided the capital and its monastery establishment. However, the fact remains that throughout Hakuin's career, the provinces were his main theater of operations, not the large and historically important temples in Kyoto or Kamakura.

The first and only time Hakuin is known to have conducted lecture meetings in Kyoto is during the visit mentioned above, which occurred in his midsixties. The main event was the series of formal Zen lectures (*teishō*) on the *Blue Cliff Record* held at the Yōgen-in subtemple of Myōshin-ji. At the time, Myōshin-ji was the most vigorous branch of Rinzai Zen, the headquarters of a nationwide network of temples that included Hakuin's Shōin-ji. Whatever Hakuin's own thoughts on the matter might have been, these lectures can at least be seen as confirmation of the stature he had achieved in Rinzai circles by this time.

For most of his three months in Kyoto, Hakuin seems to have stayed at the residence of his student Yotsugi Masayuki, a wealthy layman who lived near Sanjō Street in the central part of the city. It appears that Hakuin used Yotsugi's residence for teaching purposes as well, since the well-known painter Ike Taiga is reported to have "studied Zen" with him there.

Hakuin also met with the two abbesses, Jōshō from Hōkyō-ji and Jōmyō from Kōshō-in, who at that time were only twenty-six and twenty-two years old, respectively. The first meeting seems to have taken place at the Yōgen-in lectures, and afterward the abbesses invited Hakuin to their temples, where he says he was accorded an "extremely courteous reception." This led to a series of talks over a period of days at one of the convents (which one is not known) on *Precious Lessons of the Zen School*, a Chinese collection of Zen anecdotes.

Hakuin, inspired by what he saw on his visits to the convents, wrote the abbesses an extremely long letter later that year. In the letter, he presents an exposition of his Zen teachings, but he also directs some rather severe criticism at the abbesses for deviating from the austere principles traditionally observed in Zen temples.

Particularly disturbing to him was their habit of hiring servants to perform the manual chores.

The letter was later published under the title *Horse Thistles*, and became one of Hakuin's major works. The publication date of autumn 1751 given at the end of the first edition must surely refer to the date Hakuin finished composing the letter. The actual date of publication, although it apparently occurred not too long afterward, is unknown, a feature *Horse Thistles* shares with *Poison Blossoms* and a number of Hakuin's other works.

In the second volume of *Horse Thistles*, Hakuin remarks on the abbesses' fragile health. This would account for the gifts that the villagers of Hina and the daughters of Yamanashi Heishirō sent them, one a painting of a popular folk deity, the other an image of the Bodhisattva Kannon, both believed to be efficacious in curing illness.

When Hakuin refers to the *Ten Phrase Life-Prolonging Kannon* (*Emmei Jikku Kannon*), he probably means an image consisting of Emmei, or "Life-Prolonging Kannon," with the text of the brief *Ten Phrase Kannon Sutra for Prolonging Life* inscribed above it (see p. 198). This was a combination he himself used in some of his paintings of Kannon.

Yamanashi Heishirō's daughter Shiga was fourteen at the time; his youngest daughter Suma was twelve. The dramatic account of their father's attainment of satori after only a few nights of intense practice was recounted in the previous chapter, "Letter to a Certain Layman" (pp. 68–70). Here Hakuin confirms that Heishirō continued his Zen study after the initial breakthrough. It might also be mentioned that Heishirō's wife also studied under Hakuin, his daughter Shiga continued her study after Hakuin's death with his successor Suiō, and the younger sister Suma achieved some fame for her poetry in the *waka* form (*Priest Hakuin*, 217).

Kongō Stupas are small pagoda-shaped stone tablets carved with images of Green-faced Kongō (Shōmen Kongō), a guardian deity of Buddhism depicted with three eyes, six arms, and snakes curled around his arms and legs; sometimes only the characters of Shōmen Kongō's name were engraved on the stupas. The Kongō Stupas were common sights on the roadsides of Edo-period Japan. People worshipped Kongō—who is also known as Kōjin—as a folk deity who protected against disease and other calamities. Taoist lore held that three wormlike creatures (*san-shi*) inhabited the human body, and that once every sixty days, on the day set aside for the worship of Kōjin, the creatures would wait until the person was sleeping, and then report the person's misdeeds directly to the Lord of Heaven. Because of this, worshippers of the Shōmen Kongō cult would gather on those days and engage in an all-night vigil.

The "Senior Monk Jo" mentioned here is Daishū Zenjo, one of Hakuin's most important disciples. Beginning in about 1757, Daishū spent several years in Kyoto overseeing the various publishing enterprises outlined in "Six Letters to Senior Priest Zenjo" (Section 12). Daishū's reason for visiting Kyoto at this time is unknown, but since a number of Hakuin's works appeared at around this time, it may have been related to publishing negotiations of some kind.

Reizei Muneie (1701–69) was a high-ranking member of the imperial court. He was one of two courtiers who chaperoned the imperial abbesses on their visit to Yōgen-in (*Chronological Biography*, 217). The plan to have Muneie write a preface, probably for the projected collection of Hakuin's Zen records, later published as *Poison Blossoms from a Thicket of Thorn*, seems never to have materialized. The standard edition of the work contains a preface by Sugawara Tameshige, another member of the imperial court.

9

To Murabayashi Koremitsu

LETTER 9, 1755

Hakuin was seventy when he wrote this letter to Murabayashi Koremitsu (also Shirōbei), a lay Zen student from the Asakusa district
of Edo. Having penetrated the One Hand koan in an initial kenshō,
Koremitsu was attempting to cure an eye complaint of some kind
through the practice of the therapeutic meditation known as *Naikan*, which he must have learned from Hakuin or his writings. Recent editors of the letter have titled it, "A Miraculous Cure for Eye
Disease."

In the letter Hakuin quotes Chinese medical texts and invokes
principles of medical theory to explain both the underlying cause of
Koremitsu's disorder and the way in which he can achieve a cure.
Hakuin says that Koremitsu should cease any further koan study
for the time being, and focus on the Naikan meditation until he is
able to regain his strength. Readers of *Idle Talk on a Night Boat* may
recall that this is precisely the advice the hermit Hakuyū gave young
Hakuin when he taught him the Naikan meditation.

Hakuin sent the letter from a temple where he was conducting
lectures on the *Ancestral Heroes Collection,* an anthology of religious
verse of exceptional difficulty by the Sung master Hsueh-tou
Ch'ung-hsien (980–1052). The lectures are mentioned in passing
in Hakuin's autobiography *Wild Ivy,* but not in the *Chronological*

Biography, although the latter work does record lectures in 1756 on the *Heroic March Sutra,* a text he says he was boning up on at this time.

SINCE MY SENIOR MONK Eboku had to return to his home province on personal business, I took the opportunity to have him drop this letter off at your residence on his way through Edo.* I received and read with pleasure the two or three letters you sent recently, and I was glad to learn that you, Shūshin-ni, and Sōkichirō are all in good health. Although you write that your eye disease shows some improvement, I am nonetheless concerned about it. As I have told you before, one should never attempt to cure such an illness quickly with large doses of medicine for cooling the body. Many people have damaged their health by doing just that. But it is indeed admirable that you are diligently engaged in practicing Naikan meditation.†

In most cases, eye disease is caused by a lack of water in the system and a debility in the liver or Wood phase.‡ It is important not to harm the liver by putting too great a strain on the mind. As you are steadily engaged in religious practice, it is possible for you to exhaust yourself without even being aware of it. Also, the

---

* Eboku, later Suiō Genro (1717–89), Hakuin's successor at Shōin-ji, was from Shimotsuke Province (present Tochigi Prefecture), north of Edo. He was thirty-eight at the time.

† The Naikan (introspective) meditation is set forth in most detail in *Idle Talk on a Night Boat* (see *Hakuin's Precious Mirror Cave,* 83–114).

‡ The ancient system of five phases (*gogyō*)—Wood, Fire, Earth, Metal, and Water—used to elucidate interactions and relationships in many traditional fields of traditional Chinese thought, proceeds in a cyclical movement that is sometimes, as here, characterized as a "mother-child" relationship. This is explained as: Wood feeds Fire, Fire produces Earth, Earth produces Metal, Metal produces Water, Water nourishes Wood. In Chinese medicine, these five phases are allied to the five major organs: liver with Wood, heart with Fire, spleen with Earth, lungs with Metal, kidneys with Water. Maintaining the correct balance between them is essential for maintaining good health.

growing inner strength a person experiences after breaking through the great doubt into kenshō can cause an elation in the mind that will harm the liver or Wood phase as well.

Generally in the case of eye disease, it is important above all to avoid overtaxing the mind. The mind accords with the Fire phase, so overexertion that excites the mind and Fire phase and causes it to rise upward will, on the principle that Fire overcomes Metal, harm the lungs or Metal phase. The lungs are sometimes referred to as "mother Metal," and on the principle that Metal produces Water,* they are regarded as the mother of the Water phase. When the mother is emaciated and produces only a thin flow of milk, the child will invariably be weak.

When the lungs are damaged, a shortage of water in the kidneys will inevitably result. Since Water acts as mother to the liver or Wood phase, on the principle that Water nourishes Wood, a lack of Water in the kidneys weakens the liver (the child). Since in the system of the five phases, the Wood phase corresponds to the liver among the bodily organs and to the eyes among the five sense organs, the liver governs the eyes. Hence you must try to keep the mind or Fire phase calm and tranquil so that a lack of Water in the body, causing parching of the liver or Wood phase, does not occur.

It is said in a work titled *A Treatise on Nourishing Life*,† "The mind is nourished by silence; the eyes are nourished by darkness." The words "nourishing the eyes in darkness" mean becoming just like a plodding, dull-witted ignoramus. His eyes are shut, he is oblivious of all considerations, pro or con, good or bad, he has nothing to do with the ups and downs, prosperity and decline, of worldly existence, and he pays no heed to the next life or to becoming a Bodhisattva either. In other words, a simpleton of the first order, someone who steers clear of social contact and becomes like a newborn infant that is unaware when people come

---

* That is, moisture forms on the surface of metal.

† This work has not been identified.

and unaware when they depart. Like a wooden man, or a stone woman. If you continue to practice in this way for one or two years, you will one day discover that your eye complaint is completely cured.

When those who have yet to experience kenshō undertake this exercise, it becomes extremely pernicious, the dead, dried-up practice of silent illumination Zen. But when undertaken by those who have already experienced satori, it becomes a great and good activity, nourishing to the Dharma bones and marrow, that focuses and concentrates all the body's primal *ki*. The great teachers of the past all devoted three to five years to tempering and refining their attainment in practice of this kind.

I had poor eyesight when I was young. My eyes often gave me trouble. Then one day in Gifu, Mino Province, I heard some words from an elderly physician named Imagawa Junshō that greatly intrigued and stimulated me: "If you want to have eyes like a hawk," he said, "you should take as your teacher the owl that roosts in the daylight." I took these words, and Layman P'ang's saying, "an eighty-year-old man enters the market with both ears deaf and both eyes blind,"* and worked on them during my practice. I focused on cultivating my mental *ki* in mute silence while continuing my daily fare of Naikan meditation on the side. Before I realized it, the primal *ki* throughout my body had concentrated and filled the sea of *ki* below my navel, and my eyesight began steadily to improve.

I have been sitting up through the night writing this letter in the dim light of a paper-covered lamp (*andon*) without using spectacles. I am presently also engaged, in response to the wishes of students in the area and my own monks, in formal lectures (*teishō*) on the *Ancestral Heroes Collection*, a text teachers in the past have shied away from using because of its extreme difficulty. Every day, in preparation for the talks, I read the text three or four times over. I read twenty or thirty pages of the *Heroic March Sutra* every

---

* These words are not found among Layman P'ang Yun's (d. 808) sayings.

day as well. I carry these books with me even when I am invited somewhere, and I hardly ever have to use my spectacles to read them. If people ask me for a painting, I oblige them. Although seventy years old, I rarely have to use my spectacles when I paint either. Mentally I grow steadily more vigorous, and I am continually traveling around the country to spread the Dharma teaching. Even though I may become tired, I never consider curtailing these efforts. If you would like to be as active and vigorous as I am, it is important that you religiously follow the steps I set forth below, carefully cultivating your primal *ki* so as to retain Water in your system.

Last year you wrote in a letter: "I have resolved to stop taking large doses of medicine that cool the body. Losing four or five eyes wouldn't bother me, as long as I am able to stay alive." As it sounds as though you have arrived at a state of pure concentration in your practice this past year and are steadily gaining strength from it, I feel obliged to remind you that your eyesight is extremely important as well. Here is why: there is a saying, "A student who has not penetrated fully should concentrate on the meaning rather than the words; a student who has penetrated fully should concentrate on the words rather than the meaning."* This means that once you have acquired a bit of strength from your initial attainment, you will be unable to go on and study the words and teachings of the Buddhas and patriarchs, gain a mastery of the circumstances of post-satori practice, and grasp the fundamental principle of the Buddha Way, unless you avail yourself of the power of verbal prajna.†

That is why I earnestly hope that your eyes will be completely

---

* Based on a statement by Zen master Fu-shan to the effect that those who have yet to achieve kenshō should concentrate on grasping the essential principle of Zen, and once it is achieved should confirm their understanding through the study of words and letters (*Blue Cliff Record*, Case 100).

† Verbal prajna (*moji-hannya*). A term, perhaps coined by Hakuin, emphasizing the importance that learning and book knowledge have in his program of post-satori practice.

cured. For the time being, you should stop reading Buddhist writings so avidly, drastically reduce your dealings with others, and set as your foremost priority keeping your eyes shut and working to concentrate your primal *ki* in the cinnabar field.

Chih-i's *Great Cessation and Insight* speaks of two "cessations,"* the cessation of phenomena and the cessation of ultimate truth. In the first cessation, one draws the mind down and concentrates it in the cinnabar field—the area from the lower back down into the feet—and becomes like a dead person, mute, utterly quiescent, oblivious of all external phenomena. The primary object of the cessation is to quiet the mind and *ki* energy. It is the ultimate key to cultivating life. In the second of the cessations, one keeps the mind constantly focused on the basic principle of the true aspect of all phenomena, and the truth of the one, solitary vehicle.† The Buddha taught, "If you concentrate the mind in the soles of the feet and constantly keep it focused in that one place, any illness can be cured."‡ Zen Master Huang-lung Hui-nan often told his assembly, "I always keep my mind down, filling my lower belly."§ This is similar to the cessation of phenomena in Chih-i's work.

Master Shih-t'ai said, "The key to disciplining the body lies in gathering ki. The key to gathering *ki* lies in concentrating the mind. When the mind is concentrated, *ki* gathers. When ki is gathered, cinnabar is produced. When cinnabar is produced, the

---

* *Cessation* and insight (or contemplation), *shikan* in Japanese, are the two chief elements in the program of Buddhist meditation Chih-i sets forth in *Great Cessation and Insight* (*Mo-ho chih-kuan*).

† The *Lotus Sutra* (Expedient Means chapter) teaches that changing phenomena are all ultimately manifestations of truth, and that it is through the vehicle of Buddhahood alone that this is grasped. A similar passage describing the two cessations appears in *Idle Talk on a Night Boat* (see *Hakuin's Precious Mirror Cave*, 106).

‡ Based on the theory that illness, which is caused when the function of one of the four great elements (earth, water, fire, and wind) making up the physical body becomes too strong or too weak, can be rectified by concentrating the mind.

§ These words are not found among Huang-lung's records. In *Wild Ivy* (103), Hakuin attributes them to an unidentified priest named Po-yun.

physical frame is strong. When the physical frame is strong, the life force is full and replete. When the life force is replete, a person can expect to live three hundred years. His eyes and ears will be strong and healthy to the end, and he will enjoy other benefits as well, commensurate with the quality of his practice. Such are the secret methods the sages have employed to refine the cinnabar elixir."*

In the *Treasure Mirror*,† it is written that "the key to refining cinnabar is contained in the teaching of the five nonleakages or nondefilements: eyes not seeing falsely, ears not hearing falsely, nose not smelling falsely, mouth not speaking falsely, body and mind not functioning falsely."‡ This signifies that the five sensory organs—eyes, ears, nose, tongue, and body—correspond to the five phases—Water, Fire, Wood, Metal, and Earth—and refining the cinnabar elixir, the great matter of the ancient sages, to concentrating the five phases down in the ocean of *ki* and the cinnabar field.

Now as we know, the human body is constantly functioning and being made to function, assimilating energy from food and making the blood circulate, all of which are necessary for sustaining life. Since the *Treasure Mirror* refers nonetheless to the body "not functioning falsely," those words must have some deep meaning. It is an important matter students should carefully scrutinize on their own.

"The mouth not speaking falsely" is a means for concentrating the mind and gathering *ki* in the lower body. The best way to go about concentrating the mind is to close your mouth and remain silent. Hence it is said, "In Zen, silence is good; noise, raising a din is not good."§

---

* Neither Master Shih-t'ai nor the passage in question has been identified. In his various works, Hakuin attributes this quote to five different people. See *Idle Talk on a Night Boat* (in *Hakuin's Precious Mirror Cave*, 95).

† I have been unable to identify this work.

‡ The teaching of five nondefilements (*go-muro*, a term that connotes the pure wisdom of Bodhisattvahood and Buddhahood) is a matter of stilling the evil passions by means of the five senses.

§ *Blue Cliff Record*, Case 6.

There is a scripture titled *The Silent Child Sutra*. Its contents may be summarized as follows:* Superior students who practice diligently and achieve kenshō feel an initial joy of great intensity that makes them want to dance around ecstatically. When this happens, if they give in to the selfish desire simply to enjoy the experience, the energy in their minds will inevitably rush upward into their head and shoulders. In many cases, this brings on a condition known as "Fire melting Metal," an almost incurable malady.† Hence students must quiet these initial transports of joy passing through their minds, and make themselves as speechless as newborn infants. An infant intent on sucking its mother's breast utters not a single sound. Its five sensory organs are in perfect working order, but it is as though they are not functioning. Students must become like that, nurturing their Dharma bones intently as their meditation imparts growing strength to them. This is essentially the same as the "infantine practice" taught in the *Nirvana Sutra*.‡

In order to achieve strong and healthy eyes and ears, a steadfast regimen of meditation coupled with the study of texts is essential. The two should complement and strengthen one another. Although such a regimen does not of course belong to the ultimate reaches of the Zen school, it is nonetheless indispensable for a student once he has attained kenshō.

It will be the same with your practice as well. At first you will feel discomforted or gloomy, and you will chafe at the lack of freedom. You will have to buckle down, continue striving assiduously

---

* *The Silent Child Sutra* (*Mugon dōji-kyō*), T401. Hakuin is not summarizing the sutra's contents, but rather recasting them in terms of his own teaching.

† Literally, "the Fire phase at the left pulse point (located at the inner side of the left wrist) melts the Metal phase at the right pulse point (at the inner side of the right wrist)."

‡ Infantine practice (*yōni-gyō*). One of sixteen practices of the Bodhisattva Kannon that are set forth in a chapter of the same name in the (Mahayana) *Nirvana Sutra*. In this practice, the student becomes like an infant that has not yet begun to talk.

for two or even three years, never forgetting the great matter of acquiring strength from this practice of *dhyana* you are engaged in. Instead of pleasures you might be experiencing—meeting and conversing and debating with friends, exchanging pleasantries with acquaintances, pursuing illusions with no more substance than dreams or flowers in the air—you will be returning into the mountains of your fundamental being, the fastness of your self-nature. You will be seeking that native place, simple and un-adorned, where you gaze over fields extending as far as the eye can see, a landscape universally illumined by the bright moon of unchanging suchness, and resplendent with the flowers of prajna wisdom and the cherry blossoms of the other shore. Beneath those trees, you will discover Mani jewels numerous as Ganges sand shining brightly from Indra's Net, each one reflecting all the others.* Yet it will all be as calm and tranquil as the surface of a lake of utterly placid water. It will be like a landscape in the Pure Land of Nirvana, where streams, birds, trees, and forests are all intoning the Buddha's Name and preaching his Dharma.† Not even the wonderful reward of acquiring birth as a human being or deva can compare with it.

Consider this carefully. You received human rebirth so diffi-cult to obtain, you came to believe in the Zen teaching so difficult to encounter. As a result of merit accumulated through contin-ued practice, you entered the samadhi that is beyond comprehen-sion, and you suddenly and unexpectedly grasped, in full and clear realization, the sound of one hand. As this is a rare achieve-ment, it is natural that you would have difficulty restraining your elation. But you are now at a point of essential importance. You must suppress such feelings and quiet your emotions. You must

---

* The metaphor of *Indra's Net*, a net that extends throughout the cosmos with a jewel in each of its meshes, each jewel reflecting all the others in an infinite process, is used to explain the interconnectedness and interpenetration of all phenomena, and the infinite variety and virtues of a Buddha and his teachings.

† Descriptions in the *Amida Sutra* of Amida's Pure Land of Bliss.

cast both the elation you feel and the satori you have attained aside. The Sixth Patriarch said, "If your mind retains a single trace of satori, you're better off back in the state of delusion."* This is what is meant by "transcending both the disease and the medicine"†—once the illness (delusion) is cured, the medicine (satori) must be discarded as well. It is also why it is said that "Students unable to break free from their fixed positions fall back into the poisonous seas of illusion."‡

Years ago a beginning Zen student training under Gudō Rōshi devoted himself assiduously to his meditation practice,§ gradually accumulating merit until his attainment reached maturity. One day he experienced a sudden satori. Beside himself with joy, he began dancing mindlessly about, sobbing and laughing and hooting like a crazy man. Watching him, Gudō's heart filled with joy. He said:

"Unless a person starts waltzing about like that as though he was out of his senses, he can't be said to have truly acquired the strength of kenshō. Still, you mustn't be content with this minor attainment. To reach the ultimate ground of genuine tranquillity, there are still many final and difficult barriers to be be negotiated. Though the sutras say that the initial awakening of the Bodhi-mind is itself genuine awakening, the place you have attained is only at the beginning of the Fifty-two Stages of Bodhisattva-

---

* This saying is not found among the records of the Sixth Patriarch; a similar one by Zen master Hsin-chou Chih-ch'ang appears in the *Records of the Lamp* (ch. 5).

† From the Record of Lin-chi. Lin-chi addressed the assembly and said: "The Zen school doesn't see things that way. What counts is this present moment—there's nothing that requires a lot of time. Everything I am saying to you is for the moment only, medicine to cure the disease. Ultimately it has no true reality" (*The Zen Teachings of Master Lin-chi*, 34).

‡ From the "leakage of views," one of Zen Master Tung-shan's three kinds of delusion, in which a student who adheres to a fixed position "falls into the poisonous seas of illusion" (*Blue Cliff Record*, Case 15).

§ Gudō Tōshoku (1577–1661), an eminent Rinzai priest to whose lineage Hakuin was affiliated. This story is not found among Gudō's published records.

hood.* You have gone beyond the first ten stages, the Stages of
Faith, and have entered the second ten stages, the Stages of Secu-
rity. You have opened the eye of great wisdom that enables you to
discern the oneness of sentient beings and Buddhas, phenomena
and ultimate reality; to see the vast radiance shining gloriously
forth from mountains, rivers, and earth, so that each of the myr-
iad forms arrayed throughout the universe, down to the smallest
maggots, gnats, and blackflies, will tower up before you like a
precipice ten thousand feet high. The irrepressible joy you feel is
thus perfectly understandable. However if you intend to plumb
the profoundest depths of the great ocean of the Dharma, you still
have a long journey remaining before you. The patriarchal gardens
lie beyond the most distant horizon. It is here that many students,
those of middling or inferior capacity, stop, contenting themselves
with a smaller attainment. But you must strive diligently. Do not
give up partway to your goal!

"Resolve that you will muster a spirit of great courage and
dauntlessly turn forward the wheel of the four universal vows,
carrying out the Bodhisattva's great and endless work of seeking
self-attainment while helping others; that you will amass a
boundless store of Dharma assets to use in teaching and benefit-
ting sentient beings.†

"If you fail to penetrate the great matter that furnishes you
with all the virtues of Nirvana, and you remain satisfied with
what you have attained today, you will fall without even knowing
it into the comfortable old nest of a small, partial attainment—a
plausible but incomplete Nirvana of the kind espoused by those
of the Two Vehicles. If that happens, you will end up wasting
your life in the mistaken belief that the wretched state you have

---

* A division of the Bodhisattva's practice into fifty-two stages: ten each of faith, se-
curity, practice, devotion, and development, and the final two stages, enlightenment
and final enlightenment.

† The original text is more specific, naming four virtuous attributes (*shitoku*) that are
acquired on entering Nirvana or enlightenment: abiding in truth, enjoying a state of
bliss, enjoying perfect freedom, and remaining free from all defilement.

attained, inferior by far even to the ignorance of the unenlightened, is great and supreme realization.

"The Buddha once scolded a student for this very reason. 'I'd
sooner you be reborn into the mange-ridden body of an old fox,'
he said, 'than as someone with the meager attainment of the Two
Vehicles.'*

"An old verse says:

> *A clear pool, fathomlessly deep*
> *With a sheer unruffled surface,*
> *Why should a valley stream*
> *Send waves rippling out*
> *Through the shallows?*†

"This is something Zen monks should emulate. It is a verse
they should have constantly on their lips."

After hearing Gudō's remarks, the monk immediately performed a prostration before him. His mind, which had been in a
state of such jubilant excitement, was now perfectly calm and
clear. Afterward, he devoted himself with even greater intensity
to his practice.

What does Gudō mean by "final and difficult barriers"? That
large accumulation of poisonous fox slobber the ancient teachers
in their infinite mercy left behind to enable future generations of
students to overturn the virulent seas of satori fixation, to stomp
the hellish defiling filth of dogmatic views into the dust, to rise
free of the adamantine net of satori elucidation, and to bore out
of the constricting coop of conceptual understanding. Thus the
great Zen Master Yun-men said, "With countless corpses lit-
tering the ground, those who make it through the thicket of

---

* A similar statement appears in Zen Master Bassui's *Covered with Mud, Steeped in
Water* (*Wadei-gassui*), apparently based on a reference in Chih-i's *Great Cessation and
Insight*.

† By the early Heian poet-priest Sosei Hōshi, found in the *Kokinshū*.

thorn and briar are the genuine article, men of the greatest accomplishments."*

"Nan-ch'uan's Death," "Huang-po's Gobblers of Dregs," "Yen-t'ou's Final Word," "Chao-chou's Two Hermits," "Te-shan's Begging Bowl," "Su-shan's Memorial Tower," "Wu-tsu's Buffalo through the Window," "Yen-kuan's Rhinoceros-horn Fan," "Tung-shan's Thirty Blows," "Ch'ien-feng's Three Kinds of Illness," "Yun-men's Examine!" "Secretary Ch'en's Traveling Monks," "The Lady Burns the Hermitage." Every one of these hard-to-pass koan barriers is a briar bush snarling upward beyond the heavens, a growth of razor-edged beach-thorn reaching out far as the eye can see. Any true and authentic weeds that sprout up in the gardens of our school will take these mortally poisonous stories one by one, chew them into submission, and swallow them whole. Then, with the skill of a singing girl performing miraculous feats atop a pole, or a street urchin juggling his gems with marvelous aplomb, they will proceed forward, sporting on their arms divine death-dealing amulets, and crush between their jaws all the poisonous fangs and claws of the Dharma cave. They will trip up packs of plodding donkey-chinned dunces and horse-jawed dolts, and tie them in close knots. They will poison the brains of venerable demon-faced, lop-headed shavepates. They will level the waves of the true tradition rising up from the eastern seas, and scatter the virulent smoke of the transmission wafting in from the west.† In so doing, they will requite the profound and boundlessly vast debt owed to the Buddhas and patriarchs. What a glorious moment it will be!

However, having now learned of these difficult koans I've enumerated, if you immediately take it into your head to start

---

* From the *Comprehensive Records of Yun-men* (*Yun-men kuang-lu*).

† The physiognomy of these "dunces" and "dolts" marks them out as priests of the highest caliber. An anonymous annotation in Hakuin's *Poison Blossoms* adds, "If someone hit them a blow with a stick, they wouldn't even turn their head." The feats listed here that young Zen adepts perform in the post-satori phase of their training exemplify the total freedom of which they are capable.

boring your way through some of them, it will only make your eye complaint return, cause a hazy darkness to rise up on all sides. Before you set about penetrating these koan barriers, you must first cultivate your strength through the practice of Naikan meditation.

I was a young monk of twenty-three when I finally succeeded in stomping underfoot the life-roots that held me to birth and death. I could see the essential matter that negates the great void and smashes iron mountains to dust as though it was in the palm of my hand. But I was still moving as though in the shadow of a lamp, and I was unable to lay either hand or foot on any of those virulently poisonous difficult-to-pass koan stories. Then I was taught the secret method of Naikan meditation. After practicing it constantly both day and night, I suddenly grasped all those difficult and complicated stories. They vanished like ice in a cauldron of boiling water. I felt like a traveler in a strange and remote land who had suddenly encountered his wife and children.

How can others have these same experiences? Empress Lu's Chen.* Mencius's mother's loom.

A MIRACULOUS PRESCRIPTION FOR EYE DISEASE

- Sincerity—dosage: 2 measures
- No words or speech—1 measure
- Total dedication—1 measure
- Untroubled mind—1 measure
- No divertissement—1 measure

---

* Lu Hou, the consort of the Han emperor Kao Tsu, a masculine woman with an iron will, helped her husband consolidate his power. On becoming regent after his death, she murdered her young son's rival with poisoned wine made from the deadly feathers of the Chen-bird, described in the *Book of Former Han* (*Han-shu*) as having a black body, red eyes, and living on venomous snakes. *Empress Lu's Chen* is apparently a reference to the virulence of the hard-to-pass koans, which also bring instant death to students.

As a youth, Mencius decided to give up his studies and return home. When he got there, he found his mother at her weaving. Without a moment's hesitation, while continuing her work, she reproved him severely for his lack of resolve.

+ Patience—5 measures
+ Cloddish ignorance—1 measure
+ Unsociability—1 measure

TEN TABOOS FOR EYE DISEASE

1. Passion and lust
2. Irritation and anger
3. Thinking, discriminating
4. Monetary concerns
5. Running off at the mouth
6. Reading and writing
7. Addiction to Buddhist writings
8. Discussing religious practice
9. Social obligations
10. Fretting

If you scrupulously avoid these ten taboos, your eye disease will be completely cured.

HOZ, 6:441–52; HHZ, 14:201–28

From a brief inscription bearing the date 1746 that Hakuin wrote on a document awarding Koremitsu the Buddhist name "Mumon," we know Koremitsu's study with the master started at least ten years prior to the time this letter was written. The statements Hakuin makes in the letter and the difficulty of the teaching he imparts to Koremitsu would seem to confirm that Koremitsu was an advanced student well conversant with the intricacies of Zen literature.

Hakuin was evidently on familiar terms with Koremitsu's family as well. He asks after Koremitsu's ex-wife Shūshin-ni (*ni* meaning "nun") and his son Sōkichirō, suggesting that Hakuin had probably visited their Edo residence.

Koremitsu also seems to have been related in some way to Murabayashi Erin, also a resident of Asakusa in Edo, who appeared in the first letter in this book ("Letter to Watanabe Sukefusa"). It may be remembered that Hakuin wrote Murabayashi's son Tokusaburō a letter scolding him for unfilial behavior.

Hakuin's diagnosis of Koremitsu's affliction and the recommended cure that he outlines in this letter have similarities to those he sets forth in *Idle Talk on a Night Boat*, the story of his struggle against "Zen sickness" that he had published ten years earlier.

Hakuin himself seems to have suffered from poor eyesight throughout the latter half of his life. He declares on more than one occasion how wonderfully his eyesight improved when he starting practicing Naikan meditation. Yet he owned, and presumably used, a pair of spectacles, and though some of the inscriptions he wrote dating from late in his life end with the boast, "I didn't even need my spectacles to write [or paint] this," there are others in which he excuses his "poor brushwork" by saying, "I wrote it without using my spectacles."

This is one of half a dozen or so long letters that Hakuin wrote to advise students who were suffering from illness. Among the letters were several addressed to people like Koremitsu who were plagued by eye complaints, and to them Hakuin prescribes the Naikan meditation. To those afflicted with more serious maladies, he advises recitation of the *Ten Phrase Kannon Sutra*. In one letter, addressed to the lay Zen practicer O-Satsu, who was caring for a sick but disobedient teacher, Hakuin describes the mental attitude that the person engaged in nursing the patient should assume.

10

To Yoda

LETTER 10, 1755

This letter is addressed to Layman Yoda Takanaga, a wealthy farmer and landowner of Izu Province. Dated the eleventh month of 1755, Hakuin's seventieth year, the letter attempts to resolve a feud between two elderly female members of the Yoda family.

The Yodas, one of the most influential families in the province, had enjoyed close ties with Hakuin from his early years at Shōin-ji. The letter does not supply a given name, but in as much as Mr. Yoda's father and grandfather both adopted the hereditary name "Takanaga" on becoming head of the family, we may assume he did as well. He and his father both studied Zen under Hakuin, appearing in his records as patrons of nearby Kiichi-ji, where Hakuin taught on a number of occasions, and as donors to some of Hakuin's building projects.

I AM GLAD to hear that everyone in your family is well. Nothing has changed here, either.

I became worried last year when I heard rumors about discord in your household. On further thought, knowing what fine people you all are, I dismissed them as a piece of baseless gossip.

Recently, however, Tenkoku Oshō of Kiichi-ji made a special

trip here all the way from southern Izu.* He wanted my help in healing a family quarrel that he said was causing you and your family serious distress. He is eager to get things patched up before the upcoming seventeenth-death-anniversary ceremony for Daizō-in [the posthumous name of Takanaga's father].

I was impressed by the compassion Tenkoku Oshō has shown in trying to reconcile the two parties so that the memorial ceremony can be carried out successfully. Listening to him describe the strained relations that presently exist, it didn't seem to me that either party was acting in a totally unreasonable or outrageous manner.

I am sure that Daizō-in in the other world sees all these goings-on as clearly as if it was in the palm of his hand. If both sides will take into account the considerable trouble Tenkoku Oshō has gone to in making the long trip here to see me, reconcile their differences, forgive and forget all that has happened in the past, and participate in the ceremony in a warm and friendly spirit, the event will be a much greater success than could ever be attained by mere offerings of food and drink, even if ten thousand priests came and performed the services. Imagine how pleased the deceased would be to see that happen!

But if they do not do this, if they continue bickering and stubbornly refuse to budge from their own selfish views, and separate ceremonies have to be held, then no matter how elaborate they are and how rare and lavish the offerings, the fires of their wrathful thoughts will separate them from the deceased by a barrier more formidable than hellish sword-leaved trees and razor-sharp mountains. Not even a single drop of water will reach him. They will achieve nothing except to wreck his hopes for attaining the other shore of enlightenment, and totally eclipse his aspiration for the full moon of ultimate suchness. If you went through the Buddhist sutras and commentaries, vernacular writings, and

---

* Nothing is known about this priest.

even the stories and books of foreign lands, I think you would find clear agreement that in such a case there is no alternative for the deceased but to suffer intense torment and agony. That is the reason the sutras say, "The fire produced by even a single thought-instant of anger becomes a conflagration that consumes the merits of good deeds however infinite in number."*

In *Tales of Past and Present*, the story is told of a dream that a Tendai bishop had one night long ago on Mount Hiei in Kyoto.† He beheld splendid Buddhist halls and pavilions richly decorated with gold and silver, filled to overflowing with shelves upon shelves of scripture. There were groups of five, ten, fifty, and a hundred scrolls of the *Lotus Sutra* embellished with precious jewels and pearls, set out in beautifully serried rows. Suddenly, he saw flames appear from one of the scrolls. They spread with tremendous speed, becoming an inferno towering into the sky. The bishop was astonished. "Why would they burn like that?" he asked himself.

An elderly priest standing nearby said, "Forty years ago, a priceless scroll of Buddhist scripture just like those was discovered in this temple. People were beside themselves with joy, and came to pay homage to it. Then, unaccountably, the scroll suddenly burst into flames. The fire spread quickly to the other sutras stacked on the shelves. Bishop, are you aware that the number of sutras now on the shelves of this hall is exactly the same as those you have read during your forty years of residence here? What is to be dreaded above all else are the fires of wrath.

"Proclaim a resolute vow that from this day forth you will conduct yourself like the Bodhisattva Never Despising, always retaining a tranquil mind and never succumbing to thoughts of

---

* Similar statements appear in the seventh-century Buddhist encyclopedia *Fa-yuan Chu-lin* (*Forest of Gems from the Dharma Gardens*) and in the poems of Han-shan.

† *Tales of Past and Present* (*Konjaku monogatari*), ch. 8, "Words of Dōjō, Priest of the Sonshō-in of Hosshō-ji."

anger, regardless of the difficulties you may encounter.* Unless you can do this, you should give up reading sutras altogether.

"You yourself saw how the flames that appeared from the sacred scriptures rose into an uncontrollable conflagration before they could be stopped and rapidly spread and consumed all the sutras you read in your tenure here. And not only the sutras either, for the flames of anger will consume every bit of merit you have obtained from all the good deeds you have performed."

With that, the Bishop woke up.

It should be clear from this story that if the Buddhist services and other good works you and your family perform for the deceased are carried out in a spirit of harmony and mutual understanding, they will have the virtue and merit of a benevolent act of the highest order. If, on the other hand, they take place in an atmosphere of enmity and anger, those evil thoughts will turn into flames as surely as the fire that appeared from the sutras the bishop had read. They will grow and spread until they become a raging conflagration. If that happens, not only will you fail in your attempt to offer help to the deceased; you will inflict terrible damage and suffering on him.

From the time Daizō-in was a young man, he taxed flesh and bone, endured ten thousand difficulties of every kind, in order to ensure that his children and everyone in his family would be provided for and never have to suffer want. He assumed that after his death you would all come together on his memorial days in a spirit of good will and perform the proper rites for his repose in the next world. Even in his dreams he could never have imagined that members of his family would become so alienated toward each other, harbor such bitter resentment—as though they were perpetually warring states.

---

* Never Despising (Sadāparibhūta), a Bodhisattva who appears in the *Lotus Sutra*. He bowed to everyone he met, declaring, "you will become a Buddha." Thinking he was making fun of them, people beat him with sticks and threw stones at him. But he still kept bowing to people and telling them they would become Buddhas.

Any good acts performed in such circumstances could never be in accord with the mind of the deceased. Memorial services conducted in the absence of such accord will do nothing to aid him in reaching enlightenment. If Daizō-in were alive today, would he be pleased to witness this squabbling? Wouldn't he be angered? Wouldn't he be moved to tears? If he was alive and received separate invitations issued by the two sides asking him to attend their ceremonies, what do you think he would say? Surely, whether alive or dead, he would decline them. If you want your actions to be in accord with the wishes of the deceased and assist him to enlightenment, nothing you could do would be more beneficial than to conduct a single harmonious ceremony with your hearts and minds at peace.

For someone of Daizō-in's virtue and benevolence, wise men and women will begin working together several years prior to the funeral rites to make sure they will be conducted in a fitting manner. They will pledge to spare neither themselves nor their purses, nor to shrink from the performance of any austerities—even mutilating their bodies, arms, or fingers, or holding a burning wick in lamp oil in the palm of their hand. They will hasten tearfully about carrying out the preparations, oblivious of the physical and mental hardship—copying sutras using their own blood, offering large donations, carving and enshrining images of Buddhas and Bodhisattvas, erecting sutra mounds,* holding meager feasts, undertaking strict observance of the precepts, chanting and copying out sutras—there is no end to the efforts and self-sacrifice they will undertake.

---

* The creation of *sutra mounds* (*kyōzuka*), normally by burying a sutra in the ground in a metal vessel to preserve it for posterity, was done to accumulate merit. Usually the sutras were copied out on paper, although sometimes copper, clay, tiles, and shells were used. Making the mounds with pebbles was popular in the Edo period, with the devotee writing one character from a sutra text on each of the pebbles, until he had inscribed the entire text. The stones were then buried in the ground, covered by a mound of earth, and, in some cases, capped by a memorial stone.

Recently, some of the women who visit my hermitage from the Negata area around Mount Fuji walk down along the beach a mile or so away, gather up a basket of the flat pebbles they find on the shore, and carry them here on their backs. Then for the sake of their father, mother, or husband, they create a "pebble sutra" by inscribing a single Chinese character from the *Lotus Sutra* on each of the stones. When the text is complete, they bury the stones in a sutra mound. Two of them summoned a priest when the sutra mound was finished, and had him perform rites before it. In the past, women have sold themselves into slavery in order to be able to conduct these services for their parents' repose in the next life.

What are those family members of yours thinking? Performing virtuous acts like these never seems to have entered their minds. Without any consideration at all for the deceased, they just persist in their hostility, exchanging meaningless insults. Even if they go through the motions of holding Buddhist services, with minds filled with such malicious thoughts, there is no possible way they could respond to the needs of the deceased.

Please make sure that the elderly ladies at Yoshida and Matsuzaki read the contents of this letter carefully.* Tell them that Hakuin said they should cease their bickering. They should overlook matters that are of no real consequence, and show understanding for each other's views. Layman Daizō-in's seventeenth death anniversary will not come again. They must remember the brevity of human existence—"brief as the morning dew, brief as a lightning flash." Since they are over sixty and seventy now, no one can guarantee they will be around for the next services on the twenty-fifth anniversary or on the thirtieth anniversary after that. No one lives forever, so they should make up their minds that this is the last chance to take part in services for Daizō-in, and resolve that for his sake they will exert every effort, undergo any hardship, forgiving and forgetting everything that has trans-

---

* These are two small villages, now incorporated into the town of Matsuzaki, not far from the main Yoda residence.

pired in the past, and do their best to make the ceremony a complete success.

Now, having come to the end of this letter, I am going to address a few words directly to the priest at Gyokurin-an.* I don't know about more distant provinces, but I am sure any of the inhabitants of Suruga or Izu would be delighted to enjoy the Yoda family's wealth and prosperity, which provides them an abundance of all that the world has to offer. Do you suppose this success proceeds from the gods and Buddhas? Isn't it all the result of the virtue and benevolence of the deceased, Daizō-in? Since this will be his seventeenth death anniversary, preparations should have begun several years ago. You should have been encouraging people to give their unqualified support, working together with them to create and enshrine Buddhist images, to copy passages from the sutras, or, since that is popular now, to erect a pebble sutra mound, so people who see it will pause and pay reverence, remarking that it was donated on the occasion of Daizō-in's seventeenth death anniversary. Isn't it your responsibility to promote activities of this kind? But even without going to such lengths, it shouldn't be too much trouble to arrange for a smaller ceremony, ten or twenty people gathering for services at Gyokurin-an and performing meritorious acts such as offering food and drink to the attending priests, reciting and copying sutras, and the like. No one would refuse to take part in such meetings if they know it is for Daizō-in.

I find it hard to understand why you have shown no concern or involved yourself at all in this death anniversary. It is completely at odds with the purpose and aspiration you have always shown. I cannot understand it at all. Daizō-in's seventeenth anniversary will not come again. Everything is now dependent on you. You should go and visit as many people as possible, plead with them for their support, on bended knees if need be, so that the event will be carried out successfully from first to last. This is

---

* A small subtemple belonging to Kiichi-ji located near the Yoda residence.

something no one can do for you. It is extremely negligent for a priest of your capacity, who resides so close to the home of the deceased, to behave in this manner. Once the death anniversary passes, whatever you do will be for naught. No help whatsoever to the deceased. Everything depends on your resolve. The matter is entirely in your hands.

If you come up with some good ideas, you can tell me about them in person, since I will probably be visiting Matsuzaki before long. Or you can tell Tenkoku Oshō, and I can learn the particulars from him. It should be possible for the two of us to meet at Enashi, Tabi, Kuchino, or some other nearby port, and make the passage to Izu in the same boat. My powers are limited, but my counsel may still be of help to you. That said, I have a great many obligations. It is not always possible for me to go where I want and do exactly as I wish. Still, inasmuch as Tenkoku Oshō made a special trip all the way here to see me, and considering the importance of straightening out the troubles in the Yoda household, neither am I able simply to sit silently by.

I am sorry to put you to the bother of reading this long letter, but I didn't know how else to convey my thoughts to you. I stayed up all night, rubbing the fatigue from my old eyes, to compose this long and useless sermon. I hope you will give these matters your careful consideration, and I hope that everyone concerned will find their way to set their past grievances aside, get together and talk things over, and finally put this quarrel behind them.

AN AUSPICIOUS DAY, THE FIRST MONTH OF FIFTH YEAR
OF HŌREKI (1755), THE OLD PRIEST HAKUIN

PS: To the Yoda family. You should regard the priest of Gyokurin-an as a messenger from Daizō-in, dispatched to transmit his views to you all from the other world. Please accord him the utmost hospitality.

HOZ, 6:432–40; HHZ, 14:157–66

This letter, like the one scolding Watanabe Sukefusa (pp. 1–14) for failing to carry out his filial obligations, deals with the kind of moral correction Hakuin, as a village priest, was probably frequently called on to perform. The precise nature of the ladies' quarrel is not specified, though it sounds like a classic wife and mother-in-law feud. Hakuin entered the picture because the enmity between the women had poisoned family relations to the point of causing obstacles in conducting an important religious ceremony for Takanaga's father, referred to here by his posthumous name, Layman Daizō-in, who died in 1739.

In Japanese Buddhism, ceremonies for the deceased are held periodically following the original funeral, which is regarded as the first yearly observance. Although the intervals between observances vary according to sectarian and local customs, ceremonies are generally held several times during the first year following the death, then in the third, fifth, seventh, thirteenth, seventeenth, thirty-ninth, and fiftieth years, though here Hakuin mentions services in the twenty-fifth and thirtieth years as well. All the meetings are conducted in a similar fashion, with a Buddhist priest or priests chanting from a sutra while family and guests offer incense in front of the altar, usually followed by a meager or vegetarian feast. The merit that accrues from these activities is believed to facilitate the deceased's liberation from the cycle of birth and death, and eventual attainment of Buddhahood.

In addition to encouraging Takanaga, as head of the family, to convince the two parties to forgive each other, Hakuin also takes to task the head priest of Gyokurin-an, who will officiate at the ceremony, for not taking a more active role in preparing for the event. Gyokurin-an was a subtemple of nearby Kiichi-ji and had been built by the Yodas as a family temple. The identity of this head priest is unknown.

Yoda's father's relationship with Hakuin is known from "A Record of the Sutra Repository at Kiichi-ji," a document, included in the *Poison Blossoms* collection, that Hakuin wrote in his forty-eighth year (1733). In it he describes the circumstances surrounding the construction of a sutra repository to house a set of the Buddhist scriptures, praising Takanaga for providing funds to complete the project at a time when work had come to a standstill, and for donating a full set of Buddhist sutras. He then writes:

> Yoda Takanaka, the head of one of the wealthiest families in southern Izu, lives in extremely affluent circumstances. By donating a small fraction of his wealth, he was able to procure with great dispatch a full set of sutras and commentaries, and to assure that the construction of a sutra repository was completed as well. To maintain the gift, he also donated some rich rice fields with a yield of several *koku* of rice.* In the *Sutra of Forty-two Sections,* the Buddha said, "There are twenty things that are difficult for human beings. One is for a person of great wealth and position to develop an aspiration for the Way." A person like Takanaka, it would seem, has been exempted from a prophecy that issued from the golden mouth of the Buddha himself. An exception of inestimable value! (*Poison Blossoms from a Thicket of Thorn,* 5)

Hakuin made frequent trips up and down the Izu peninsula, visiting temples and lay residences for practice meetings, lectures, and talks. He also spent time recuperating from his travels at some of the hot springs for which the peninsula is famous. The Yoda residence was located in a particularly remote area of the peninsula about ten miles up the coast from its southern tip. Hakuin probably took the most direct route on his trips to Izu, traveling by small boat straight across Suruga Bay to avoid the long coastal road that winds interminably along the deeply indented western side of the peninsula.

The large and stately Yoda residence overlooking the Naga River that flows through Matsuzaki is in more or less the same state it was when Hakuin visited, although it is now the Ōsawa-ya, a large inn and hot springs.

---

* One *koku* was about five U.S. bushels.

11

Two Letters to Sakai Kantahaku Sensei

LETTERS 11–12, C. 1755

Sakai Kantahaku ("Sensei" is a term of respect) is known to history solely from the information in these letters. He was a member of what seems to have been a sizable community of Hakuin's lay followers in Edo who took part in the practice and lecture meetings that Hakuin conducted on his trips there. The city was only a few days' journey from Hara, eighty miles east on the Tōkaidō Road, and on occasion many of these students also made the trip to Shōin-ji to continue their study with the master.

Hakuin's visits to Edo, some of which lasted for many months, evidently were more frequent than the handful recorded in the *Chronological Biography*. The evidence of Hakuin's acquaintance with the city, its inhabitants, and its vibrant cultural life is found scattered throughout his writings, suggesting that he found the bustling new metropolis well suited to his own irrepressible personality.

Although it seems likely that both letters to Sakai belong roughly to the same period, only one of them can be dated, so there is no way to determine their sequence. I will start with the one that provides the most information about Sakai's life, since it will help introduce him.

We learn from this letter that Sakai was a samurai, unmarried, and living in Edo, with a strong interest in the martial arts. He had not yet entered service but had some experience studying Zen, probably with Hakuin, apparently without much success. That he was unmarried and not yet in service suggests he was also young. The letter is filled with the admonitions and exhortations typical of Hakuin's teaching letters, but the personal tone found in his more private letters is evident as well.

LETTER 11

As I had not had any news or letter from you for a while, I was glad to hear that you are now in Edo, healthier and heartier than ever. As for this old monk, I'm almost ashamed to admit the fine fettle I'm in.

I cannot commend you too much for your determination to continue koan practice while you pursue your martial arts training. I heard from En Zōsu that your study in that field is more or less completed.* Now is thus an excellent time for you to carry out your long-cherished desire, and focus solely on resolving the great matter of essential importance to you. To continue procrastinating as you have in a world as fleeting and transient as a lightning flash or morning dew, your mind constantly fixed on affairs of a purely mundane nature, reveals a total and woeful lack of the resolution necessary for the task. Even if you train in the martial arts until you are as proficient as Kyūrō with the sword or Sanada with the lance, in the end it will be worth no more than a vision in a dream or a flower in the air. Practice of the martial arts prepares one for the moment of conflict. Koan practice prepares you to face death. As long as the world is at peace, warriors have no

---

* Zōsu is the title for the monk who holds the post of temple librarian; it seems also to have been used more loosely to refer to a senior monk generally. En Zōsu appears in both letters, but unfortunately he cannot be identified.

need to reach for their weapons. But not a single person anywhere in the world can avert the coming of death.

Should conflict break out, it is only natural for those trained in the military arts to receive stipends to carry out their duty as vassals of a lord. But you are not in that position. You do not owe a single debt of loyalty to a lord, and you still happily enjoy a carefree bachelorhood. Although in your present circumstances you are in no way different from a young monk who has left home for the priesthood, I can't avoid the impression that your aim is to be ready, should hostilities occur, to run out and take a few heads so your exploits will be recognized and rewarded with a position and regular stipend. If that is indeed what is in your mind, it is contemptible in the extreme. And if things were to go against you, there is no assurance your own head would not fall.

From now on, what is essential for you is to begin focusing single-mindedly on your koan practice in the safe, utterly riskless pursuit of kenshō, setting your sights on rewards that are eternal and never ending. There is an old waka,

> *Wisdom in this floating world*
> *Urges us to discard that self*
> *We'd discarded once before,*
> *Surely no one can rely at all*
> *On a self of such little worth!*

Repeat this poem over and over, so that the next time we meet, it will describe your own state of mind.

The second letter was written to enlist Sakai's help in an urgent project Hakuin was involved in. He wanted to have a woodblock engraved with an image of the deity Akiba Gongen, so that prints could be made and distributed to participants at a ceremony he was scheduled to conduct at the Kannon-ji Zen temple in Hara. An illustration of the print is found on p. 113.

The ceremony is mentioned in the *Chronological Biography,* which enables us to place the letter in Hakuin's seventieth year: "In the ninth month of 1755, Hakuin's neighbor Uematsu Suetsuna donated a statue of the deity Akiba Gongen to the Kannon-ji Zen temple in Hara and asked the master to perform enshrinement rites for it" (*Hakuin's Precious Mirror Cave,* 221). We know from another earlier entry that in 1736 Uematsu had established the Kannon-ji on the site of a former Hara temple.

LETTER 12

WITH ALL THE FIRES we have been having recently, and more and more people turning to Akiba Gongen for help, someone has proposed that printed images of the deity be produced so they can be freely distributed to ordinary citizens.

I include with this letter a drawing I did of Akiba Gongen. I am sorry to trouble you, but I would like you to take the drawing to a skilled woodblock cutter in Edo and have him use it to engrave a wooden block from which printings can be made. This should be done as quickly as possible. Villagers here in Hara have built a small Akiba Shrine, and an enshrinement ceremony for a wooden image of the deity has been scheduled for the seventeenth of next month. Since at that time I would like to present each of the participants with a woodblock print of the deity, I am anxious that the work be completed with all speed.

As soon as you receive this letter, if you set out on horseback and locate an engraver, it might even be possible for you to deliver the finished woodblock and prints to me here in person. I would appreciate it much more than any gift you could bring me from Edo. You can stay here at Shōin-ji, and remain as long as you like, one year, two years, doesn't matter. I'll see to it that you aren't treated the way you were on your last visit, when they put you to work cleaning and sweeping and drawing water. Brother En has been talking about you. He said he is looking forward to your

Woodblock print of Akiba Gongen. Private collection.

arrival, and that this time things should work out just fine. No need to worry about shivering from cold or going hungry while you're here.

But it is of the utmost importance that the completed prints arrive here by the seventeenth of the ninth month. Since I want to be absolutely certain that they do, if you should become sick or some other unavoidable circumstance arise to prevent you from performing your task, I want you to wrap the painting, this letter, and the money I am enclosing together, bind it all up very securely, and send it to Mr. Iseya Shirōemon in the Kuramae area of Asakusa. Tell Iseya to hire a skilled woodcarver who he is sure will do a good job. I will send money to recompense him for his time and trouble. Tell him that if it is not enough, I will send more.

Please exercise the greatest care in carrying out these instructions. Regard this as being a once-in-a-lifetime request directly from me. As soon as the prints are done, send them by regular *sando* post.[*] I will take care of all charges at this end. As all these efforts will be meaningless if the prints do not arrive by the seventeenth of next month, the donor has told me to impress upon you the necessity for all possible haste. I must add that although speed is of the essence, the woodblock must not be carved in a hasty or slipshod manner, since it will become a treasure of the temple, to preserve and to use for future printings.

I apologize for bothering you with so many troublesome details, but do not doubt that your efforts will be for an extremely worthy cause. You will be performing an act of devotion of very great merit. So I ask that you move expeditiously and bend your steps through the streets of Edo to carry out my request.

---

[*] An express postal service between Edo and Osaka that carried official documents, letters, and parcels, left three times monthly (*sando hikyaku*), on the second, twelfth, and twenty-second. There was also a private courier service, *santo hikyaku* (mentioned below), between the three main cities (*santo*), Edo, Kyoto, and Osaka. This courier service took about eight days to cover the distance from Edo to Osaka; the time for an ordinary pedestrian was closer to two weeks.

If you would rather someone else deliver the painting to Mr. Iseya, that will be quite all right too, providing the person you select can be depended on. In that case, be sure to include a letter in your own hand politely requesting the assistance. Iseya Shirōemon and I go back quite a way and have a regular correspondence, so I cannot imagine that he would receive you with anything but the greatest courtesy. If by any chance he does not, however, you will have to turn elsewhere for help. It is hard to imagine it would come to that, but if it does, feel free to make use of the piece of silver I have enclosed.

But whichever way you decide to do it, given the importance of this printing, I must earnestly request that you proceed with the utmost diligence and greatest care. When the prints are completed, if you find there is not enough time left to send them by regular *sando* post and you need a faster method, use a commercial carrier. They can deliver it to us in two days. But you must be careful, because occasionally they run behind schedule. Make sure if you use them that the package will arrive in time. Either method you choose, we will pay the postage at this end.

Write and confirm receipt of this letter as soon as it arrives. I await your reply.

HZB, *165–66*

Uematsu Suetsuna (1701–71), who donated the funds for the printing project, was the head of one of wealthiest families in Suruga Province. A close lifelong friend of Hakuin, his large and beautiful residence was (and is) located literally right around the corner from Shōin-ji. Uematsu was a great patron of the arts, and he kept picture albums filled with paintings and inscriptions that celebrated writers and artists of the time, such as Ike Taiga and Maruyama Ōkyō, painted at his request while stopping over to enjoy his hospitality on their way through Hara on the Tōkaidō Road.

There is an underlying sharpness to this second letter (more pronounced in the original than in the translation), undoubtedly a reflection of Hakuin's great concern with getting the job done on time. It is interesting to see him ordering a member of the samurai class around as he might a servant, while simultaneously using fairly polite language.

The letter also allows us to make the additional inferences that Mr. Sakai may have been sickly, and so unprepossessing that Mr. Iseya, probably a merchant, might treat him rudely. Iseya's identity (the name actually refers to his business or shop) cannot be traced, in part because this name was so popular at the time that it figured with other phenomena frequently encountered in Edo in a popular saying: "Fires, quarrels, Iseya, and dog turds." The final item on the list, it should perhaps be mentioned, was a remnant of the policies of Tokugawa Tsunayoshi, the infamous "Dog Shogun."

Shrines to Akiba Gongen, a protective deity worshipped by followers of Shinto, Buddhism, and Shugendō, seem to have started appearing around the beginning of the Edo period, though the main center of the Akiba cult was the large Shinto Shrine on Mount Akiba in Tōtōmi Province. The word *gongen*, "temporary manifestation," refers to the various forms the Buddhas and Bodhisattvas that were imported into Japan assumed as indigenous Shinto deities. Akiba Gongen was believed to be an incarnation of the Bodhisattva Kannon.

According to one legend, Akiba was originally a Buddhist monk named Sanjakubō; through rigorous ascetic practice he sprouted birdlike wings that enabled him to fly freely through the air, sometimes riding astride a white fox. Revered even prior to the Edo period as a deity who protected against fire, it was during the shogun Tsunayoshi's reign (1680–1709), a period of tremendous conflagrations, that worship of Akiba reached its peak.

Woodblock prints of Akiba Gongen like the one shown here, mounted in scroll form to be hung up as charms or amulets, still can be found, usually in rather battered condition, in bookseller's catalogues, with a frequency that suggests Shōin-ji issued multiple printings during the later Edo period. Hakuin attempted to spread Akiba worship among the populace in other ways as well, depicting the deity not only in countless ink drawings, but in large and elaborate paintings, some of which rank among his most impressive artistic works. But in sheer numbers, Hakuin's greatest contribution in this line were the single-line inscriptions bearing the name "Akiba Gongen," which he was constantly writing and giving people to hang in their homes as protective charms against fire (see p. 184).

For Hakuin, of course, Akiba Gongen's powers were not limited to protecting against fire. Like his Buddhist counterpart Kannon Bodhisattva, Akiba was capable of bringing Buddhist practicers endless blessings of every kind: "Properly speaking, the custom of hanging up scrolls of painting and calligraphy, even great masterpieces, achieves nothing in the end but to gratify temporarily the vulgar eyes of the viewer. There is no real benefit. However, if you have the inscriptions of the sacred names of Akiba and Kompira mounted, hang them in your alcove, and from time to time place some incense before them and venerate them while doing *gasshō*, you will immediately dispel the seven calamities and beget the seven kinds of good fortune. What act of goodness could exceed this?" (HHZ, 6:95).

12

Six Letters to Senior Priest Zenjo

LETTERS 13–18, 1757–58

These six letters to Hakuin's disciple Daishū Zenjo (1730–78) in Kyoto, where Daishū had been stationed to steer his teacher's manuscripts through the publishing process, chronicle the long saga of the vicissitudes encountered in getting one of Hakuin's most important works, *Poison Blossoms from a Thicket of Thorn*, into print.[*]

Addressed to Zenjo Shuso, or Senior Priest Zenjo, the letters reveal the great importance publishing came to assume in the final decades of Hakuin's life, and provide fascinating insights into this important aspect of Hakuin's teaching activity, whose strategies and inner workings would otherwise be almost completely unknown. In just the two years during which these letters were written, in addition to the ten volumes of the *Poison Blossoms* collection (which included a one-volume *Supplement*), two other important works, *Idle Talk on a Night Boat* and *Precious Mirror's Lingering Radiance*, appeared as well.

---

[*] The translations and commentary in this chapter are based largely on the article "Hakuin no kambun goroku Keisō dokuzui hankō no kei-i" [Circumstances surrounding the publishing of *Poison Blossoms from a Thicket of Thorn*, Hakuin's Zen records in Chinese] by Yoshizawa Katsuhiro, in the periodical *Hanazono daigaku kokusai zengaku kenkyūsho ronsō* vol. 2 (2007): 97–129.

Daishū, who one prominent Zen historian has ranked along with Tōrei, Suiō Genro, and Shikyō Eryō as one of Hakuin's four major disciples, practiced under Hakuin for more than ten years. A native of Hōki Province (in present Tottori Prefecture), Daishū returned to western Japan in 1764 and was installed as head priest at Jishō-ji in Buzen Province (present Oita Prefecture) on the island of Kyushu. Although few details are available about Daishū's later teaching career, it was apparently a fairly distinguished one, since after his death he was awarded a Zen master title. Modern art historians have focused on Daishū's friendship with the well-known Nanga painter Ike Taiga, a lay follower of Hakuin, who on an extended visit to Jishō-ji executed a number of noteworthy *fusuma* and screen paintings. Most of the fifteen letters that Hakuin wrote Daishū have been preserved at Jishō-ji, mounted together as a horizontal scroll.

Despite Daishū's importance in Hakuin's Dharma lineage, his name appears only briefly in Hakuin's Zen records. Two anecdotes are recorded in *Stories from a Thicket of Thorn and Briar,* a nineteenth-century collection devoted to the leading priests in Hakuin's line. One of them describes Daishū's arrival at Shōin-ji as a young monk:

Daishū Zenjo, from Hōki Province, was a man of great natural intelligence. He acquired an extensive knowledge of the Buddhist scriptures and Confucian classics. However, being still unversed in the teachings of the *I Ching,* he set out for Edo with the intention of studying with the leading Confucian teachers there. He stopped over at Hakuin's temple on his way through Suruga Province. Hakuin asked his reason for going to Edo. "I haven't been able to make much headway with the *I Ching,*" he replied. "I thought I'd seek instruction from some of the teachers there." "You won't be able to understand the *I Ching,*" said Hakuin, "unless you first acquire the power that comes from kenshō. Why don't you stay here and practice for a while. If you achieve kenshō, I will personally explain the *I Ching* to you." That is how Daishū came to join the assembly at Shōin-ji, and eventually achieved kenshō. He stayed on at the temple as Hakuin's attendant for ten years. He compiled and edited the master's *Poison Blossoms from a Thicket of Thorn*.

—STORIES FROM A THICKET OF THORN AND BRIAR, 39–43

Poison Blossoms from a Thicket of Thorn, a ten-volume compilation of Hakuin's Zen records, contains material in a wide variety of Zen genres produced in the course of his teaching career, such as religious verse, comments on koans, instructions to students, Dharma talks, remarks delivered at death anniversaries and funeral services, letters, prefaces, painting inscriptions, lengthy essays, a treatise on the Five Ranks, and a commentary on the *Heart Sutra*. Although it is unquestionably one of the major works of Hakuin Zen, the difficulties involved in reading *Poison Blossoms* have kept it from being more widely known, even to priests in Hakuin's own Rinzai school. One of the chief difficulties is the topical nature of many of the pieces, which were written for a specific person or occasion—events and names that had been known to Hakuin's immediate followers were gradually forgotten and much of their underlying meaning rendered unintelligible with the passage of time.

The circumstances surrounding the publishing of *Poison Blossoms* are involved, and can no longer be known with certainty. One version of the events is given in the colophon to the work. It is attributed to Kida Ganshō (n.d), a wealthy Osaka merchant and Zen student (also referred to here by the sobriquet "Kurogane-ya"), although it appears likely that Hakuin had at least a hand in writing it:

On my way through Suruga Province to the northeastern provinces in the winter of the sixth year of the Hōreki era (1756), I stopped at Shōin-ji and had an audience with Zen Master Hakuin. He was suffering from illness at the time, so I waited and received his instruction when his condition had improved enough to allow it. During my stay, I read a manuscript of Hakuin's Zen records in nine fascicles that was kept in the attendants' quarters. It was compiled by the Zen man Daishū of Hōki Province. In it, master Hakuin vigorously attacks sham Zen teachings that have sprung up around the country with words and phrases of great power and lofty, penetrating Zen thrusts. It was like hearing the howls of the lion king, or ground-shaking thunder. At times he points out errors in the *Blue Cliff Record*, at times he clarifies the meaning of the Five Ranks. Anyone who reads it is certain to cast false teachings aside and turn to the authentic path of Zen. Here in these pages his guidance for negotiating the secret depths emerges with a great strength and vigor that is totally beyond ordinary unenlightened understanding. If such a work did not exist, how could a student know the genuine path of Zen practice?

It started me thinking. If this manuscript were published, students would be able to more readily attain the Zen source. When I mentioned this to the Rōshi, he replied, "No, don't do that. If notions my mouth was allowed to mumble off in my sleep were published, it would only steer future generations off course. I want you to burn that manuscript. I see no need to go out of my way to humiliate myself." Despite my best efforts to make him change his mind, he remained adamantly opposed to the idea.

When it came time for me to leave Shōin-ji, I bundled the manuscript secretly in with my belongings, took it back to Osaka with me, and began to arrange for it to be published as quickly as possible. There was no time for the text to be properly edited, so it is possible that some of the Chinese characters may be mistaken, and for that I must beg the reader's indulgence. I can only hope and pray, however, that these records now published will become a standard against which future generations of Zen students will measure themselves.

As the true story seems to have been quite different from this, Kida appears to be playing, or being made to play, his part in another of Hakuin's fictions. We will see in reading the following letters to Daishū that it was Hakuin himself who conceived the idea of publishing *Poison Blossoms*. Hakuin played a central role in compiling the original manuscript, then pressed forward with great determination, in the face of many setbacks, until the project was finally completed.

It is not known exactly when *Poison Blossoms* first appeared. The publication date is sometimes given as 1758, but it was likely the spring of 1759, when the one-volume *Supplement* was also published.

LETTER 13, EIGHTH OF THE FOURTH MONTH, 1757

Although he was now seventy-two, this period was one of the busiest of Hakuin's career. For much of 1757 he was on the road moving from temple to temple in order to conduct lecture meetings at locations in Suruga, Kai, Tōtōmi, and Shinano provinces (detailed itineraries are given below, as well as in the section on the Hakuin-Tōrei letters.

The first of the six letters is a response to a progress report on the printing of *Poison Blossoms* that Hakuin had received from Daishū in Kyoto. The letter is mainly concerned with a preface to the work that Hakuin had requested from the Confucian teacher Yanada Zeigan. One of the leading scholars of the age, Zeigan, employed by the Himeji clan of Harima Province (present-day Okayama Prefecture), resided in the castle town of Akashi on the coast of the Inland Sea, southwest of the present-day city of Kobe.

Hakuin first met Zeigan during in the winter of 1750 while he was visiting Ryōkoku-ji in Akashi to deliver a series of lectures. They apparently kept in touch over the following years. Evidence of their growing friendship is found in the letters and verses they exchanged, which were filled with expressions of mutual admiration and respect (see *The Religious Art of Zen Master Hakuin*, 17–18).

Unlike many prominent Confucian teachers of the period,

Zeigan had a keen interest in Zen. He had engaged in Zen practice as a young man, and references to Zen and Zen writings occur quite frequently in his works. He even refers to himself at times as "Layman Zeigan." He also had a reputation as one of the finest contemporary writers of *kambun* Chinese, so when Hakuin was looking for someone to write a preface for *Poison Blossoms*, Zeigan was a logical choice.

In reading through Hakuin's manuscript prior to writing the preface, Zeigan noticed a short piece titled "Reading Razan's *Study of Our Shinto Shrines*." In this piece, Hakuin vigorously attacks the anti-Buddhist views of the Confucian Hayashi Razan, founder of the Hayashi school of neo-Confucianism, who had been a trusted adviser to the early Tokugawa shoguns and had played an important role in establishing neo-Confucianism as the orthodox creed of Tokugawa governance. Razan's criticisms of Buddhism were based on his belief that it had been a harmful influence on native Japanese traditions such as Shinto, and that its principles of monasticism subverted basic Confucian ideals such as filial devotion.

Zeigan, concerned about the intemperate language Hakuin used in criticizing Razan, mentioned that it might be wise to delete the piece from the collection. Any attack on Razan and Tokugawa orthodoxy would be sure to attract the attention of government censors. Zeigan must also have known that Hakuin had been in hot water with authorities several years previous to this. In Hakuin's work *Snake Strawberries*, he had broken the taboo of mentioning the first Tokugawa shogun, Tokugawa Ieyasu, and as a result the text had been placed on the government's list of banned books. Zeigan's advice, offered out of concern for his friend and undoubtedly the commonsense view of the matter, elicited a strong reaction from Hakuin.

I RECEIVED YOUR LETTER on the third of the third month, but have had nothing from you since. Tōrei still has not shown up, and I would like to know when he is going to come.

I don't care if Zeigan does think the essay on *Study of Our Shinto Shrines* should be cut from *Poison Blossoms*; I had good reasons for writing that piece, which he is completely unaware of, so I want you to leave it in. If his complaints continue, we will just have to delete his preface. It is probably better to leave it out anyway. It won't be much help. Let's just forget about the preface. As I myself will not be writing to them, would you tell Kurogane-ya (Kida Ganshō) and other concerned parties in Kyoto of this decision? I hope the preparations for publishing the work are going forward. Please confirm this as soon as possible. I am busy with a number of different things now, so I am afraid I'll have to stop here.

PS: I no longer have the slightest inclination to include Zeigan's preface in the collection. Please make sure Layman Kida is aware of this. And please be sure, be absolutely sure, that the preface is *not* included in the work.

HZB, 152–53

It appears that Hakuin, in asking Daishū to inform Layman Kida "and others" (possibly donors) of the decision to delete the preface, is in fact calling on him, or them, to break the news to Zeigan that his advice will be ignored and his preface scotched. Kida was also in Kyoto during this period, presumably in connection with the publishing project, and he appears to have been in contact with Zeigan.

Hakuin's reference to Tōrei's failure to appear at Shōin-ji can be better understood by reading the section dealing with the Hakuin-Tōrei correspondence (see section 13).

Two months later, when Hakuin wrote this second letter, he was still busily conducting lecture meetings at temples in Suruga, Kai, and Shinano provinces. We find that he seems to have given more consideration to Zeigan's advice. We also learn of another difficulty, likely related to the Zeigan affair, that Hakuin is now facing: it seems that Kida has not yet come up with the funds he promised to cover the printing costs.

LETTER 14, TWENTY-FIFTH OF THE SIXTH MONTH, 1757

[THE FIRST PART of the letter is missing] . . . You should know that I have directed the bursar at Shōin-ji to send you the money to pay for the fair copy [to be used for engraving the printing blocks for the *Poison Blossoms* text].

Regarding "Reading Razan's *Study of Our Shinto Shrines*" [the piece Zeigan had advised him to delete]: I want you as a precaution to move it to a separate section at the end of the *Supplement*. It will then be easier to delete in the unlikely event some trouble should arise. Also as a precaution, I'm thinking of making this a private edition published by Shōin-ji. Please write and tell me how much the entire printing costs are going to come to. Be sure to include a written invoice.

Also, so there will be no misunderstanding, you should meet privately with Shinzaemon [one of Kida's given names], apprise him of what we have been discussing, and make repeated and earnest requests for the donation [he has promised]. I have been going around telling people that a praiseworthy layman has come forward and volunteered to donate the funds to publish my Zen records. It would be an utter disgrace if the project had to be abandoned at this point. Keep that well in mind, and exercise the greatest prudence in dealing with him on this matter. Explain carefully that in Zen works such as this, a few mistakes in the text, wording, and the like are of no concern whatever. I should write a letter myself, but as I am weighed down by a great load of work (not to mention the infirmities of age), it will have to be put off till another day.

HZB, 173–74

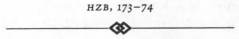

In the printing process, a fair copy was made of a manuscript, usually by a professional scribe, in the exact format in which it would appear in the final book. Each page of the manuscript was glued to a block of wood, and the wood was cut away, leaving the written words in relief. The printing was done by placing a sheet of paper on the inked block, and pressing it down to apply the inked image to the paper. As the making of the fair copy was the very beginning of the process, we know that the printing of *Poison Blossoms* still had not advanced beyond the editorial stage.

Hakuin sounds ready to go elsewhere for donations since Layman Kida seems disinclined to provide the funds he promised. Kida's reasons for dragging his heels are not stated. Kida knew Zeigan and must also have been aware of the concerns he had raised, so Kida may have been worried that his involvement in the project might land him, and the family business, in hot water with the authorities. Although clearly exasperated at this turn of events, Hakuin seems to have harbored no enmity toward Kida: the colophon Kida had composed for *Poison Blossoms* was still in place, with his name attached, when the book finally appeared.

Hakuin did not delete the piece on Razan, but he did direct Daishū to take a few precautionary measures. One of them was to turn the book into a private, temple edition, a step that could be accomplished very simply by stating this fact in the *kanki*, the space at the end of the book where the date, the place of publication, and the publisher are given. This would presumably offer some protection to donors and to the bookseller who printed the work.

The rare first edition of *Poison Blossoms* bears the publisher's imprint "Ganshō-tei," a name found nowhere else in Hakuin's writings or in the printing records of the time. Although the word *ganshō* appears in the *Book of Changes*, I suspect Hakuin took the name "Ganshō-tei" from the Sung poet Su T'ung-po, who used it as a sobriquet in some of his writings. Since the name can be rendered literally as "Holding the [offending] piece in one's possession pavilion" (containing the nuance that it will eventually be published), Hakuin would seem to have appropriated the name and included it in his first "temple edition" as an allusion to the Zeigan affair.

Very few copies of this first edition are known to exist. In most early editions, the publisher is given as Ogawa Gembei, the bookseller and publisher Daishū had been working with in Kyoto. As the actual publisher of the work, Ogawa could have easily inserted his own name as soon as it became clear that government censors would take no action on the book.

The second precaution Hakuin directed Daishū to take was to remove the piece criticizing Hayashi Razan from the main body of *Poison Blossoms* and put it at the end of the one-volume *Supplement*. It could then, if necessary, be easily deleted without the cost of having new blocks carved. For some reason this directive was not carried out, and in the edition of the *Supplement* that finally appeared, the problematic piece is found in the middle, not at the end, of the volume.

LETTER 15, END OF SIXTH MONTH (?), 1757

Hakuin sent this next letter from Iida, in Shinano Province, where he was conducting lecture meetings. After mentioning the success of the meetings he had held so far that year (a subject also dealt with in the section on the Hakuin-Tōrei letters, p. 163), he notes the arrival of the newly published *Idle Talk on a Night Boat* (another project Daishū had probably supervised), which had been sent from Kyoto. This would turn out to be Hakuin's most popular book, remaining in print almost constantly up until the present day. But Hakuin's main reason for writing this letter, and the problem still uppermost in his mind, was the continued lack of progress in printing *Poison Blossoms*.

Here Hakuin's criticism of Yanada Zeigan reaches its highest pitch. Exasperated at learning that not even the fair copy of the *Poison Blossoms* text had been made, Hakuin lays the blame on Zeigan, since his suggestion to scratch the piece on Razan made Layman Kida have second thoughts about financing the project. Although Hakuin has apparently not given up on Kida completely—he tells Daishū to make one more appeal to the layman—Hakuin now sounds as if he is hedging his bets, fairly confident that donations can be procured from other sources.

Ironically, on the seventeenth of the seventh month, only weeks after Hakuin wrote these harsh words about Zeigan, the old scholar passed away at his home in Akashi at the age of eighty-five. It is not known whether he was even aware of the extent of Hakuin's displeasure.

ON READING YOUR LETTER of the twenty-ninth of the fifth month, I was glad to learn that you reached Kyoto without incident and that you are taking good care of yourself. I am in quite good health, too. I have carried out very successful lecture meetings at seven different locations on the road between here [Daiyū-ji in Iida] and Kai Province. I have just finished the *Three Teachings of the Buddha-patriarchs* today with a talk on the *Sutra of the Bequeathed Teaching*. I leave here on the fourth of the seventh month for Kōzen-ji in Fukushima in Kiso Province, where I am expected to conduct a lecture meeting on the *Lotus Sutra* after O-bon.

Before going any further, let me say how extremely delighted everyone here was to see how beautifully *Idle Talk on a Night Boat* has been printed. We received with deep gratitude the fifty-five copies publisher Ogawa Gembei sent us from Kyoto. Please convey our best regards to him.

Next is the matter of *Poison Blossoms*. I had been waiting day and night expecting to receive the joyful news that the printing was completed. First Zeigan's carping and caviling held things up, and then because of that, Kurogane-ya [Kida] said he wanted to withdraw his pledge to donate the funds. These unexpected setbacks took me totally by surprise and thoroughly disappointed me. You should not worry yourself about it in the least. It was an unavoidable set of circumstances due entirely to my own lack of virtue.

Let's leave things as they are for the present. If Kurogane-ya doesn't want to put up the money, that can't be helped. If we solicit donations from senior priests in temples around the country and from the elderly laymen who come to my lecture meetings, I don't think we will have any trouble making up the deficiency. I intend to make a donation myself. Please tell me how much it is going to cost overall to print the entire work. Make the necessary inquiries, carefully total up the amount, and then send me a written estimate. Also, although I am sorry to add this to your burden, while you are there in Kyoto I want you to engage a good scribe to write out a fair copy of the text so that we'll at least have that stage of the work finished.

I understand that in going through the work, Zeigan pointed out a number of mistakes—portions of text that had been inverted, Chinese characters written incorrectly, and so forth. But none of that makes the least bit of difference. You should take no account of the objections of a dull, ignorant scholar who lacks the eye of kenshō, has no real understanding of Zen, and who merely bandies words about while feeding on the dregs of the ancients. You shouldn't be concerned even if a million others like him came forth and raised similar objections. In the future, this work will receive the admiration and praise of those clear-eyed Zen masters who emerge from the ocean of the true Dharma, and of the truly superior students who have fought their way through the thicket of thorn and briar.

I want you to convey all these sentiments to Shinzaemon [Layman Kida], too. If even then he can't understand and doesn't want to help, then the matter is closed. But be sure to have the fair copy made, and please let me know how much it will cost. I will have that amount sent to you. Make the necessary inquiries as quickly as you can. I will be waiting for the information.

Even if you answer this letter as soon as it reaches you, we will be into the O-bon season and I will have left for Fukushima in Kiso, so please send your letter there. Fukushima is situated at a crossroads on one of the main routes between Kyoto and Edo, and is served by a system of regular couriers. You should be able to locate one that goes to Fukushima. If you can't, then use the same address as before—Daiyū-ji in Iida.

I want you to sell all fifty-five copies of *Idle Talk on a Night Boat* that Gembei sent me. Be sure you keep every *sen* of the proceeds. They will be used for the printing of *Poison Blossoms* . . . [The final section of the letter is missing.]

HZB, 175–76

<hr />

LETTER 16, TWENTY-SECOND OF THE FOURTH MONTH, 1758

There is a gap of almost eleven months between the previous letter and this next one, which was sent from Rurikō-ji in Mino Province, although there may of course have been others that have not survived.

Having returned to Shōin-ji at the end of the previous year after many months of strenuous travel, Hakuin set out again the following spring (1758). His primary destination was Rurikō-ji in Mino Province, where he had been invited to deliver lectures on the *Blue Cliff Record*. Noting that it had been approximately one hundred years since the death of Gudō Tōshoku (1579–1666)—the eminent Myōshin-ji priest who Hakuin regarded as his great-grandfather in the Dharma—Hakuin decided to dedicate the lectures to Gudō's memory. Gudō, a native of Mino Province, had served several stints as abbot of Myōshin-ji and had founded a number of important temples, including Rurikō-ji in 1616.

Hakuin's itinerary after he left Rurikō-ji, as recorded in the *Chronological Biography*, is astonishing for a man in his midseventies:

At the end of the Rurikō-ji meeting, the master received invitations from Kakurin-ji, Zuiō-ji, Seitai-ji, and Bairyū-ji in Mino Province. After visits at each of those temples, he headed for Sōyū-ji in Takayama for lectures on the *Blue Cliff Record*, stopping off along the way to teach at Saigen-ji and Gyokuryū-ji as well. En route to Sōyū-ji, his exasperation at the failure of his fellow priests to support a printing of Gudō's *Records* prompted him to compose a work titled *Precious Mirror's Lingering Radiance*. When he arrived at Sōyo-ji, he wrote out a fair copy of the text and showed it to the monks.

Before returning to Shōin-ji, he responded to teaching requests from Ryōmon-ji, Rinsen-ji, and Myōraku-ji, then traveled south by small boat to Kuwana Castle, and from there went straight to Ryōgen-ji in Shiroko. He lectured at Ryōgen-ji for over a month on the *Treatise on the Precious Storehouse*, then returned to Kuwana for several days of lectures at Tenshō-ji. More teaching requests arrived, resulting in visits to the training halls of Ryūtaku-ji and Hakurin-ji in southern Owari Province for several days. He also lectured on *Hsu-t'ang's Verse Comments on Old Koans* at Chizō-in in Tōtōmi Province. In winter he was back at Shōin-ji.

Hakuin's activity in this line seems to have reached its peak during these years. From this time on his teaching efforts would be confined to sites closer to home, mostly in his native province of Suruga.

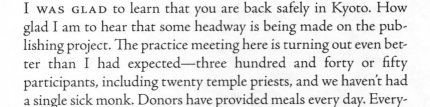

I WAS GLAD to learn that you are back safely in Kyoto. How glad I am to hear that some headway is being made on the publishing project. The practice meeting here is turning out even better than I had expected—three hundred and forty or fifty participants, including twenty temple priests, and we haven't had a single sick monk. Donors have provided meals every day. Everyone is extremely pleased, saying that there has never been such a splendid meeting of this size in recent memory.

Gifu-ya is here, as is his elderly mother, the nun Ritei-ni. I was able to have a long talk with her for the first time in many years. She kept repeating over and over that it would be a fine op-portunity, since I had already travelled this far west, to continue on to Kyoto after the meeting ended. I told her I would like to visit Kyoto once more, but that I couldn't consider making the trip without some legitimate reason. When we discussed the matter with the temple priests who had assembled here, they all said, "Since *Poison Blossoms from a Thicket of Thorn* is scheduled to appear in the seventh month, why not deliver lectures (*teishō*) on it in Kyoto?" Itsudō Oshō consulted privately with Gifu-ya. He said Gifu-ya supported the proposal, and that when Gifu-ya returned to Kyoto, he would contact fellow laymen in the Kansai area and try to assemble donations [to cover the cost of such a lecture meeting]. I gladly accepted these proposals, and warmly encouraged him to do what he could. If things work out and a meeting takes place as planned, it will help make *Poison Blossoms* much more widely known.

Kurogane-ya and Fukairi-ō had mentioned a similar plan when they visited Shōin-ji two years ago. They and four or five others were going to travel all the way to Kiso (in central Honshu where I was scheduled to conduct a meeting) to meet me and ac-company me to Kyoto. But owing to the unexpected troubles we encountered in printing *Poison Blossoms*, the plan never material-ized. Everyone says that with Gifu-ya's support (he is the man who donated the precious relic stupa to Muryō-ji) we can now rest assured that the necessary arrangements will be made in Kyoto.

I want you to visit Gifu-ya and try to find out, as discreetly as possible, whatever you can about the plans for the Kyoto lectures. I will have no knowledge of the matter, so be sure that you do not mention this letter. I learned privately from Itsudō Oshō that Gifu-ya does not want to proceed with the arrangements until he has obtained the agreement of Tōgai Oshō, and he would like someone to write Tōgai requesting his help.

PS: I am sorry to burden you with yet another request, but I have enclosed a few pieces of silver that I want you to use to buy some writing brushes. The brushes should be shaped like this: [at this point Hakuin adds a brief sketch of the two brushes].

Send them to me in one of those boxes for carrying fans. Be sure to pack them securely to keep them from being damaged.

HZB, 174–75

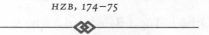

The letter shows that Hakuin used these lecture meetings and his contacts with the laymen who attended them to good advantage. "Gifu-ya" was a hereditary name used by the wealthy merchant Yotsugi Masayuki ("Gifu-ya" also being the name of his business), who resided at Sanjō and Takakura in Kyoto. Although family obligations had prevented Yotsugi from entering the priesthood, he devoted himself to lay practice throughout his life. Like his friend Tōrei, whom he helped in various ways during the difficult years Tōrei was practicing in Kyoto, Yotsugi was a native of southeastern Ōmi Province, and it was probably Tōrei who influenced him to begin studying with Hakuin.

Yotsugi became a close friend of Hakuin, and a supporter to whom Hakuin knew he could turn for financial help. Several short pieces about Yotsugi that Hakuin wrote are included in *Poison Blossoms from a Thicket of Thorn*. The story of the stupa containing precious Buddha relics, which Yotsugi donated to Muryō-ji when Tōrei was installed there as head priest, is told in the Hakuin-Tōrei letters.

In 1750, eight years prior to this letter, while attending a meeting Hakuin conducted at Ryōkoku-ji in Akashi in western Honshū, Yotsugi had passed Hakuin's One Hand koan. On his return trip the following summer, Hakuin stopped at Yotsugi's residence in Kyoto to rest up from the long journey, and ended up staying there for three months. It was on this trip that Hakuin delivered the Zen lectures at the Yōgen-in subtemple of Myōshin-ji that were described in connection with Letter 8.

Other names that appear for the first time in this letter: Itsudō Oshō (Itsudō Ekō, n.d.) was the head priest at Hōfuku-ji in Bizen Province, another one of the temples where Hakuin had lectured during the 1750 trip. One of Hakuin's most important disciples, Daikyū Ebō, was from Hōfuku-ji, and later succeeded Itsudō as its head priest.

Tōgai Oshō is Tōgai Ryōgi (n.d.), who was probably the head priest at Yōgen-in when Hakuin lectured there. There is no information about Fukairi-ō, although the suffix ō suggests he was an older man, and we may assume he was a friend of Layman Kida and probably also a lay student of Hakuin.

Hakuin seems to have been partial to writing brushes made in Kyoto. There is another letter to Daishū in which he asks for "three medium-sized brushes. Not the narrow ones."

LETTER 17, TWENTY-SECOND OF THE SIXTH MONTH, 1758

This brief letter was probably sent from either Saigen-ji or Gyokuryū-ji, which were two of the fourteen stops Hakuin had made earlier in Mino upon leaving Rurikō-ji. It tells us that although work on *Poison Blossoms* remained at a standstill, progress had been made on the printing of the one-volume *Supplement*, no doubt due to the donation (which is mentioned in the letter) that had been pledged to pay for it.

IN MY LETTER of the sixteenth, I said I would send you four additional pages for the *Poison Blossoms* text; they are included here. Although I realize what a burden this work has been to you these months, I must ask that you do everything possible to have it completed as soon as possible. The lack of progress is very discouraging.

There wasn't money enough to pay for the one-volume *Sup-*

plement, but when I approached Gonzaemon and Heishirō of Ihara village, Gonzaemon sent word to my attendants that if it was only a matter of a single volume, there was no need to bother Heishirō. He would take care of it by himself. They were unable to tell him how much money was needed because they themselves did not know. In any case, he will provide the funds as soon as the book is printed. You don't have to be the least bit concerned about it.

As for *Poison Blossoms* itself, what is holding things up now? If things turn out for the worst and we are simply unable to publish it, that can't be helped—the responsibility is entirely mine. But if that happens, be sure to get the fair copy back from the printer and make certain that not a single page is missing. Since we can always publish it later, it is extremely important that we have this copy.

In any case, in order for me to discuss the matter with people and seek their help, I need detailed answers to my questions. I await your response.

PS: I repeat: there is no need to be concerned about the money for the *Supplement* volume.

HZB, 153

Yamanashi Heishirō, the lay student who achieved satori after only two nights of intensive zazen practice (pp. 68–70), lived in Ihara in Suruga Province, as did Shibata Gonzaemon (n.d.), the other Hakuin student mentioned here. Said to have been Ihara's wealthiest citizens, their large residences were located on opposite sides of the small stream that flowed down the village's main street. Shibata came through with the money he promised for the one-volume *Supplement*: a brief dedication he wrote is printed at the end of the work. It is unclear when the one-volume *Supplement* was actually published, but it was probably in 1759, at or around the same time the first nine volumes of *Poison Blossoms* appeared.

LETTER 18, THIRTEENTH OF SEVENTH MONTH, 1758

This was apparently sent from Sōyū-ji in Takayama, Hida Province. Hakuin ended up staying at this temple for two months, a visit that led to the writing of one of his most unusual works, *The Tale of Yūkichi of Takayama*, which was published several years later. A translation of this work and an account of the Sōyū-ji meeting can be found in *Hakuin's Precious Mirror Cave* (39–82).

YOUR LETTER DATED the twenty-first of the sixth month arrived at the beginning of this month. I was very glad to hear that you were back safely in Kyoto. I am also in good health. I have successfully conducted lecture and practice meetings at various temples in this area, and now will be setting out for Mino Province once again for more of the same.

I continue to worry from afar about the lack of progress in getting *Poison Blossoms* printed. Can you explain to me what the problem is?

I sent you the manuscript of *Precious Mirror's Lingering Radiance* by the previous post. Priests and laymen in this area who have ties to Master Gudō all agree that it is an important work both for the Dharma and the world at large, and have pledged to help have it printed so its message can be more widely known. That is why I sent you the manuscript. I have heard nothing from you. Did it arrive safely in Kyoto? Have arrangements been made to have it published?

As I explain in the work itself, I decided to write *Precious Mirror's Lingering Radiance* at Rurikō-ji while I was in Mino Province to conduct lectures on the *Blue Cliff Record* in commemoration of the one-hundredth anniversary of National Master Gudō's death. During the meeting, it occurred to me that to honor his memory, we should also publish the manuscript of his Zen records. Although I broached the idea at the meeting, many priests in Gudō's lineage were not present. I should visit each of them to discuss the plan in person, but at my age that is not possible. I decided to transmit my ideas on the subject to temple priests and elders around the country by writing this work. I completed it in the space of six or seven days, as I was traveling in a palanquin between Mino and Hida provinces. It grew to a length far beyond my expectations. I was prompted to do it solely from the sadness I feel in witnessing the decline of the Buddha Way and the degeneration of true and authentic koan Zen. A number of other delusory thoughts that came into my mind are included in it as well.

As I believe I mentioned to you in my letter a few days ago, people here have promised to provide, and send to you, whatever funds are necessary to have *Precious Mirror's Lingering Radiance* printed.

I have learned that they reached a decision at Jikei-ji (in northern Mino Province) to publish Gudō's Zen records. Fortunately, Librarian Zenna has business in Kyoto around the week of O-bon,* so he will be able to take the complete manuscript of the *Records* with him. I told him that he should visit you on arriving in Kyoto so the two of you can discuss how best to have it published. He should certainly be there by the end of O-bon.

I also want Zenna to take a revised manuscript of *Precious Mirror's Lingering Radiance* and a colophon I wrote for Gudō's *Records* with him. I will give them both to him when he leaves for Jikei-ji, and he will then deliver them to you in Kyoto along with the manuscript of the *Records*.

Since we are now well into the seventh month, the manuscript of *Precious Mirror's Lingering Radiance* that I sent you earlier is probably ready to be printed. Many people here who have made donations toward the printing costs eagerly await copies of

---

* Nothing is known about Zenna Zōsu ("Zōsu" is a title normally reserved for the monk in charge of the temple library, but is also applied as a term of respect to senior monks in general). The monk Shūi and the layman named Kaga-ya, who appear several paragraphs below.

the work. You should know that I have instructed Zenna that it can be printed as an independent work, not together with Gudō's *Records*. You will find that the revised manuscript of *Precious Mirror's Lingering Radiance* I am now sending contains some additions to the text I sent previously. I know it will be bothersome, but when the new version arrives, would you very carefully compare the two texts and have a new fair copy made for the block-carvers? When I learn from you what the additional cost will be, I will immediately send you the money. So please do not worry, and proceed with the work.

As for running out of money for the printing of the *Supplement* to *Yōen Dokuzui:*[*] Shūi was here not too long ago and suggested asking Shibata Gonzaemon of Ihara village for a donation, so I sent such a request to Gonzaemon, filling him in on all the particulars, but it seems he never received it—it must have been held up somewhere. Then recently Gonsui-ō told me that I had only to ask, and Mr. Shibata would willingly provide whatever I needed, so I gladly sent several more applications to him, which I imagine he has received by now. As you already know, when I asked Shibata to donate funds together with Yamanashi Heishirō, he volunteered to supply the entire amount himself.

Gonzaemon's son Gombei-rō has gone to Kyoto for his health, and is staying not far from you. Have you heard if he has fully recovered? The elderly nun Myōju-ni,[†] the mother of Yoza-emon of Okitsu (she is in extremely fine fettle and taking an active part in our summer retreat here) worries about Gombei day and night. If he is still in Kyoto, please ask him to write her. I've been wanting to send him a letter myself, but have been holding off because I wasn't sure whether he was still in Kyoto or

---

[*] Hakuin refers here to his Zen records as *Yōen Dokuzui* (*Poison Blossoms from a Strange Garden*), the title he had considered using before finally settling on *Keisō dokuzui* (*Poison Blossoms from a Thicket of Thorn*).

[†] Judging from her concern for Shibata Gonzaemon's son Gombei, the nun Myōju-ni was evidently related in some way to the Shibata family of Ihara.

had started for home. If he is still there, please give him my best regards.

As for the confidential matter regarding Gonzaemon, I wanted to write to him about it, but there is no mail service between here and Suruga Province. If you place this letter securely in an envelope and send it to Gonzaemon with a cover letter of your own, it will be the same as if I had sent it. Please do this without fail.

After O-bon I will rest for four or five days, and then I am scheduled to go stay for a spell at Myōraku-ji in Hikumi village, Mino Province. I have received an endless series of teaching requests from other temples as well. Letters should be addressed to Ryūju-ji in Atsuta, Owari Province. Write on the envelope that the post-runner should deliver the letter to me wherever I am staying in the area; also that all necessary fees will be paid at this end. Ryūju-ji is situated on some well-trafficked roads, so you don't have to worry about doing this.

Kaga-ya just sent a very courteous letter as well as a bag of [sweets?] rarely seen in these parts, which I enjoyed immensely. Please be sure to convey my sincerest thanks to him.

It is wonderful, the eagerness with which the priests and nuns and laypeople in this area devote themselves to *sanzen*. They take up all my time, day and night. I'm on the verge of collapse. I hope you will sympathize with me.

You say your eye trouble has cleared up. Please take good care of them. Also, please confirm receipt of this letter by return post as soon as it arrives; if you are too busy to write, have someone else dash off a note for you. I have a mountain of other things to say to you, but am, as you can no doubt imagine, extremely busy. I will write again soon.

HZB, 154–56

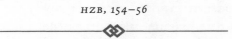

At the Rurikō-ji meeting earlier that year, when Hakuin had tried to convince the temple priests in attendance to assist in publishing an edition of Gudō's Zen records, he had also sent a letter to other senior priests in the area to solicit their help as well. The general response, even from those belonging to Gudō's own Dharma lineage, was at best lukewarm.

Incensed, Hakuin immediately began to dash off a tract, titled *Precious Mirror's Lingering Radiance* ("Precious Mirror," Hōkan, is Gudō Tōshoku's National Master title), criticizing their indifference and contrasting it with the effort Gudō had always devoted to promoting the ideals of koan Zen. Most of the work is taken up with stories and anecdotes that chart the course of what Hakuin believed to be the authentic Rinzai tranmission that had passed to him through Gudō, Shidō Munan, and Shōju Rōjin.

After composing this work (he said) while being carried in a palanquin through mountainous Hida Province, Hakuin made a fair copy of the text on arriving at Sōyū-ji in Takayama, and was able to dispatch the completed manuscript to Daishū for the printer in Kyoto at the end of the sixth month or the beginning of the seventh month of this same year. *Precious Mirror's Lingering Radiance* appeared in the eighth month, having been whizzed through the entire publishing process—fair copy, woodblock carving, printing, and binding—in about a month, showing how quickly and easily books could be produced under favorable circumstances.

The first edition, bearing the joint imprint of Ogawa Gembei (the Kyoto bookseller who had published *Idle Talk on a Night Boat* and was scheduled to do *Poison Blossoms from a Thicket of Thorn*) and the Osaka publisher Funatsu Shinuemon, states that *Precious Mirror's Lingering Radiance* was paid for by "donations from the lay community of Sōyū-ji in Takayama." The title strip on the cover identifying the book as "a supplement to *Poison Blossoms*" shows that Hakuin originally intended it as part of that collection. Actually, it appeared before *Poison Blossoms* and in a totally different printed format. Perhaps because of that, and also due to its length, *Precious Mirror's Lingering Radiance* has come to be regarded as a completely independent work.

Hakuin's plan for publishing Gudō's Zen records was unsuccessful at the time, but thirty-nine years later in 1797, after his death, it was printed under the title *Hōkan-roku* (*Records of Precious Mirror*).

13

The Hakuin-Tōrei Letters

Tōrei Enji's (1721–92) eminence as a Zen teacher in his own right imparts a special interest to this correspondence. Although complete texts of only three of Hakuin's letters to Tōrei survive, they all date from a critical period in Tōrei's study under him—between 1757 and 1760—and reveal many fascinating details of their sometimes difficult relationship, including Hakuin's desperate attempts to entice his recalcitrant student, who had fled to far-off Kyoto, to return to the roost.

Also included here are the three surviving letters that Tōrei wrote to Hakuin. To explain the connection between the various parts of this correspondence, I have placed the letters within a narrative structure that sketches out Tōrei's study under Hakuin as it unfolded from their first meeting, continuing to Tōrei's appointment as Hakuin's Dharma heir, and then to Tōrei's abbotship of the newly acquired Ryūtaku-ji. The story is pieced together primarily with information from their chronological biographies, *The Chronological Biography of Zen Priest Hakuin*, compiled by Tōrei, and the *Chronological Biography of Zen Priest Tōrei*. The latter is an especially valuable source, since it presents an account of events from Tōrei's side, providing a more detached view of Hakuin's actions at the time.

When viewed together in this way, in the correct chronological context, this correspondence provides a rare, behind-the-scenes look at the fascinating interaction between these two great, intricately related figures, revealing them each individually, the issues that concerned them, and their at times puzzling master-disciple relations.

When twenty-two-year-old Tōrei first arrived at Shōin-ji to study under Hakuin, he had already experienced several satoris. Hakuin, at fifty-eight, was at the peak of his powers, with a reputation that was beginning to reach beyond the confines of the Buddhist establishment alone. His late sixties and seventies, when these letters were written, were an extremely busy time for him. He was traveling a great deal more, visiting temples in distant provinces to conduct lengthy lectures and practice meetings. This is also the period when most of his many literary works were written. They can be seen as an attempt to spread his Zen teaching to a wider public, and no doubt also reflect an increased desire to leave behind a record for future generations.

But of greatest concern to Hakuin was the all-important matter of a Dharma heir, someone he could count on to carry on the work of producing the superior students who would be needed to keep the traditions of his koan Zen alive. When Tōrei arrived, Hakuin had already given Dharma sanction to a handful of students, who had left to assume abbotships in temples around the country. The indications are, however, that Hakuin was quick to recognize in Tōrei the exceptional talents and potential he regarded as essential in a successor. Fiercely dedicated to the Zen path, Tōrei had broken through the initial barrier into kenshō, and he also possessed special intellectual and literary gifts that enabled him to express with powerful eloquence the understanding he had achieved. As we will see, however, Tōrei was not so sure of the plans Hakuin had made for him.

Born and raised in Ōmi Province on the eastern side of Lake Biwa, at the age of eight Tōrei was ordained as a Zen monk at a temple not far from his home. He spent the next eight years as an acolyte, learning the ways of temple life, familiarizing himself with Buddhist texts and Confucian classics, and acquiring a proficiency in Chinese composition that would later draw the attention of Hakuin. At sixteen Tōrei traveled to Hyūga Province on the island of Kyushu to seek instruction from the well-known Rinzai teacher Kogetsu Zenzai. The choice seems to have been influenced by a visit Kogetsu made to Tōrei's family home while passing through Ōmi on a trip to Edo, though Tōrei was four years old at the time.

Tōrei left after less than two years in Hyūga. It is said he was disillusioned by the insufficient focus on zazen practice that he found at Kogetsu's temple. Tōrei returned to the Kansai region and studied under several Rinzai masters, although for the most part his training seems to have been undertaken on his own, in a series of long, solitary practice sessions. These exertions brought results, including an experience, a year prior to his visit to Hakuin, described as a "great satori" (*daigo*). Tōrei visited Hakuin to seek his evaluation of this enlightenment, and his subsequent study under Hakuin's guidance can perhaps be seen as his post-satori practice, a matter of maturing and deepening the original kenshō.

On the fourteenth of the second month of 1743 when Tōrei arrived at Shōin-ji, Hakuin greeted him by saying, "What took you so long? I've been hearing about you." Hakuin then turned the new arrival over to a senior monk named Gangoku (Gangoku Zenko, d. 1794) to teach him the ropes. It didn't take long for Hakuin to discover Tōrei's ability in Chinese *kambun*, for within months of Tōrei's arrival we find Hakuin entrusting him with the responsibility of editing his *Talks Introductory to Zen Lectures on the Record of Hsi-keng*, an important work that Hakuin was readying for publication.

After only a month at Shōin-ji, Tōrei came down with diarrhea and was obliged to leave. He repaired to his native Ōmi Province to recuperate, and was able to return and resume his study later that year. The *Tōrei Biography* records that "On the first of the twelfth month, while sitting in zazen, he [Tōrei] thought, 'Master Hakuin must think I'm a very mediocre student. He seems to make a point of not using his iron hammer and tongs on me. It is possible he doesn't know what is in my mind?'" (p. 103). Tōrei composed a letter explaining his reasons for coming to Shōin-ji and presented it to

Hakuin. He titled it "A Request to Kokurin Rōshi [Hakuin] for His Iron Hammer and Tongs," alluding to the severe means Zen masters use in tempering the students who train under them.

LETTER 19

[To: Master Hakuin]

OFFERING INCENSE and performing nine bows, with profound respect, your student Dōka [Tōrei's name at the time] writes the following to present to you:

Great Zen master, it is said that the practice of Zen must be genuine practice and that satori must be genuine satori, that if a student wishes to stay with a teacher and study under him he must begin by divulging everything that is in his mind, and only then ask about the Way, and into this not the slightest bit of self-concern must be allowed to enter. Although I have wanted to lay bare to you what is in my heart, I have not had an opportunity to do so. Hence I have sketched out on this paper some notion of what I would like to say.

I left home to be ordained at the age of eight. I thought, "I am now a child of Buddha. I must understand the Buddha's Dharma and work to benefit all living beings. Few in the present day are actually able to accomplish this goal, so it must be an extremely difficult task. How can I achieve my purpose unless I am prepared to lay down my life in the struggle?" From then on, I stopped speaking to people, keeping my mind focused solely on my religious quest. Even if there had been questions I wanted to ask, there was no teacher around to answer them. Even if I had wanted to talk with others, there were no friends with whom to converse. I entered a dark room and concentrated all my efforts on my practice. At times I lifted up my eyes to heaven in woeful supplication. I had read about the various methods for reaching the truth. They seemed to be limitless in number. I didn't know what to do or how to proceed.

One day I read a passage in *Ta-hui's Letters*: "If in practicing the Way you obtain no results, you should make earnest supplication to the Buddhas and Bodhisattvas, pledging to them that your resolve will never slacken. If with their help you encounter a good teacher who gives you a turning word that enables you to realize supreme enlightenment and leave birth and death suddenly behind, you will succeed to the eternal life of Buddha-wisdom, and thereby requite your incalculable debt to the Buddhas. When that happens, the causes that had kept you from reaching enlightenment for so long will vanish altogether. You will acquire great strength and ability in all your activities, whether you are practicing zazen or actively engaged in everyday life, and it will all—everything—proceed directly from that primary vow."

I was not yet fifteen when I decided that the time had come for me to set out on a Zen pilgrimage. I desired it most ardently, but circumstances did not allow me to leave the temple. In spring of the following year I once again went to my teacher. "If I just go on wasting my time like this," I entreated, "it is sure to undermine my original resolve." Finally, deciding that the only option remaining to me was to slip away in secret, I shouldered my traveling pack and set out in the direction of Hyūga Province on the island of Kyushu, hoping that the teachers there would give me thorough instruction in the ways of Zen practice. My first stop was Tafuku-ji in Bungo Province, where I stayed for the summer retreat. Then I went on to visit Zen Master Kogetsu, and his Dharma heir, Zen Master Zuigan. I received the benefit of their guidance, and once or twice during my practice was able to attain some insights. In the end, however, I felt a dissatisfaction I had not experienced before.

I sought out a spot remote from human habitation, fashioned a small hut, and practiced diligently for a period of twenty or thirty days. First, I lost all sense of home and family, then suddenly the teachings of the self-nature, the mission of the Bodhisattva, dhyana, wisdom, and the other paramitas were all immediately manifested before my eyes. I saw the lofty and precipitous principle of direct pointing espoused by Shakyamuni, Bodhidharma, Lin-chi, and Te-shan.* Yet I was still unable to firmly grasp this within the marvelous realm of differentiation. Whenever I entered a place of commotion or excitement, it seemed I had lost everything I had attained. This troubled me. I got out some books and began poring over the words and phrases of the Buddha-patriarchs. I also engaged in a month of intensive practice, in the course of which I once again experienced occasional insights.

Then I recalled some advice that Zen Master Zuigan in Kyushu had given me: "When you leave here and head eastward, you will no doubt pass through Suruga Province. I have heard of a teacher there named Hakuin. I have not met him myself, but it is said that the means he employs in guiding students are quite different from those of other teachers." Why, having received such advice, hadn't I been more prompt in acting upon it?

The winter practice period was approaching, so I made my way to Ryōgen-ji in Ise Province to participate in a three-month Dharma assembly being held there.† "No matter what happens," I thought, "I am indeed fortunate to have this chance to concentrate on my training. No Zen student worth his salt can allow even a short period of one hundred days to go to waste." Sitting diligently day after day, night after night, staring pebble-eyed, teeth clenched vice-like in my jaw, I suddenly grasped my self-nature—as if it was lying there in the palm of my hand. "I've got it!" I thought, beside myself with joy.

I wanted to leave for Suruga Province as soon as possible so I could ask you about the attainment I had achieved. I found a companion, and we set out together. But on the way here I kept

---

* *Direct pointing* (*jikishi*) is a shortened form of the saying "direct pointing at the mind of man, seeing into the true nature of self (*kenshō*), and attaining Buddhahood," which is said to express the basic standpoint of Zen.

† According to the *Tōrei Biography*, he was there in 1742 for the winter retreat, a three-month period of zazen.

up a constant conversation with my companion, offering him advice and encouragement, and in so doing, I seemed to lose all the power I had acquired.

That is how I came to visit Shōin-ji. The first time I saw you I was mentally shouting, "This teacher truly possesses the Dharma eye." But as I listened to you speak, I just smiled and kept my thoughts to myself.

When I heard you deliver Zen lectures on *Ta-hui's Arsenal* [held that year in the third month], the priests and others that appeared in the stories were all exactly the way I had imagined followers of Zen would be—they corresponded perfectly. At the age of eighteen, it seemed to me that someone practicing the Way should imitate the virtue of Bodhidharma, and emulate Lin-chi's and Te-shan's refusal to remain content with the attainment they had achieved. Looking around, however, I soon realized that there were no teachers like them anywhere in the country, and that the best I could do would be to just hang up a drawing of Bodhidharma, the first Zen patriarch. So I did that, and performed a hundred prostrations before it every day, making the following vow:

> I entrust myself completely to the great priest, teacher, and Bodhisattva Daruma Engaku, first of the Zen patriarchs. I vow to attain your Dharma eye. I vow to attain your Way. I vow to acquire your virtue. I vow to acquire your transcendental powers. I vow to acquire your wisdom. I vow to acquire your expedient means. I vow to acquire your eloquence. I vow to carry out the Bodhisattva vow. I vow to liberate all beings unconditionally. I vow I will receive your confirmation and sanction.

I did this every day without fail for a number of years. When I saw you for the first time, Master, I was sure I had come before the First Patriarch himself. I knew that if you deemed me worthy to be your student, I would give myself totally to my training, even lay down my life if necessary. If you did not accept me, I would hide myself deep in the mountains, devote myself to a rigorous life of practice, and keep at it until such time as I received that confirmation from Bodhidharma.

But as it turned out, I had found my teacher. I could say that I had achieved one of my fundamental aspirations. I embarked on a period of practice that brought me occasional satoris.

I achieved a state of oneness with all things and my doubts completely vanished. I had it, and this time I did not lose it. I carried the *Blue Cliff Record* with me constantly during the first months at Shōin-ji, and I was able to penetrate to a clear understanding of every one of its cases.

But I was unable to put that understanding to use in my everyday life. I asked myself, "I have reached attainment. Why can't I put it to practical use?" I began concentrating steadily on this doubt. As I did, one night as I was quietly doing zazen, it occurred to me for the first time that what I had attained was not a true kenshō. From that moment on, everything throughout the four quarters turned into one great mass of doubt. I tried to bore in and get to the bottom of it, redoubling my efforts, but it turned out to be so complex I could not fully resolve it.

I had found a place to pursue my Zen study that could not be matched anywhere in the country, yet because it was difficult to see you and seek your advice in person, I was unable to forget everything else and concentrate single-mindedly on my practice. Please, great master, give me the benefit of your enlightened instruction.

I formulated a vow at the age of seventeen that has always remained in my mind: "Even if I do not realize the Way and liberate sentient beings in this lifetime, in future lives and rebirths I will never slacken my effort. If I fail, may I sink forever into the cycle of karmic rebirth." But despite that determination and resolve constantly spurring me on, I have been unable to bring my practice to completion. I beg you, master, bestow your great mercy and compassion on me and help me to reach my goal!

What else is there to say? I don't want a Dharma robe or a comfortable life in a well-to-do temple, I want only to see the true Buddha-nature. I'm not attached to words and letters, I want only to see the true Buddha-nature. I don't covet reputation or fame, I want only to see the true Buddha-nature. I'm not concerned with physical well-being or living a long life, I want only to see the true Buddha-nature. I don't crave peace and tranquillity, I want only to see the true Buddha-nature. I have no interest in calligraphy and painting, I want only to see the true Buddha-nature.

In soliciting your help like this, I am aware that I am far from being a person of exceptional ability. Yet I am unable to cease my quest. If thanks to your guidance and teaching I succeed in completing the great matter of Zen, I will do everything in my power, grudging neither my health nor my life itself, to producing one or two courageous fellows of superior capacity, flinging dippers of foul, stinking water over their heads until they open up a thousand eyes and transmit the vital pulse of wisdom. I hope in that way to requite the enormous debt of gratitude I owe the Buddha-patriarchs. Here is a verse:

> The first kenshō, I believed my mind finally was at rest,
> Closer study revealed to me the full extent of my shame.
> Beseeching men and gods, relying greatly on your help,
> I seek neither peace nor comfort, only the path of Zen.

THE TWELFTH MONTH OF THE THIRD YEAR OF KAMPŌ (1743)
HOZ, 7:7–10

At that time, there were over a hundred students assembled in or around Shōin-ji, most of whom were no doubt engaged in koan work with Hakuin, so it is not surprising to learn that Tōrei had only limited access to Hakuin, especially the informal kind of contact that he was seeking.

Hakuin's response on reading Tōrei's letter is recorded in the *Tōrei Biography*:

"Dōka, is your aspiration as strong as that? In the past I tried using tongs and hammer on a few of my students, but they soon found it intolerable. They couldn't take it. Some of them ran away. Some went into hiding. I learned from this that Zen monks in this day of the degenerate Dharma are not possessed of superior capacity. Not one of them was a vessel for the Mahayana teaching. No matter what you feed them, they seem unable to receive it. Hence I refrain from using such strong methods on them. From what you've written here, I don't think there's any doubt that you possess the capacity for the Mahayana teachings. Only I'm a bit afraid that you may not be up to it physically."

Bristling at this, Tōrei replied, "Don't say I'm weak. I appear complaisant outwardly, but that is because I have kept apart from the frivolous concerns of mundane life. But within, my resolve in seeking the Way is such that I would willingly lay down my life in the effort. Why do you judge me by ordinary worldly standards?" (*Tōrei Biography*, 108)

In spring of the next year (1744), Tōrei experienced his first great satori at Shōin-ji. It came suddenly while he was engaged in an extended period of rigorous solitary practice in a small room behind the temple which, he said, had "totally exhausted" him and left him "deeply troubled." Tōrei ran to Hakuin's chambers and explained to him what he had experienced. "I've been residing at Shōin-ji for thirty years," said Hakuin. "At the present time there are a hundred monks in training here. None of my students has ever seen what you have."

In the twelfth month, Tōrei returned to Ōmi Province on receiving word that his mother had fallen seriously ill. For the next three months he nursed her while performing six hours of zazen each night as well. Tōrei was back at Shōin-ji later that year (1745), but stayed only a month or two, then returned once again to the Kansai area, lodging in a room near the Hall of the Great Buddha in the Higashiyama area of Kyoto, close enough to his mother to make frequent visits. That winter Tōrei engaged in a solitary retreat of a hundred and fifty days, during which he achieved another satori, enabling him "to grasp the enlightened activity of Hakuin's everyday life."

On New Year's Day, Tōrei wrote Hakuin from Kyoto. He begins by describing his practice during the previous year, then he sets forth the particulars of the attainment he had just achieved.

LETTER 20

[To: Master Hakuin]

MOST RESPECTFUL GREETINGS:

I hear that your health remains good and that you are raising your Dharma standard higher by the day—surely it is a cause of profound joy among men and gods alike.

Although in the past I was satisfied with the attainment I had achieved, I still lacked the realization that the Buddha's disciples Mahakashapa and Ananda had experienced. I felt constraints when engaged in the doings of daily life. When I engaged the difficult-to-pass koan stories, it seemed as if I was grasping at them in the dark. I thought to myself, "I am certain I have penetrated to a clear understanding of these koans. What did I need to do to overcome this lack of freedom?" Finally, I realized that although I possessed the eye of kenshō, the strength that comes from dhyana was not yet fully mature. Vowing that I would perfect my practice, I strove mightily, mustering every effort, but after maintaining continued concentration for many days, my lack of freedom still remained unchanged.

Last winter, in the tenth month, I borrowed a small dwelling that I intended to use for a desperate struggle to the death. I pledged, "I will not leave this hut until my goal is achieved." I locked the gate, secured the door, cutting myself off from all contact with the outside world. I began counting off days and nights filled with pain and suffering, like a man under sentence of death. I took the bright gem [of my Buddha-nature] and sported with it endlessly, never once putting it down. At times, I had it right before me; at times, I lost it completely. I found it extremely difficult to keep my mind continually focused. No matter what I did, I was oppressed by sad and fearful thoughts, my mind in a disturbed and uneasy state. I continued that way for fifty days.

Suddenly, all the constrictions fell away, the bright gem smashed into oblivion. Now everything was totally open, fully unbared. Feeling utterly free and unrestricted, I felt the truth of the words, "putting down the onerous burden, feeling the pure wind rise up."

But since I still had not penetrated through and achieved complete freedom of activity, I set my jaw, clenched my fists, and once again whipped the dead ox forward. I plunged straight ahead and continued without stopping, not caring in the least what became of me. Even on the coldest days and bitterly frigid nights, my robe was constantly wet with perspiration. Whenever I sensed the approach of the sleep demon, I took a sharp needle and jabbed it into my thigh—right to the bone. I lost all taste for food and drink. "If I can't penetrate to a realization of the Buddha-patriarchs' heart and marrow," I thought, "I'm better off dead."

Another fifty days passed. I experienced satori eight or nine times. Suddenly, the enlightened activity of the master's everyday life was mine. *Ha ha. Ha ha!* I realized everything I had done until now had been mistaken. Nothing but dead and useless effort. I wanted to grab hold of Po-yun and give him thirty blows with my stick.* I truly understood for the first time the great and vast function of the teachings you had given me. How could I ever have done this without all that instruction you had personally granted me? I would have just continued the way I was headed, wasting my entire life attached to a dull and lifeless understanding of satori. Now, when I recall that time, I see that each of the words and phrases that came from your lips possessed the vital blood of life. How terrifying and how compassionate they were! And how wonderful that today I can say I am without question a legitimate descendent of Bodhidharma and a true son of Master Hakuin.

I had some minor doubts in the past: At the great assemblies on Lotus Peak when the Buddha preached the *Lotus, Nirvana*, and other sutras, and all the participants attained enlightenment, why did Mahakashapa alone break into a smile of understanding when the Buddha held up a lotus flower? I wondered about Ananda, another disciple of the Buddha: After serving as the Buddha's personal attendant for thirty years, he finally, during the preaching of the *Heroic March Sutra*, achieved a great many satoris. From my reading of the Mahayana scriptures, I knew that all of them are extremely profound. Why did Ananda, who had been present when many of them were preached, have to wait so long before attaining great enlightenment? Why did Mahakashapa, a much younger monk, achieve realization before him? While I understood vaguely that Mahakashapa's breaking into a smile was a case of the special teaching outside the scriptures being transmitted through mind-to-mind transmission, it

---

* Po-yun Shou-tuan (1025–72) was known for the words "You're still not there!" which he used to urge students to greater effort. "Po-yun said, 'Several Zen monks were visiting from Mount Lu. Each of them had passed the threshold into satori and very capably expressed his attainment as well. When asked about koans, they could come up with clear responses. When asked for capping words, they produced them too. But they still were not there." Tōrei is expressing his absolute certainty that his realization is full and complete.

was still not entirely clear—as though I was reading something by moonlight. But it is without any doubt true that the Dharma, the Buddha-mind, is indeed communicated in this way. The reason for the Zen sect's preeminence over all the other Buddhist schools is found in this transmission that took place to Ananda and Mahakashapa. If Zen had been content merely with attainment of satori, something that is asserted in the Tendai, Shingon, and Kegon schools as well, there would have been no need to establish a separate Zen school.

But I want you to know, my great teacher, that you need not worry. From this time on, I will not grudge my body or my life, I will not involve myself in any worldly concerns, I will do nothing but devote my life solely to holding up the great matter, entering the fire, entering the water, grinding body and bone to powder, until I succeed in returning the patriarchal gardens to verdant springtime. If I fail in this, I will vanish into the mountain fastnesses, spend my days wearing garments of woven grasses, drink water from the valley streams, and my name will never again be heard in the human world. Please understand these secret thoughts of mine.

Esteemed master, I have had the immense good fortune to receive your *inka*, a great Dharma seal of confirmation that has impressed itself deeply into my bone and marrow, inspiring the trust of all the world. I'm probably going to find life pretty busy from now on—*Ha ha ha ha!* What I have experienced today can never be fully and decisively grasped through the words of others. Buddhas of the three worlds can have no part in it. Generations of patriarchal teachers are driven back thousands of leagues before it.

I have only one desire now, great teacher, and that is to put your mind at rest. My purpose lies nowhere else.

With great respect and humble gratitude I offer this verse:[*]

---

[*] The verse alludes to "The Lady Burns the Hermitage," a koan Tōrei had struggled with during this period (*Tōrei Biography*, 117).

An old lady stood in front of her hut scolding passersby,
Mind bound in resentment, scoured by troubling thoughts.
Then one morning on happening to encounter an old priest,
She unloaded all the junk she'd been carrying around so long.

I used to think that in my satori I had obtained a gem of immaculate purity. Today I know it was a grain of sand in my eye. How immensely difficult it will be to repay even a small bit of my debt to old Buddha Po-yun. Who could have known that in this there exists a "little something" of immense importance? If anyone suddenly came up to me and said, "You're not there yet!" my immediate answer to him would be, "It's completely mine!"*

A DAY IN THE NEW YEAR PERIOD, THIRD YEAR OF ENKYŌ (1746). DŌKA
[TŌREI] PERFORMS A HUNDRED BOWS AND OFFERS THIS TO THE
ATTENDANTS OF THE GREAT AND VENERABLE PRIEST OF SHŌIN-JI.

HOZ, 7:11–13

Hakuin's response on reading this account of Tōrei's breakthrough is said to have been: "Ka [Tōrei], you've penetrated completely through!" According to Hakuin's *Chronological Biography* (*Hakuin's Precious Mirror Cave*, p. 211) the letter also meant that Tōrei was confirming his acceptance of the offer that Hakuin had made to designate him as his Dharma heir. This assertion, coming as it does right from the horse's mouth (Tōrei compiled the *Chronological Biography*) would appear to be unimpeachable.

Hakuin is described as jubilant at having secured a person of such exceptional gifts to carry on his teaching. He decided to make the letter public immediately, and silenced the senior priests at Shōin-ji who tried to dissuade him, telling them, "If you aren't able to believe in a person from reading what he writes, how are you going

---

* See footnote p. 154.

to understand the minds of the ancient teachers when you read their stories in the Zen records?" (*Hakuin's Precious Mirror Cave*, 211).

Tōrei remained in the Kyoto area for almost four more years, engaging in a series of solitary practice sessions to further mature his understanding, while fighting off recurrences of a serious illness thought to be consumption. When Tōrei finally returned to Shōin-ji in the winter of 1749, Hakuin summoned him to his chambers and presented him with a written document sanctioning him as his Dharma successor. Hakuin also awarded Tōrei the gold brocade robe symbolizing the transmission. Tōrei's account of this meeting is found in the *Tōrei Biography*:

> On the twenty-second day of the twelfth month in the second year of Kan'en [1749], I was summoned to the master's chambers. He brought out the Dharma robe. "Since I began residing here at Shōin-ji," he said, "I have worn this robe five times when I delivered formal lectures on the *Blue Cliff Record*, and a number of times when lecturing on various sutras and commentaries. I have used it for thirty years. I now pass it to you. You must devote yourself to raising up and restoring the true Zen traditions that have fallen into the dust. Do not let this Dharma transmission die out."
>
> Receiving it with gratitude, I said, "Nothing could compare with the incalculable weight of this robe. It certainly cannot be measured in so many thousands of pounds. All the words and phrases of the Buddhas and patriarchs, the most difficult of the difficult, return to me. *Hah!* When Lin-chi was given the robe, he immediately called for fire. Yun-an refused it. Now it has come down to me—this stinking carcass draped in a feculent robe! Like pouring a dipper of shit over a precious agate. In order to requite my debt to my venerable teacher, a debt that penetrates my very bone and marrow, I will cut off the tongues of anyone who voices mistaken views and attachments. Will I find a single

understanding friend?" Holding up the robe, I said, "Look,
the twelfth month is coming to an end, and all the trees are
pregnant with the spring" (*Torei Biography*, 138).

The next year (1750), Tōrei was on the road much of the time,
visiting Kyoto and Edo, while continuing his post-satori training.
He now found himself refusing students, who had started coming to
him requesting instruction. The following year Tōrei linked up with
Hakuin in Kyoto, where he served as Hakuin's attendant during the
lecture meetings that Hakuin conducted at Myōshin-ji and other
temples in the capital. Tōrei remained with his teacher the rest of
the year, accompanying him to similar meetings in Bitchū Province,
and then all the way back to Shōin-ji.

The next spring, Hakuin asked Tōrei to assume the abbotship
of Muryō-ji, a tiny temple he had recently acquired in nearby Hina
village, six miles west of Hara. It was run-down, poverty-stricken,
and not even officially registered as a temple at the Myōshin-ji headquarters. Tōrei was extremely reluctant to accept the post, believing
the responsibilities of running a temple would sidetrack him from
his primary objective, which was the completion of his training.

After much soul-searching, Tōrei finally gave in to Hakuin's
earnest appeals, although not before making Hakuin swallow the
following three conditions: (1) There would be no attempt at a later
date to make Tōrei assume the abbotship at Shōin-ji (Hakuin's intention from the first); (2) Tōrei himself would make all decisions
relating to Muryō-ji, without regard for others' (that is, Hakuin's)
opinions; and (3) Tōrei would be free to leave whenever he wanted,
and entrust the temple to the care of another priest.

Tōrei served at Muryō-ji for more than four years, although for
some of that time he accompanied Hakuin on lecture meetings
around the country. While residing at Muryō-ji, Tōrei spent the
mornings on begging expeditions in the village, and the nights
doing zazen. Hakuin urged him to visit Myōshin-ji in Kyoto and
receive accreditation as a Dai-ichiza (First Monk), which would

make it possible for Tōrei to be officially appointed as head priest at any Myōshin-ji temple. Tōrei saw this accreditation as a step toward being installed at Shōin-ji, and balked at Hakuin's request. But when Hakuin cited his own advanced age and told Tōrei how eager he was to see his Dharma heir begin teaching before he died, Tōrei was again obliged to give in. The next year when Hakuin did in fact endeavor to install Tōrei at Shōin-ji, Tōrei refused, citing the conditions he had made on accepting the Muryō-ji post.

Hakuin was not to be put off, and tried to force the issue once again the following spring. This time Tōrei, after spending the night on his zazen cushion mulling the matter over, decided that the only avenue left open to him was to leave Muryō-ji. On the sixteenth of the first month, he wrote a letter to Hakuin (see below) and set out, at the age of thirty-six, for the Kyoto area. Before leaving Suruga Province, Tōrei stopped off to visit the Zen nun Eshō-ni, another Hakuin student. "I'm fleeing from Muryō-ji," he told her. "It's hard to tell when I'll be coming back. Please take care of yourself, and don't ever give up your aspiration for the Way." In parting Tōrei gave her a waka he had written:

Having cast away my self,
My name too lies back at Hina,
In what world will I again see
The floating world of Hara?*

Tōrei then took out a notebook containing miscellaneous verses in praise of the Bodhisattva vows he had copied out. "These are a Buddha's primary vows," he said. "No one has ever attained Buddhahood without fulfilling them. I now give them to you. Practice them diligently." Eshō-ni received the gifts with tears in her eyes (*Tōrei Biography*, 163).

---

* Ukishima-ga-Hara, the "floating island of Hara," was a poetical name for Hakuin's village. Located among low-lying fields, it appeared to approaching travelers behind a strip of shallow marshland that made it seem to float over the surrounding fields.

Here is the letter Tōrei wrote Hakuin on leaving Muryō-ji:

LETTER 21

[To: Master Hakuin]

WITH DEEPEST RESPECT I write this down to send to the great and venerable Zen teacher at Shōin-ji. It has always been my earnest vow to press steadily forward until I complete the path of the Zen patriarchs. Having meager capacity and inferior endowments, I have still not achieved total freedom in my dealings with the world, and I have become unsure of my spiritual bearings. I am physically and mentally exhausted. Not only am I incapable of carrying out the Bodhisattva practice of "saving oneself and saving others," I fear that I have disgraced my Zen comrades as well.

I have been editing your *Chronological Biography* and reading details of the unstinting effort you exerted throughout your career. The suffering you endured in your travels in Echigo and Shinano provinces, which enabled you to reach attainment and to acquire the ability to teach others. The suffering you underwent in Izumi and Mino provinces, as you gradually penetrated the truths of both ultimate reality and phenomenal existence. It is something no one today can even attempt. Not to mention the tribulations you endured in more than twenty years' residence at Shōin-ji, during which you entered steadily deeper day and night until you finally penetrated the inner secret set forth by the Buddha on Vulture Peak. While concealing your virtue over the course of the months and years, you have succeeded in greatly enhancing and promoting the personal treasures that were amassed by Master Daitō.

Ahh! What trials and tribulations the path of Zen exacts from its followers! The years it takes for their virtue to attain maturity!

Unable to stop nervous sweat pouring down my body or quaking fearfully from head to foot, I make my bows to you, great teacher, begging you to recall your own doings in the past, and asking you to allow me to devote myself single-mindedly to attaining the Dharma. The words of Master Tz'u-ming that you always cite about great diligence producing a brilliant radiance remain fresh in my ears.

EAGERLY RECEIVING THE WATERS OF BOUNDLESS COMPASSION
FLOWING FROM THE MOUNTAIN HEIGHTS, YOUR DISCIPLE TŌREI ENJI
MAKES A HUNDRED PROSTRATIONS ON THIS THE FIRST MONTH OF
THE SEVENTH YEAR OF HŌREKI (1757)

HOZ, 7:40–41

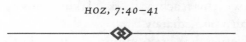

In a notation Tōrei wrote in his manuscript of Hakuin's *Chronological Biography* for the year 1757 (it was deleted from the later printed version), he quotes briefly from a letter Hakuin sent him in Kyoto. It was written some months after Hakuin learned that Tōrei had fled Muryō-ji: "In the first month a letter arrived from the master summoning me back to Shōin-ji. He said, 'I am growing older and am in dire need of my Dharma heir. Please return here and carry out your duties.' I answered only, 'I have respectfully received your command.'" This response is clarified by a passage in the *Tōrei Biography*: "On receiving the master's letter Tōrei thought, 'I've heard this argument before. Once again I'm being asked to return. I think it best to keep my distance from him.'"

The full text of this letter has apparently been lost, but it seems safe to assume that it was more or less similar, in substance and tone, to the three Hakuin letters that have survived—attempts, pleas, to convince Tōrei to come back immediately and help Hakuin carry out his teaching duties.

The first of the three letters dates from the autumn—the thirteenth of the eighth month—of this same year, 1757. At the time Tōrei was still firmly ensconced in Kyoto, and Hakuin,

following a series of successful lecture meetings at temples in Kai
and Suruga provinces during the spring and summer months,
was at Kōzen-ji, a large Zen temple in the mountainous Kiso area
of central Japan (see Letter 15), engaged in a series of lectures on
the *Lotus Sutra*.

Hakuin begins the letter on an upbeat note, with descriptions of his busy itinerary and the success of the meetings so far.
He then dwells on his dissatisfaction with the monks attending
him on the trip for acting contrary to his wishes. This leads to a
reproach of his chief disciples (no doubt meant to include Tōrei)
for quitting Shōin-ji and leaving him without a capable assistant
to help him with his teaching work. Hakuin ends by appealing to
Tōrei to return immediately.

A brief letter that Hakuin posted earlier in the year to his
disciple Daishū Zenjo confirms that Hakuin's primary frustration was Tōrei's refusal to return, despite all his persuasion and
cajolery. Daishū was in Kyoto, and presumably had some direct
contact with Tōrei: "I am very discouraged knowing that for the
time being Tōrei will not be coming back here. Ever since this
spring, each time I offered incense at my daily lectures I prayed
that he would travel to Kōzen-ji in autumn for the meeting on the
Lotus Sutra. Please tell him that I want him to attend without
fail" (HZB, 153–54).

LETTER 22

[To: Priest Tōrei]

IT SOUNDS AS THOUGH since leaving for Kyoto you have been
in uncommonly good health. I couldn't be more pleased. I am in
tolerably good condition myself. I was full of vigor and vitality
during my travels through the mountains this spring. After conducting a meeting at Nanshō-in in Kai Province, I stopped off on

my way home to teach at eight or nine other temples between Shimoyama in Kai and Nakayama in Suruga. I encountered especially fine weather in Kai Province before the O-bon observances [held from the thirteenth to the fifteenth of the seventh month, at the end of the summer retreat]. I was also pleasantly surprised at the number of devout and right-minded students I encountered there. Clerics and laypeople came together to give me a very cordial reception. The lord of the castle came by in person, and we conversed in a very warmhearted manner. I saw more large, old, and historic temples on this trip than I can describe. I can say without exaggeration that the memories of these past months will never be forgotten.

As a result of these experiences, I suddenly found that I have returned to perfect health. My appetite is even better than it was two years ago. When I read things out during my talks, my voice is always loud and clear. Great numbers of people travel long distances, as far as seven *ri*, in order to hear me teach. As the meetings have turned out to be such a success, I take great pleasure in performing my duties in the mornings and evenings. So there is no need to be concerned about either my health or my stamina.

However there is one thing I deeply regret, and that is the decision, arbitrarily made, to have my lectures on the *Lotus Sutra* open at an impossibly early date. Without so much as a word of consultation, they set it for the twentieth of the seventh month, only three days after the end of the summer retreat. This will be a big disappointment not only to participants who had planned to come from distant provinces, but also to monks and temple priests in the surrounding provinces as well, whose duties will keep them from arriving in time for the opening. I don't suppose more than a hundred and sixty or seventy people can be expected to attend. A large lecture meeting like this on the *Lotus Sutra* is something I will only be able to conduct once in my lifetime. Yet as matters stand, it's going to be like cleaning out my ears using a six-foot staff as an ear pick. It is extremely regrettable. While ultimately, of course, the responsibility lies with me, this unfortunate turn of events came about through the incompetence of attendants Ban Zōsu and Kai Zōsu.

This is how it happened. In the third month of this year, Ban Zōsu took it upon himself—no one sent him—to travel to Kōzen-ji in Fukushima where the *Lotus* meeting was to be held. He was there throughout the fourth, fifth, and sixth months— over a hundred days—troubling them with his presence and burdening them to provide for his room and board. From there, he made a long journey—twenty-eight or nine *ri*—to visit me (I was passing the summer retreat at Seigan-ji in Iijama boning up on the *Three Teachings of the Buddha-patriarchs*) in order to convince me to open the meeting on the *Lotus Sutra* earlier than had originally been planned. Armed with false logic and specious arguments, he tried to persuade me that it was essential for me to go to Fukushima before O-bon. I adamantly refused his proposal for the following reasons: If I went to Fukushima before O-bon, it would attract a great many other people there as well, and since they would be hanging around disrupting the working of the temple—something I want to avoid—I would have no choice but to begin the *Lotus* meeting early, immediately after O-bon. In that case, I would be disappointing the groups of student monks and temple priests who want to attend the meeting but would be unable to arrive in time [because they must be at their own temples during the O-bon season]. As a result the lecture meeting, an important opportunity for me to deal with the *Lotus Sutra* that will not come again, would to my infinite regret be attended by a relatively small number of people.

Fortunately, the priest of Zuiō-ji in Katagiri village, Shinano Province, which is only about one *ri* from Kōzen-ji in Fukushima where the *Lotus* meeting is to be held (four or five years back he came to Shōin-ji to invite me to deliver lectures at his temple), had strongly urged me to visit his temple before O-bon. He said I could give some leisurely talks during the O-bon ceremonies, and after that make my way leisurely to Kōzen-ji for the *Lotus* meeting. Such a schedule would be convenient for everyone concerned. And it would enable me to avoid making the long journey—seven or eight *ri*—to Kōzen-ji, a hard climb up steep mountain roads, and a return by the same route.

I told Ban Zōsu as firmly as I could that the schedule he had suggested was totally unacceptable. I was determined to remain where I was for the time being no matter what he said, and would proceed to Fukushima after the O-bon observances. Unfortunately, everyone had already been won over to Ban's plan, including the priests of Gyokusen-ji and Rinsen-an. Not a single person showed any sympathy for my feelings on the matter.

After exhausting myself ruminating over this, I hit upon a plan that, under the circumstances, seemed unavoidable. I would agree to proceed to Fukushima, but after I had conducted four or five sessions there I would plead illness, wrap things up expeditiously, excuse myself, and return as quickly as possible to Shōin-ji.

Although I was in pretty foul humor making my way those twenty-eight *ri* up the long mountain inclines to Fukushima, I was pleasantly surprised to find what a splendid place it was. It is situated in an exceedingly beautiful and propitious mountain setting, and the temple was finer and grander than I had been led to expect. So things could not have turned out better in that regard. Although I had been led to believe that I would have ten, perhaps fifteen days to leisurely rest up after O-bon, one day I was suddenly told that the opening of the meeting on the *Lotus Sutra* had been set for the twentieth of the seventh month—they had laid their plans so I would be unable to refuse.

A large number from the lay community attended. They listened intently, with great devotion, to my words. But in the end only twelve or thirteen priests and twenty or thirty student monks were able to attend. Hence what was to have been a large lecture meeting turned into a large disappointment. A significant event in my teaching career ended up a series of abbreviated talks on the *Lotus Sutra*, with me merely reading portions of the text and offering comments on some of the more important points. It is a cause of endless regret. My disappointment was intensified by the fact that the lectures on the sutra were delivered by express invitation at a large and important temple. At my age, it is extremely unlikely that a chance to conduct lectures on the *Lotus* at such a gathering will come again.

Having said this much, I will add that the reason it happened is because the people I trust to serve as my arms and legs, men like you, Ryō [Shikyō Eryō], and Jo Zōsu [Daishū Zenjo], had dispersed to other parts and were not in attendance. I might add to that the indecisiveness you have displayed. I was told you had assured people you would be here for the *Lotus* meeting around the first of the eighth month, so I was looking forward very much to seeing you. But you never showed up. All this has left me sad and discouraged. I feel powerless to cope with these matters. On top of that, I've had this endless succession of lecture meetings around the country for the past several years that is beginning to resemble a long drawn-out country farce.

So you should regard your return here as your destiny—the result of past karma. Think of yourself as being in a river you have only crossed halfway. I am entreating you to come and assist me for the next three or four years. This is the last demand I will make of you. I don't know what plans you have at this time, but you should set them aside for the time being and take up your traveling staff once again. Return and perform whatever services you can.

These are the words of an old man whose strength is steadily waning. As you are well aware, I haven't a single person here who I can count on to assist me. No one even to properly attend me. In all earnestness, I call on you to be prepared to lay down your life in this cause.

This is the path great Bodhisattvas like Manjushri and Samantabhadra followed in the past.* They worked as ordinary disciples, abandoning their own aspirations, concealing their Bodhisattvahood, using their skilful means and helping the Buddha's Dharma assemblies to achieve the great success they did.

I won't say anything further about matters such as building a temple [for you?]. At all events, as soon as this letter reaches you, there's no need to ponder the matter. Just hit the road and get back here as soon as you can. Get used to the idea that you will be spending three to five brief years as the group leader in a communal prison cell.

Regarding the Muryō-ji affair. I have held discussions with the priests of Chōzen-ji and Gyokusen-ji and with others as well about petitioning Seiken-ji [Shōin-ji's mother temple] to accept one of Kairyū's disciples as my successor here at Shōin-ji, so the matter will no doubt be decided expeditiously, with applications being made to one or two candidates. Should any difficulty arise, I am certain that the combined efforts of the priests of Ryōshin-ji, Daijō-ji, Chōfuku-ji, and Sūju-ji—all very reliable men—will assure that the matter will be resolved.†

If perhaps it is just that you don't want to return to Muryō-ji, I should be able to arrange for you to go to Rinsen-an in Nagasawa and replace the priest there. I'd like to have you somewhere in Suruga Province as long as I am alive. But in any case, as soon as this letter reaches you, don't stop to think things over. Just set right out and come straight here to Shinano Province where I am

---

* Bodhisattvas Manjushri and Samantabhadra assisted the Buddha when he preached the *Lotus Sutra*, appearing in the outward guise of Shravakas (disciples of the Buddha striving to achieve the Way): "Bodhisattvas pose as Shravakas . . . employing countless expedient means to convert the different kinds of living beings. They proclaim themselves to be Shravakas and say they are far removed from the Buddha Way, and so bring emancipation to immeasurable multitudes. . . . . Inwardly, in secret, [they act] as Bodhisattvas, but outwardly they show themselves as Shravakas" (*Lotus Sutra*, 146).

† In fact, rival factions appeared among Hakuin's followers, each pushing their own candidate for successor at Shōin-ji. The matter remained deadlocked for some time, until Tōrei finally stepped in and convinced Hakuin, and Suiō Genro, that Suiō was the right man for the post.

staying. I will be here waiting for you; even after the present lectures on the *Lotus Sutra* are over, I will remain in Shinano to finish up some lectures I started on the *Record of Daitō* at Zuiō-ji in Katagiri. I will be at Zuiō-ji until after the middle of the tenth month. You should set out the minute this letter reaches you. I will be expecting you to arrive here this month, without fail.

I don't even have to tell you that after you left Muryō-ji, the people of Hina village were greatly saddened, but it would seem that even the Buddha relics enshrined in the temple share those feelings.*

I am awaiting your prompt return. I'm enclosing a small amount—a few gold pieces—for your return trip. If it is not enough, borrow what you need and I will see that it is paid back as soon as you arrive here. I won't write any more now since I can explain everything to you in person when I see you.

PS: No matter what plans you may have, no matter what the circumstances, wherever you are when this letter reaches you, I want you to grab your traveling staff and hurry back here immediately. If you don't, whatever dignity and reputation I have attained in my lifetime will be lost. It would put me in a terrible spot, and you would be committing a serious breach of your filial obligation. So don't start mulling it over. Just consider it as something you must do for your teacher's sake. Set out at once.

THIRTEENTH OF THE EIGHTH MONTH

HOZ, 6:493–98

---

* "Relics sometimes found among the ashes of virtuous priests following their cremation [they were also found among the ashes of the Buddha] are said to be the natural result of the great merit they attained through meditation and wisdom in previous lives" (*Essential Teachings*, 77). The relics enshrined at Muryō-ji had been donated by the wealthy Kyoto layman Yotsugi Masayuki at the time the temple was reestablished and Tōrei, his longtime friend, installed as head priest. I suppose Hakuin means the relics are "saddened" because Muryō-ji is without a priest to perform proper rites for them.

One of the most striking things about this long and unusual letter is the way Hakuin goes out of his way to let Tōrei off the hook on the Muryō-ji affair. Hakuin tells Tōrei that he will no longer try to force him to serve at Shōin-ji, and if Muryō-ji is not to Tōrei's liking, other arrangements can be made, such as moving him into another temple in the Suruga area. Having acquired a Dharma heir of exceptional ability, Hakuin now finds himself in his early seventies up against someone as strong willed as himself, although Hakuin could hardly have failed to appreciate Tōrei's eagerness to avoid an abbotship and continue his practice, since that is exactly the same ambition Hakuin had aspired to at a similar stage in his career.

Be that as it may, Hakuin's overriding concern at this point was to have Tōrei close enough to assist him in his teaching work. The following spring (1758), Tōrei met Hakuin halfway, at least geographically speaking, acceding to his pleas and traveling from Kyoto to Mino Province to take part in lectures that Hakuin was conducting at Rurikō-ji on the *Blue Cliff Record* (see "Six Letters to Senior Priest Zenjo," p. 124). According to the account in the *Tōrei Biography*, Tōrei availed himself of the opportunity to apologize for his transgressions, and when Hakuin became tired partway through the meeting, he asked Tōrei to "share the teaching seat" (that is, lecture in his place) for several days. After the meeting Tōrei agreed to Hakuin's request and accompanied him part of the way back to Shōin-ji. They visited a temple together in Kai Province and ascended Mount Akiba in Tōtōmi Province. At that point, Tōrei headed back for Kyoto.

The following year, on the seventeenth of the fourth month, Tōrei received another letter from Hakuin containing some fresh enticements. In the winter of the previous year, Hakuin had decided to purchase a ruined temple named Ryūtaku-ji in nearby Mishima, seven miles east of Hara. Strict government restrictions in place at the time virtually prohibited the establishment of new temples, but it was often possible to buy an old temple or temple site that was already on the official register and rebuild on it. Hakuin told Tōrei that he wished to construct a training temple on the site and to install him as abbot.

LETTER 23

[To: Priest Tōrei]

FINANCIAL CONSIDERATIONS have obliged Shinkyō-ji to offer the site of an old temple named Ryūtaku-ji that is under its jurisdiction. Other temples in the vicinity affiliated to Kamakura monasteries have expressed interest in purchasing it, but Shinkyō-ji would rather, if it is possible, to transfer the registration to our Myōshin-ji lineage. I have had several visits from people urging me to acquire Ryūtaku-ji as my retirement temple. At first I put them off, saying it wouldn't do me much good, since at my age I can't expect to live much longer. Recently, however, priests Gyokusen, Kanjū, and Chōsen got together and made a special visit here, urging me to reconsider. They had inspected the Ryūtaku-ji site, which they described as being set in a beautiful situation, possessing an atmosphere of exceptional sanctity. A guardian deity named Azuma Gongen is enshrined in the precincts, and there is a Buddhist image carved by Kōbō Daishi.* They are believed responsible for numerous miracles that have occurred in the area, and a surprising number of pilgrims come to perform devotions to them. The original temple was on elevated land, and had the support of twenty households (*danka*). They said that it also owned fields, paddies, and a patch of mountain forest, which is probably true considering how long the temple has been there.

Shinkyō-ji is asking a hundred *ryō* in gold to have the deed transferred. I could manage fifty fairly easily, but since I had no prospect at all of obtaining the other half, I told the priests to discontinue the negotiations. They said I shouldn't worry. If I could come up with the initial fifty *ryō*, Mr. Ōhito Yasuzaemon

---

* Kōbō Daishi (Kūkai) is also credited with the founding of the original Ryūtaku-ji. Both attributions must be taken with a grain of salt.

in Izu promised that he would assume responsibility for the remaining amount.* They assured me that a hundred *ryō* is an extraordinarily low price considering the exceptional size of the building that serves as the visitors' quarters—it is nine by six or seven *ken* [approximately 18 by 13 yards]—which would be possible to use for the time being without any repair. These days it can apparently cost a hundred *ryō* just to change a temple's name. I am rather advanced in years for such a move, but you could go and reside in it. Everyone seems to agree that the location is excellent, and the large size of the building in which the kitchen and monks' quarters are housed will provide ample room for any number of resident students and visiting monks. They say it would be difficult to find another place anywhere in the country as suitable for a training hall as this. Everyone agreed that you should return from Kyoto as quickly as possible and take charge of it. Presented with all these reasons, I had little choice but to give my consent to proceed with the purchase.

Muryō-ji has become an onerous burden. It has fields and paddies, but they lie unused. Just this last year, not enough rice was produced even for the quota owed the government. It was only by purchasing two bales of rice that we were able to make up the lack and pay the land tax. If this situation continues, we can't expect any improvement in the management of the temple in the future either. People seem to accept that in the end we will have no choice but to dispose of it. However, if you come back and reside at Ryūtaku-ji as my Dharma successor, I think it will be possible to transfer the Buddha relics enshrined at Muryō-ji to Ryūtaku-ji.

In any case, as soon as this letter reaches you, please return to Suruga and inspect the Ryūtaku-ji site for yourself. I do not think it will be possible in the foreseeable future to acquire such an ideal

---

* The name Ōhito Yasuzaemon (n.d.) also appears in Hakuin's *Chronological Biography* (1759) as one of the people Hakuin consulted about the plans for establishing the new Ryūtaku-ji (*Hakuin's Precious Mirror Cave*, 225).

site anywhere in the country. So please hurry back. You can get more particulars from the priest of Denshū-ji. Given the nature of the matter, I ask that you keep the information in this letter confidential. I am unable to put down everything I wish to say to you, so the rest will have to wait till later.

SEVENTEENTH OF THE FOURTH MONTH, HAKUIN

HOZ, 6:499–500

———————◈———————

Throughout the next year, as Tōrei continued turning a deaf ear to the calls for his prompt return, Hakuin moved forward with the plans to reestablish the new site, including meeting with the parties involved in the project to confirm Tōrei's appointment as Ryūtaku-ji's first abbot.

Meanwhile, Hakuin acquired yet another temple. While he was in Edo that autumn to conduct a lecture meeting, he learned that Shidō-an, the hermitage in Edo where Zen Master Shidō Munan (the teacher of his teacher Shōju Rōjin) had formerly resided, was to be bought by another Buddhist sect. By peremptorily stepping in and promising to buy the hermitage himself, Hakuin succeeded in stopping the sale. Tōrei quotes a brief passage from a letter he received from Hakuin at the time informing him of the acquisition: "By an unexpected turn of chance, I was able to purchase the hermitage where my venerable Dharma ancestor Shidō Munan passed away, the site where my own revered teacher Shōju received the tonsure. You must come immediately and take custody of Shidō-an and look after it for me. There is talk in the government of canceling its status as a temple. We must not allow that to happen" (*Tōrei Biography*, 172).

Tōrei's response this time was positive: "Do not worry yourself about it. You can leave the matter to me. For the time being, we'll send the monk Dōgi to Shidō-an. When spring comes, I will return" (*Tōrei Biography*, 172).

Given Tōrei's track record, it is perhaps not surprising that in the first month of 1760, even before spring arrived, Hakuin sent him yet another entreaty, this time addressed jointly to Tōrei Oshō and Zenjo Shuso. Zenjo (later Daishū Zenjo) was also in Kyoto at the time attending to Hakuin's publishing projects (see Letters 13–18).

LETTER 24

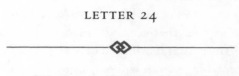

[To: Priests Tōrei and Zenjo]

YOU REPORT THAT you are both in good health and are taking care of yourselves as the New Year arrives. Considering my years, I feel extremely fit as well. Arrangements for purchasing Ryūtaku-ji in Sawachi village that I described in last winter's letter are gradually being concluded, and everyone here is waiting anxiously for you and Zenjo Shuso to return from Kyoto. Kanjū Oshō has been particularly helpful. He is dispatching Hachibe to accompany you back. No matter what plans you have made, given the circumstances you must set them aside and return. Hachibe will be informed of further details and relate them to you when he arrives. I am unable to write more now.

Sincerely yours, Hakuin

HOZ, 6:502

A ceremony was held that spring on the Ryūtaku-ji site for the purpose of designating the seventy-five-year-old Hakuin as founder of the new temple. Tōrei arrived from Kyoto in the fourth month, and was immediately appointed the new temple's first abbot. The *Tōrei Biography* includes an account of the dialogue that took place at the time—an account no doubt supplied by Tōrei himself—which goes a long way to explaining Tōrei's original reluctance to go along with the plans Hakuin had laid out for him.

In his long letter to Tōrei over a year previous to this [Letter 23], Hakuin had rambled on about the splendid surroundings of the Ryūtaku-ji site. He had probably done this because he was aware that the site itself was wet and marshy and poorly suited for a temple. When Tōrei returned to Shōin-ji and met Hakuin, Hakuin spoke to him in a slow, deliberate manner that seemed to lack conviction. Tōrei thought, "The master is ashamed of having bought the site. If I say something now, it will only cause him pain. I must stay here and do what I can to help dispel the distress he feels." He said, "Ryūtaku-ji is in a fine location. If you entrust the matter to me, I will see to it that a fine temple is built there." Overjoyed at hearing such words, Hakuin replied, "You are the only one who could accomplish it. Please do your best!" That is how Tōrei became abbot of Ryūtaku-ji (*Tōrei Biography*, 176).

In the *Chronological Biography of Hakuin* that Tōrei compiled, there is no reference to this meeting, nor is there any mention of the problematic temple site Hakuin had purchased (the name Takuchi, where Ryūtaku-ji was located, literally means "marshy land"). This is not surprising, since Tōrei would have avoided using material that cast an unfavorable light on Hakuin in the master's biography.

On being officially installed as abbot of Ryūtaku-ji two years later, Tōrei set about the work of constructing the temple. The first and most important thing he did was to move the temple from its original site to a new location, described as being "one hill away." Although this new temple was also beautifully situated among the foothills below Mount Fuji, it was on ground that would provide a firmer, more secure foundation for the temple structures. The building work completed, Tōrei assumed abbotship of Ryūtaku-ji, residing and teaching there until his final years, turning it into the important training temple his teacher Hakuin had envisaged.

The Shōin-ji succession, after years of wrangling by Hakuin's followers, was resolved when Tōrei stepped in and made the case for

Suiō Genro, a senior Hakuin student who does not even seem to have been in the running at the time. Tōrei finally was able to convince Hakuin, and then a reluctant Suiō, that Suiō was the best man for the post. After what was apparently a somewhat shaky start, Suiō developed into a fine Zen teacher in the Hakuin mold.

A section in the *Tōrei Biography* sheds further light on Tōrei's obstinate refusal to serve as a temple priest, first at Muryō-ji, and then at Ryūtaku-ji. In the winter of 1776, eight years after Hakuin's death and only a year after the main hall had been erected, Ryūtaku-ji was razed by a catastrophic fire.

> Even before the fire had been put out, Tōrei ordered a palanquin readied and set out for Shidō-an in Edo. *"Ahh!* Is this Heaven's doing, or is it man's?" he thought. "I haven't served at the temple for personal interest. I endured those long hard years only because of the commission I had received from Hakuin Rōshi. No matter how splendidly Ryūtaku-ji's buildings might be reconstructed in the future, what real benefit would result from that? The time has come for me to engage in an extended period of post-satori practice and nurture the sacred embryo of the Buddha-nature. In the coming years, my best course of action will be to find some unknown valley, hide my tracks, and devote myself to the study of the ancient sages" (*Tōrei Biography*, 239).

As it turned out, Tōrei spent most of his time in Edo, focusing on the study of the Yuiitsu Shinto tradition, so the "ancient sages" perhaps refers to the legendary figures of early Japanese history. Yuiitsu Shinto originated at the Yoshida Shrine in Kyoto, and although it stressed Shinto's original Japanese roots unadulterated by later syncretism, it actually included Buddhist elements as well. Some of Tōrei's solitary practice in Kyoto as a young monk took place in the hills adjacent to the Yoshida Shrine, and he had formed a close relationship with the Shinto priests there.

Meantime, Tōrei's Zen students back at Ryūtaku-ji seem to

have been left to fend pretty much for themselves. Some of them solicited funds and were planning to rebuild one of the temple buildings. When Tōrei learned what was afoot, he was livid with anger:

> "Didn't I make myself perfectly clear? I don't want Ryūtaku-ji rebuilt! All you men need for shelter is a bundle of thatch to cover your heads. Then you should proceed quietly to clarify the matter of your own selves. How in the world did you acquire the means to act against my express wishes? The only reason I reestablished Ryūtaku-ji in the first place was to please my teacher. If it were rebuilt now, I would be reviled on all sides as a profligate swindler. Not even to mention the debts Ryūtaku-ji has already piled up. Do you think I could shamelessly reside in such a place? I intend never to enter its gates again" (*Tōrei Biography*, 245–46).

On finally returning to the Mishima area two years later, Tōrei took up residence in a small hut he fashioned in the mountains several miles behind Ryūtaku-ji. A few years later, after his students came and begged his forgiveness and pleaded with him to return, he finally relented, and the work of rebuilding the temple began several years after that (*Tōrei Biography*, 251).

14

To Daimyo
Matsudaira Sadataka

Matsudaira Sadataka (1716–63), Oki-no-kami (Hakuin mistakenly calls him "Iyo-no-kami"), Lord of Matsuyama in Iyo Province on the island of Shikoku, was one of a half dozen or so provincial Daimyo whose confidence Hakuin is known to have gained. These men apparently met and consulted with Hakuin during stopovers at the Hara post station on their compulsory round-trips to and from Edo each year. This led to exchanges of letters that, on Hakuin's side, were often lengthy essays dealing with the particulars of Zen practice. Some of these letters were later revised and printed in book form. The most well-known are probably those he sent Nabeshima Naotsune of the Hasuike clan of Hizen Province, with whom he seems to have had a particularly close relationship, which were published as the famous *Oradegama*.

Although apparently not actively engaged in Zen practice, Sadataka sought Hakuin's advice on a number of occasions. Hakuin mentions Sadataka's previous visits in this letter, and he refers to another visit in Letter 28, which was written several years after this.

Although many of the themes Hakuin touches on in this letter—benevolent governance, sutra recitation, and Naikan meditation—also appear in his letters to other Daimyo, there is little reference to Zen teaching as such. Instead, the tone throughout is much more personal, perhaps a reflection of Hakuin's concern over Sadataka's health. Unfortunately, the advice Hakuin gives him—total abstention from intercourse with young consorts and boy servants, and a program of therapeutic Naikan meditation to strengthen his *ki*—seems to have gone for naught. Sadataka died three years later at the age of forty-seven.

Among the interesting revelations in the letter is Hakuin's more than passing acquaintance with *The Medicine Peddler (Uirō-uri)*, a popular Kabuki play that the celebrated Ichikawa Danjūrō II (1688–1758) was performing at the Morita-za, a theater located near the Daimyo's residence in the Ginza area of Edo.

NOTHING COULD HAVE given me any greater enjoyment than the long talk we had recently when you stopped over at my humble little temple. It was not like receiving a visit from an ordinary caller. I felt a special pleasure because of the benevolence you have shown in ruling your fief, giving sympathetic consideration to the common people, and because of the love and respect your vassals feel for you. I have been greatly heartened to hear almost daily reports from your area of the country telling of the respect and reverence in which you are held by subjects both high and low—rumor has it that the Daimyo of Okayama, Matsudaira, and Ōzu, in that order, are the three most generous and compassionate lords in the Chugoku Region [southwestern Honshu].

Not having seen you for some time, I must say that I noticed that you appeared weaker and in a poorer state of health than before. There was no sign of that remarkable physical strength of yours. To begin with, it appeared to me that your system was exceedingly dehydrated. This bothered me—I kept thinking about it even after your palanquin had left. Of course, it probably is connected to the hemorrhoids you suffer from, but that too is caused by a lack of sufficient water in the system. Please exercise the greatest prudence, both for your retainers' sakes and the sake of the ordinary people living in your domain, and recognize that to live a long and prosperous life, it will be vital to focus resolutely on nourishing your health.

I hesitate to even mention this, but I ask you to imagine how sad your retainers and subjects would be if something should by chance happen to you.

Although thanks to benevolent acts in a past existence you have been born into one of the three countries [India, China, and Japan], if you lose that life you will be lower than even the meanest commoner. Rebirth in the human world is said to be extremely difficult. There is nothing more wonderful than to achieve such a birth. And you were moreover born into a Daimyo's family, destined to become the ruler of an entire province. If you do not pay careful attention to preserving your health, you will fall back into your old haunts in one of the three evil realms of existence. Wouldn't that be regrettable in the extreme? From this time on, please constantly remind yourself of this. Make sincere applications to the gods and Buddhas for a long and healthy life.

I am sending you two pieces of calligraphy inscribed with the names of the protective deities Kompira Daigongen and Akiba Daigongen [see p. 184], together with thirty copies of the *Ten Phrase Kannon Sutra for Prolonging Life*. Have the calligraphies mounted, and hang them in your main *tokonoma* alcove. Give each of your attendants a copy of the sutra. At night when it is quiet, if everyone assembles and chants out the sutra with loud voices, they will invoke its benefits not only for the preservation of Your Excellency's health, but for the health of your vassals and everyone throughout the land, and of course for your son and successor Nagahisa as well.

Recently Lord Nishio died in Edo.* People of all ranks and classes of society mourned his passing in a way that is still being

---

* Nishio Tadanao (1689–1760), Daimyo of Yokosuka in Tōtōmi Province, had died earlier that year. A high official of the shogunate, he served as Jisha Bugyō (Magistrate of Shrines and Temples), finally rising to become Rōjū (Chief Counsellor).

talked about months later. Last autumn when I was in Edo I was invited to the Nishio residence, he received me most cordially. I recently sent his young son and successor a letter of condolence that ended with my attempt at a waka:

> Though knowing the ways
> Of this uncertain world,
> How unfortunate the subjects
> Who've been left behind.

You should keep this in mind and never slacken your efforts. Lord Nishio was over seventy. His passing was not unexpected. You have not yet reached the age of forty [actually, Sadataka was in his midforties]. You are still in the prime of life. How unfortunate it would be if something happened to you, and rumors started that you passed away because you had neglected your health.

I wanted to tell you all this in person when you visited the other day, but amid all the commotion and confusion I never got around to it. After your sudden departure, I felt badly about not having imparted to you what was uppermost in my mind. I even contemplated making a quick trip to Edo to visit you, but again things kept coming up and prevented me from going. Therefore I have sent one of my monks with this letter.

I feel obliged to tell you (although it is a matter I bring up with reluctance) that nothing is worse for someone suffering from an indisposition caused by a lack of water in his system than to be in a situation where he is surrounded by young women. You must at all costs separate yourself from them. The same goes for that young catamite who accompanied you to the temple last time.

If the ladies in your seraglio get wind of this, I realize that some of them might get angry, but if they do, even though they may be your specially chosen consorts, they are being disloyal to you in the extreme.* They must be made to understand that the

---

* Loyalty to one's master (*chū*) was an essential concept of Confucian ethics.

measures are being taken for the sake of your health. If one of them fails to come around even then, I'll have to drop by from time to time and have a word with her in your stead—reenact the tea-priest Chinsai's role in Danjūrō's *The Medicine Peddler* that is being performed near your residence.

But unless you distance yourself from your young consorts and preserve your vital energy, you will probably never completely recover your health. It is said that good medicine is bitter, and that faithful advice offends the ear. You may be displeased by the words I have written here. If so, please forgive me. I have spoken out with your best interests at heart, and only because I am seriously concerned about your health. As I said, I deeply regret that my teaching duties kept me from visiting Edo during the summer and autumn and saying these things to you in person. I should be able to find some free time for a visit next spring. I will look forward to seeing you at that time. I am writing this at night, rubbing my old eyes to shake off the fatigue. Please understand my concerns and begin a regimen to improve your health so that you will be as fit as you used to be.

When I was twenty-four, I depleted the Metal in my lungs by pushing myself too strenuously in my zazen practice. It caused the Water in my lungs to dry up, resulting in a serious illness that turned out to be extremely difficult to cure. None of the physicians I consulted could do anything to help me. I had a terrible time. Died ten times over. Then I heard about a sage named Hakuyū who was living in the mountains of Shirakawa, east of Kyoto. He had attained the age of three hundred and seventy and was said to be fully conversant with the secrets the ancient sages had devised for preserving health. I made the long trip to Kyoto and paid my respects to him in his mountain cave.

He instructed me in the great matter of achieving long life, teaching me the Naikan method that the sages used to return the cinnabar elixir to its source in the cinnabar field below the navel. After leaving him I devoted myself assiduously to practicing this meditation, and gradually I returned to perfect health. I turned seventy-five this year, but since that time I have never been sick. I have much more energy than any of the young monks here. I am able to take up my brush and scribble away letters and such at night, even without putting on my spectacles.

Some years back, at my attendants' request, I wrote down the methods of Naikan meditation and published them under the title *Idle Talk on a Night Boat*. Seasoned old physicians around the country are said to read it with elation. More than twenty of my Zen students have also benefited from the book. It has kept them free of sickness and other calamities as well. Fortunately I still have a copy of this book at hand, so I will have one of my attendants take it to you. Please read it carefully, then refine the cinnabar elixir that you have within you so you too can reach a marvelous old age of four or five hundred years.

The title of the book alludes to master Hakuyū's dwelling in the mountains of Shirakawa. It was taken from the proverb "A night boat on the Shirakawa River." If there is anything you have trouble understanding, you can have one of your physicians explain it to you. The book was published by Ogawa Gembei of Kyoto, whose store is located on Sanjō Street. He still has plenty of copies in stock, so if you contact him you can obtain as many as you want.

The young women in your seraglio might not appreciate this book, it might put them out of humor, so please do not show it to them. There's no need even to tell them about it. Toasted rice-cakes (*yaki-mochi*) are enjoying a great vogue in Edo these days, but if any of your ladies should succumb to them, it might cause trouble for you.* If after reading the book you find my arguments convincing, please send me a short note to let me know. I will be waiting to hear from you.

---

* Hakuin is playing on a double meaning of the word *yaki-mochi*: (1) dried rice-cakes that are toasted until soft on a charcoal grill; and (2) to become jealous, since at that time *yaki-mochi* came to be used for a jealous wife. A well-known *senryū* (a short satirical verse) of the time went "*Yakimochi de nyobō fukurete atsuku-naru*"—which had the double meaning: "Eating toasted rice-cakes, / My wife / Bulges and thickens" and "Becoming jealous / My wife / Boils and grows sullen."

I do hope that somehow I will be able to visit Edo this winter or the following spring so that I can see you.

HZB, 177–78

Kompira Daigongen and Akiba Daigongen (also see Letters 11 and 12) were Shinto deities who devotees also regarded as manifestations of the Bodhisattva Kannon. Hakuin inscribed the names of these deities in countless calligraphic works—a single line of large bold characters—and distributed them, usually in pairs (see the images on the following page), so people could hang them in their homes as charms against fire and disease.

Kompira, the tutelary god of seafarers and travelers, was the object of an extremely popular cult in the Edo period, drawing droves of pilgrims to the main Kompira Shrine on the island of Shikoku. Akiba was worshipped primarily as a god of fire; the tremendous vogue his cult enjoyed is probably accounted for by the catastrophic conflagrations prevalent at the time.

Yet as we saw in Letters 11 and 12 (pp. 116–17), Hakuin attributed the same extensive powers to the two deities as he did to the Bodhisattva Kannon whose manifestations they were. Devotees who hung their images or inscriptions bearing their *myōgo*, or sacred names, in the tokonoma and worshipped them assiduously would immediately be able to "dispel all the seven calamities and beget all seven kinds of good fortune." (HHZ 6:75)

Another interesting point in this letter is Hakuin's mention of the tea-priest Chinsai and the play *The Medicine Peddler*. Although the influence of Edo Japan's vibrant popular culture is clearly evident in many of Hakuin's writings, this letter is the only time he mentions Kabuki, which was enormously popular at the time. *The Medicine Peddler* (*Uirō-uri*) was a smash hit when it opened earlier in the century, and it was still being performed to full houses with Ichikawa Danjūrō II (1688–1758) in the lead role, astonishing audiences with his remarkable displays of rapid, tongue-twisting oral virtuosity as the medicine peddler touting his cure-all medicine.

Left: Kompira Daigongen; right: Akiba Daigongen.
Private collection.

Hakuin parodied street spiels of this kind, using rhyme and alliteration and fast-talking wordplay, in short vernacular chants such as "The Penetrating of the Self-Nature and Becoming a Buddha Pill," in which he touts Zen as a miraculous panacea for all one's ills.

The comment Hakuin makes here about the *chabōze* (literally "tea-priest") Chinsai shows him to be thoroughly conversant with the libretto of *The Medicine Peddler*, raising the possibility, unverifiable though it may be, that he himself attended a performance on one of his trips to Edo. Chinsai, a supporting character, is described in the playbill as "a tea master dressed as a buffoon." Other characters include the handsome medicine peddler's lady love and various adoring courtesans. When Hakuin says in good humor that he will take Chinsai's part and speak to the Daimyo's young consorts, he sets Sadataka in the role of the medicine peddler, surrounded by adoring females attendants, and himself as the fawning, jester-like tea-priest Chinsai.

Hakuin also recommends his Naikan meditation in this letter. As a young monk on pilgrimage, Hakuin was greatly troubled by an ailment called "Zen sickness," which was caused by "a lack of Water in his lungs." His condition became so serious that he was no longer able to continue his Zen practice. He visited the ancient sage Hakuyū in the mountains of Shirakawa east of Kyoto and learned from him a secret therapeutic meditation known as Naikan (literally, "introspective meditation") that enabled him to regain his health, and through continued use, to live a long and healthy life. The story of his visit to Hakuyū and a description of the Naikan meditation he learned are the subject of *Idle Talk on a Night Boat* (translated in *Hakuin's Precious Mirror Cave*, 83–114), which he had published three years previously in 1757.

This letter, which was not published until quite recently, confirms that Hakuin took the title *Idle Talk on a Night Boat* from the popular saying *"Shirakawa yobune"* ("A night boat on the Shirakawa [River]"). Used for a person who only pretends to have been somewhere or to have done or seen something, it is based on the story of a country braggart who tells his friends that he has visited Kyoto and seen all its marvelous sights. However, he hedges when asked about Shirakawa (the name given to both an area in Kyoto's eastern suburbs and to the shallow stream that flows through it), and replies that he didn't see anything because it was nighttime when his boat sailed down the river. In other words, Hakuin chose the title to alert readers to the fact that he was engaging in fiction. This had long been suspected, but until this letter came to light in 2010 and established that the title is indeed based on the saying, only circumstantial evidence had been available to support this suspicion.

15

Two Letters to Katayama Shunnan

These two letters, written six months apart in 1761, Hakuin's seventy-seventh year, are in response to ones he had received from Katayama Shunnan (n.d.), a physician and Zen layman from the Takayama area of Hida Province in central Honshū. Hakuin had been in Takayama for several months in 1758 to conduct a practice session and deliver lectures on the *Blue Cliff Record* at the Sōyū-ji Zen temple. It was only one of the many lecture meetings Hakuin conducted in the course of that busy year, which have been described in the sections containing the letters to Daishū (pp. 130–131) and Tōrei (p. 142). The lectures were, by Hakuin's own account, a great success, with more than two hundred people attending the one held at Sōyū-ji.

The letters are concerned with donations made by lay followers in the Takayama area to help cover the expense of publishing Hakuin's books, and with the extraordinary story of the young boy Yūkichi's possession by the deity of the large Takayama Shinto Shrine. Both letters are connected with Hakuin's Takayama visit, and they also provide rare firsthand information about his relationship with the practice groups his lay students had formed in the towns and cities where he had taught, something found nowhere else in Hakuin's records.

Although not much is known about the recipient Katayama Shunnan, the letters suggest his relationship with Hakuin was close and had continued for some time. Katayama probably attended the Sōyū-ji meeting in 1758, and may at that time have achieved the kenshō or satori Hakuin refers to in the letters. Katayama evidently became a leading member of the Takayama lay community, and he had a central role in collecting donations from his colleagues to help Hakuin pay the printing costs for three of his books: *The Tale of My Childhood*, *The Tale of Yūkichi of Takayama*, and *Precious Mirror's Lingering Radiance*.The last of these was a work Hakuin had written only several months prior to his visit to Takayama. From a letter Hakuin's disciple Tōrei sent Katayama (still unpublished), we know that Katayama continued to play an active role in the Zen group in Takayama after Hakuin's death.

LETTER 26, TWENTY-FIFTH OF THE FIFTH MONTH, 1761

I WAS EXTREMELY GLAD to learn from your letters that you are all in good health and that everyone is gathering and practicing diligently mornings and nights. Nothing could give me greater pleasure. This is something that has not been seen in most other lay groups. Soon I leave to hold practice sessions at several locations in neighboring provinces. I often think how nice it would be to see everyone in Takayama once again—though I realize, considering the long journey and the increasing infirmities of age, that such a visit will probably not be possible.

Last winter when Iiyama Kiemon from Shimohara village stopped by Shōin-ji on his way back from Edo, he told me that you and your comrades who had received Dragon Staff certificates expressed a desire to have my Dharma words on post-satori practice published, and he also informed me of the amazing oracles the deity of the Inari Shrine had delivered to the citizens of Takayama. He gave me the five *ryō* that you had entrusted to him. I was deeply moved and extremely pleased by everyone's kindness.

Since I was obliged to visit Edo at the beginning of this year in order to renew my credentials with the government,* I took the manuscript of my Dharma words on post-satori practice [later published as *The Tale of My Childhood*] and the money you sent with me, and took it to a bookseller to inquire about having it printed. The manuscript runs to a hundred and sixty or seventy pages, so I have divided it into three separate volumes. Which means that, according to the bookseller's estimate, the money I have assembled will not cover even half the printing costs. I'm afraid that I have to turn to you once again for help. I was extremely grateful when I read in your letter last spring that you were willing to provide additional funds should they be needed. Is it possible for you and your fellow students in Takayama to send an additional four or five *ryō*?

I had intended to hand the finished manuscript over to the bookseller when I was in Edo, but by last spring so many people had borrowed it to make their own copies that the original became soiled and damaged—some of the pages had even disappeared. Moreover, I decided, acting on the recommendation you made in your previous letter, to delete from the manuscript the list of the people to whom I had awarded my Dragon Staff certificates. I also wanted to add five or six pages to the text. All this has made it necessary for me to write out another fair copy of the book to send to Edo. I am busily engaged in doing that now.

I tried contacting a number of people around here to raise the additional funds, but I was unsuccessful. I am deeply sorry to

---

* This trip to Edo to renew his credentials as head priest at the Bureau of Shrines and Temples was made necessary by the succession of the new shogun, Ieharu (r. 1760–86). Tokugawa Ieshige (r. 1745–60) died the previous year.

impose on you like this once again, but if you are able to send an additional five *ryō*, I would greatly appreciate it. I am well aware that this may be difficult on such short notice. If so, would it be possible for you to send me a promissory note as soon possible? I can use it to borrow the money here.

I will tell the publisher to send you five or ten copies as soon as the book is printed, together with a receipt for your donation.

I was utterly astounded to hear from Kiemon about the oracle the Inari deity of the Takayama Shrine delivered through the young boy Yūkichi. We must join together and all work diligently to carry out the deity's wishes.

Sincerely yours, Hakuin

HHZ, 7:294–307

LETTER 27, SECOND DAY OF THE ELEVENTH MONTH,
1761

I WAS EXTREMELY PLEASED to hear that you and your Dragon Staff comrades and all my other students in the Takayama area are getting on so well. I am still in good health, so please do not worry on that account.

I was surprised and delighted to receive the five *ryō* Mr. Iiyama brought to help cover the publishing costs of my work on post-satori practice. I have no doubt that it is yet another example of the divine working of the great deity of the Takayama Shrine. I am deeply grateful for all the help you have given me. I meant to write thanking you for the money as soon as I received it from Mr. Iiyama, but one thing after another has come up and I am only now able to sit down and put brush to paper.

Iiyama recounted the entire Yūkichi story to me from first to last, including all the particulars of the deity's possession of

Dragon Staff certificate. Private collection.

the young boy. I was deeply moved, and at the same time the story filled me with a feeling of the humblest gratitude. Just as this was taking place, however, a chance presented itself for me to post the manuscript of my work to the publisher in Edo, so I was obliged to give the text a quick check and send it off, together with a letter and the money you had sent. All of this has kept me so occupied that I was unable to write and thank you earlier. Please forgive me.

Not long after that, the two additional *ryō* you sent arrived. It was so totally unexpected that in my happiness I just left it lying there in its envelope for a while. In any case, thanks to Mr. Iiyama, I now know all about the Yūkichi incident and the prodigious wonders wrought by the Takayama deity. Nothing like this has ever happened before; it is totally unprecedented. I was so pleased and stimulated that the idea occurred to me to write a detailed account of Yūkichi's story, and publish it together with my manuscript. I intend to add it as a separate section following the first part of the work that I have already finished dealing with post-satori practice. It should help promote firm belief in the Zen teaching among future generations of students as they engage in their quest for kenshō. I was initially hesitant about composing the work, knowing that it would mean many more pages of text would be added, and of course an even greater expense. I didn't feel I should put such a burden on my students in Edo.

But then the two *ryō* you sent arrived, and I immediately set about composing Yūkichi's story. It grew longer and longer, until finally it was over seventy pages, much longer than I had originally intended. A day or two ago, I finally succeeded in finishing it, and it too has now been sent, along with the two *ryō*, to Edo.

However that was not the end of the matter, for the priest of Sōyū-ji in Takayama then showed up, bringing with him yet another three *ryō* in gold. That made ten *ryō* in all, easily enough to print the entire work and ensure that it will appear before the end of winter. While the delight of this unexpected turn of events was still fresh in my mind, a large group of visitors from a distant province suddenly arrived at the temple. Attending to them and their needs occupied me so completely that the Sōyū-ji priest was obliged to look in at least three times during the afternoon and remind me to write out a receipt for the money he had brought. Even then, I wasn't able to sit down and write this till now. It is late at night and I am afraid I have miswritten some of the characters in the darkness, so you may have trouble deciphering parts of it.

With all these distractions, my plans have fallen behind schedule. I should have written separate letters to thank each of the donors for the contributions they sent. Please tell them all how grateful I am. Thanks to them, the Dharma words will soon be published. I will send you ten or twenty copies as soon as the first batch arrives from the printer.

Yours sincerely, Hakuin

PS: Those who contributed to the publication of my Dharma words have, by virtue of their selfless act, provided help to generations of Zen students far in the future, keeping them from straying into false practices and saving them from the terrible misfortune of falling into the evil paths. It is a Dharma gift greater by far than thousands of ordinary good and benevolent acts. Sitting here in far-off Suruga Province, I envy the donors, who have now linked themselves karmically to the wonderful wisdom of prajna for a thousand lives and ten thousand kalpas. Even as I write these words, I am unable to stop the tears from flowing down my old cheeks. Please convey my feelings to everyone concerned.

HHZ, 7:287–93

The Dragon Staff certificates, which from his late sixties on Hakuin began presenting to students who passed his One Hand koan, consisted of an ink painting of a priest's staff, usually in the process of transforming into a dragon, an inscription giving the recipient's name, the place and date it was awarded, and words certifying that he or she had passed the two-stage koan Hakuin gave beginning students: "Hear the sound of one hand," followed by "Put a stop to all sounds."

From *The Tale of Yūkichi of Takayama*, we know that during the meeting in Takayama, Hakuin awarded these certificates to a surprising number of the participants, perhaps Katayama Shunnan among them. Although the certificates themselves do not equate passage of the two-stage koan with the attainment of satori, elsewhere in Hakuin's writings he quite often does just that.

According to *The Tale of My Childhood*, Hakuin awarded the certificates to over seventy participants at meetings held earlier in Edo. The letters to Katayama mention a list containing the names of all students who had so far received these certificates from Hakuin. Such a list was included in the manuscript version of *The Tale of My Childhood*, but was deleted from the printed text, apparently at Katayama's suggestion. The reason for this is unclear, but it may have had something to do with the events that had been taking place in Takayama, where Hakuin's followers were being subjected to criticism from members of the other Buddhist sects.

What is most surprising in these letters is their corroboration of the strange, not to say incredible events described in *The Tale of Yūkichi of Takayama* that Hakuin had published the previous year. Since knowledge of these events is essential to understanding the letters, here is the version Hakuin gives in that work, which is, it should be added, the only one we have (see also *Hakuin's Precious Mirror Cave*, 40).

Iida Yasuemon, a samurai from Takayama in Hida Province (the northern part of modern Gifu Prefecture) visited Hakuin's temple and described to him the mysterious disappearance of one Kojima Sōsuke, an upstanding citizen of that city who had apparently absconded with a consignment of valuable merchandise that his fellow merchants had entrusted to him. Sōsuke was a gifted Zen student who had experienced satori during the lecture meeting on the *Blue Cliff Record* that Hakuin conducted while visiting Takayama. Sōsuke came to assume a leading role in the close-knit lay community that had subsequently formed in the area. However, Sōsuke ceased practicing Zen after achieving his satori, in the belief that he had already achieved a final and ultimate enlightenment. Priests of the local Pure Land temples, jealous of Hakuin's success with their citizenry, used Sōsuke's suspicious disappearance as a pretext to unleash attacks on Hakuin and his teaching that caused considerable embarrassment to Hakuin's followers in the city.

While all this was taking place, the deity of Takayama's largest Shinto Shrine took possession of a fourteen-year-old boy named Yūkichi. Speaking through the boy, the deity summoned townspeople to Yūkichi's home, where he delivered a series of teachings and pronouncements over a period of days, during the course of which he revealed Sōsuke's present whereabouts and explained the real reason for his disappearance. In a series of talks delivered in the formal Zen manner that followed, the deity stoutly defended Hakuin and his koan Zen, while denouncing the local priests who had criticized him.

Sōsuke's mistake, the deity declared, was in assuming that the Dragon Staff certificate Hakuin had awarded him, which confirmed that Sōsuke had passed the One Hand koan and attained kenshō, meant that his Zen training was over and he was now a full-fledged Dharma successor, entitled to teach others. Kenshō, the deity explained *à la* Hakuin, is merely an entrance into the Buddhist life, a gateway students must pass through once if they are to undertake ongoing post-satori practice, deepening their self-attainment while teaching others.

Hakuin compiled this version of the story based on reports he received from people in the Takayama area. He wrote it immediately after finishing *The Tale of My Childhood* with the intention of adding it as a supplement to that work, explaining in the preface that he decided to publish the two works together because Yūkichi's story presented such a wonderful opportunity to dramatize the teachings he had focused on in *The Tale of My Childhood*, his "work on post-satori training." *The Tale of Yūkichi of Takayama* was thus intended as a case example dramatizing the importance of post-satori practice, with Sōsuke's troubles an object lesson on the dangers of neglecting it.

In a postscript attached to *The Tale of Yūkichi*, Hakuin says that those who had read the original manuscript—evidently they were people from the Takayama area—had pointed out "mistakes" in his telling of the story. This Hakuin readily concedes, and he even admits to embellishing the text in places, though justifying this as necessary in order to bring the story's underlying significance into better focus. This confession of mistakes and embellishments, combined with the incredible nature of the tale itself, was more than ample reason for people to read *The Tale of Yūkichi of Takayama* as a fiction Hakuin had written to promote his Zen agenda, something he was thought to have done four years earlier in *Idle Talk on a Night Boat*.

However, these two letters, which only became available quite recently (*Hida-ro to Hakuin*, 1983) seem to confirm that in the year in question, 1760, a youth named Yūkichi was believed by Takayama's citizens to have been possessed by the deity of the Takayama Inari Shrine, and had indeed delivered a series of talks of the type described in Hakuin's work. Hakuin's astonishment when he learned of this is evident from the letters. Moreover, the lay community in Takayama, in response to the deity's appeals to his audience to help Hakuin publish the manuscript of a work on post-satori practice (*The Tale of My Childhood*), had assembled donations and sent the money to Hakuin to cover the cost of printing the work.

So whatever else is said about the story, and even if *The Tale of Yūkichi* does not relate events exactly as they took place, the letters show that the tale is not just a product of Hakuin's fertile imagination, which in the absence of these letters, is surely how it would have been regarded.

The translations of these letters are revised from an earlier version published in the introduction to my translation of *The Tale of Yūkichi of Takayama* in *Hakuin's Precious Mirror Cave.*

16

To a Donor

LETTER 28, 1762—63

This letter, dating four or five years before Hakuin's death, was written at Ihara, five miles west of Hara, where Hakuin had gone to stay with an unidentified layman and government official after teaching at nearby Myōzen-ji. Though the recipient's identity cannot be determined, he was a layman and obviously a close friend of Hakuin who lived somewhere between Hina village and Hara. As he was also suffering from an unspecified illness, Hakuin spends the first half of the letter urging him to recite the *Ten Phrase Kannon Sutra for Prolonging Life*, the brief text of only forty-two characters we have seen him recommending in several previous letters, whose miraculous benefits and curative powers he was tirelessly promoting in his final decades.*

In the second half of the letter, Hakuin thanks the recipient for a donation he had made toward the publication of a Chinese Zen work, *Spurring Students through the Zen Barrier*, which had just appeared. Hakuin goes on to explain how the work had inspired him

---

* "Kanzeon! I venerate the Buddha, with the Buddha I have my source, with the Buddha I have affinity—affinity with Buddha, Dharma, Sangha, constancy, ease, assurance, purity. Mornings my thought is Kanzeon, evenings my thought is Kanzeon, thought-after-thought arises in mind, thought after thought is not separate from mind" (Translation by Robert Aitken, *The Morning Star* [Washington D.C.: Shoemaker and Hoard, 2003], 106).

to continue his training when, at a crucial point in his early career, he was on the point of abandoning it.

Hakuin writes that the printing of *Spurring Students* was made possible by donations from laymen Hayashi and Watanabe. Although nothing is known about the former, except for the fact mentioned here that he was the local magistrate (*jin'ya*) of Harada (a village not far from Hara), Layman Watanabe is probably Watanabe Heizaemon, head of the wealthy family that operated the main inn at the Hara post station, who had donated to some of Hakuin's other projects. In a colophon Tōrei wrote for this edition of *Spurring Students* (translated below), he also states that the project succeeded "thanks to donations by laymen Hayashi and Watanabe and other patrons of the master." It appears then, that the recipient of the letter was either Hayashi or Watanabe, or perhaps a third patron who for some reason did not want his name to be made public.

Further explanation of Hakuin's connection with the *Ten Phrase Kannon Sutra for Prolonging Life* and *Spurring Students through the Zen Barrier* is given following the letter.

HOW IS YOUR ILLNESS? I hope you have improved and are feeling better now. I have been worried about you and have been reciting sutras mornings and evenings on your behalf. I also took it upon myself to inquire discreetly into your situation using a method of divination. It turns out that your illness is one that must not be taken lightly. There are apparently a number of difficult problems implicated in it. It is important that you begin sutra recitations. You must perform them diligently and without fail. It seems that a total cure will be extremely difficult to achieve if you rely on physicians and herbal remedies alone.

You and members of your family should all recite the *Ten Phrase Kannon Sutra*. You should do this five hundred times in the morning and five hundred times in the evening, so that each person does one thousand recitations a day. One hundred recitations can be performed in about forty minutes, the time it takes a stick of incense to burn down. If five people engage in this practice twice daily, each one should be able to perform a thousand recitations each day. If this is done, in due course you will find yourself completely and joyously restored to health. You must not treat this illness lightly. Regard your recovery as the most important matter of your entire life.

There is a saying, "Even if someone takes extra precautions against calamity, the country will not fall into ruin."[*] So even if you were not ill and were free from any misfortune or difficulty, the *Ten Phrase Kannon Sutra* possesses such marvelous efficacy that if you take this opportunity to encourage those in your household and others as well to recite it without fail mornings and nights, it will be the greatest meritorious act you could perform, and the source of good karma of the most wonderful kind. Please, if you urge both members of your own family and other families as well to recite this sutra, it will be an act of devotion that will surely bring benefits not only to the villagers around you, but to people throughout the country as well.

This sutra is not found among the more than five thousand sutras that Shakyamuni preached during his lifetime. It seems that long ago, there was a government official in China named Sun Ching-te who for some reason or other was thrown into prison. He was sentenced to be executed the next morning. He began that night to recite the *Kannon Sutra*, intending to continue throughout the night, but a little after midnight the Bodhisattva Kannon appeared to him in the form of a young monk. "It will be difficult for you to save yourself from this great peril merely by reciting the *Kannon Sutra*," he said. "There is a shorter sutra called the *Ten Phrase Kannon Sutra for Prolonging Life*. If before morning you can recite it a thousand times, you will be spared." The Bodhisattva then proceeded to teach Sun the forty-two words that make up the sutra. He memorized them and by

---

[*] *Yōjin ni kuni horobizu*: "The country will not fall to ruin because you are (too) careful."

continuing his recitations throughout the night, he was able to complete the one thousand recitations.

He was led to the execution ground and made to sit on a leather carpet. He stretched out his neck to receive the blade. The executioner slowly raised his great sword high over his head, and then, with a loud shout, struck downward. The blade suddenly broke into three pieces, astonishing the officials who had gathered to witness the punishment. One of them got up, drew his sword from its scabbard, and attempted to carry out the sentence himself. His blade also broke into three pieces. Further attempts by other officials ended in the same result.

When the news reached the emperor, he was astounded. He summoned Sun Ching-te and asked him to explain what had happened. Sun told him about the appearance of the Bodhisattva and the *Ten Phrase Kannon Sutra* he had been given to recite. The emperor ordered five or six prisoners awaiting execution to recite the sutra a thousand times each. He then ordered their sentences to be carried out, but in every case the executioner's blade broke into three pieces before it could strike the victim's neck. The emperor thereupon pardoned them all, and issued a proclamation ordering each of his subjects—high and low, young and old alike—to recite the *Ten Phrase Kannon Sutra* a thousand times. From that moment on, the country was blessed by bountiful harvests, there were no incidents of arson, murder, or theft, and everyone lived long lives, enjoying perfect health and happiness ever after. The details of the story can be found in *Extensive Records of the Buddha-patriarchs* and other Sung dynasty Buddhist works.

In more recent times, this sutra has been responsible for a number of miraculous occurrences in our own country as well. A few years ago, at the request of a Daimyo in southwestern Honshu, I assembled accounts of these miracles into a book titled *Accounts of the Miraculous Effects of the Ten Phrase Kannon Sutra for Prolonging Life* that was published in Edo. I will have a copy sent to you as soon as I get back to Shōin-ji. If you are strong enough to do it without compromising your health, please read carefully through this work several times.

You too have now joined the ranks of the elderly, so from day to day, please try to establish and maintain a firm and resolute faith in your mind. The merit it will bring you will enable you to achieve a full recovery. It is with this in mind that I am staying up through the night, rubbing my tired old eyes in the lamplight and writing this long letter. Desiring nothing but your full recovery, I am diligently reciting the sutra and performing devotions for you mornings and nights, and I am telling my monks to do so as well.

While I was at Myōzen-ji in Takikawa, I heard that twenty copies of a new edition of *Spurring Students through the Zen Barrier* sent from Kyoto by Ogawa Gembei had arrived at Shōin-ji, so I had two copies brought to me. It was such a great surprise. I hadn't the slightest idea of the plans to have it published. When I inquired about it, I was told by a priest who knew the circumstances that the idea had originated with Priest So-and-so (he comes to Shōin-ji for *sanzen*), that he had contacted you and the magistrate at Harada, and that together you had ordered a reprinting from Mr. Ogawa in Kyoto. When I first saw a copy of the work, I was speechless. I took it and raised it over my head several times in reverence, my eyes filling with tears. When I was a young monk, this book exerted a wonderful and powerful influence on my life. The gratitude I feel for it is beyond measure. I believe it has been more important to me than my teachers or even my own parents, more important to me than the Buddhas and tutelary deities enshrined in the temple.

In my youth when I was on pilgrimage, I kept it with me as I walked along, never letting it leave my side. Twenty or thirty years ago, I heard that some half-baked priests got together and decided to burn the wooden printing blocks of *Spurring Students through the Zen Barrier* so they could keep it out of circulation. I was in tears when I heard that, it upset me so much. But now through some uncanny turn of fortune, thanks to the donations provided by laymen Hayashi and Watanabe, the inexhaustible lamp of the Buddha-patriarchs will once again emit its divine radiance. The joy I feel is impossible to express in words.

I imposed on the magistrate by visiting him and expressing my thanks in person. I am now staying at his residence. I have been meaning to visit you for a leisurely chat, both to find out how you are doing and also to express my gratitude to you. However, I have been putting it off since I did not know whether you are strong enough yet for such a visit. Now something I must attend to will take me to Myōzen-ji, near Sena village [slightly east of Hara], so your health permitting, I would like to come for a quiet visit so I can tell you about *Spurring Students through the Zen Barrier* . . . [Some words are missing from the text here.]

Just now I learned that the priest of Iō-ji in Hina village will be going to visit you today, so that gives me a chance to send you this message. I will also send you a box of somen noodles from Iyo Province in Shikoku that I received from Matsudaira Iyo-no-kami, the Lord of Matsuyama Castle. Please accept them with a smile.

I'm afraid my elation in seeing this new book has led me to write too much. I'm afraid it may be a burden for you to read it all. To avoid expending unnecessary energy, please put it aside for the time being. You can read it over slowly when you have completely recovered your strength.

Your illness will not be easily cured, so I implore you to regard it as the one great and important matter of your life, and to be sure that you and everyone else in your household appeals to the gods and Buddhas for their help and recites the *Ten Phrase Kannon Sutra for Prolonging Life* mornings and evenings without fail. If you do that, not only you yourself but also your children and the other members of your household will enjoy good health and live long and happy lives. I am sending you three copies of *Accounts of the Miraculous Effects of the Ten Phrase Kannon Sutra for Prolonging Life*, which I would like you to read. Please regard this as an opportunity to establish firm belief in your mind by diligently reciting the *Ten Phrase Kannon Sutra*. It will enable you to sustain your life for many more years.

But I've just been rambling away, writing down one senseless and tedious word after another. It smacks of blarney, or worse, shameless flattery. But have no doubts about what I said concerning *Spurring Students through the Zen Barrier*, for I am overjoyed at being honored in this way. There is nothing whatever that could give me greater pleasure in my old age. Nonetheless, I understand that you might be worried that rumors of one kind or another might start up if your role in the publication became widely known. Please do not worry about that. Rest assured that I will make no reference to it, nor will I show this letter to anyone. But in any event, I want you to understand how deeply I felt about the sutra recitations, and to promise that you will recite it mornings and evenings without fail so that you can achieve a complete and joyous recovery. I will do my part by diligently reciting it on your behalf as well.

This current trip, conducting meetings at various temples, has kept me away from Shōin-ji too long. I am old and growing steadily feebler. I regard each of these visits as my final one. I will be here a bit longer, probably until after the Double Nine Festival [held the ninth day of the ninth month]. When I return, I will have my palanquin stop briefly at your door so that I can see your face and express my gratitude to you in person. I am unable to put everything I have to say down here. The monk to whom I have entrusted this letter has also been given a few more details to transmit to you verbally.

Well, that is about all. From your great friend [Hakuin]

HZB, 340

Matsudaira Sadataka's (1716–63) gift of somen (thin noodles) may have been the *goshiki* "five-colored" variety for which Matsuyama is famous. He also gave Hakuin a decorated fan at that time, which is still extant. Hakuin later wrote an inscription explaining the fan's provenance: "I received this round fan from Matsudaira Oki-no-kami as a token of thanks for [sending him a copy of] *Spurring Students through the Zen Barrier*." (See Letter 25.)

Hakuin began promoting recitation of the brief *Ten Phrase Kannon Sutra for Prolonging Life* in his sixties, following a visit he received from one Inoue Hyōma. The fullest account of the strange story Hyōma related to Hakuin at this time is the one in the *Chronological Biography* (*Hakuin's Precious Mirror Cave*, 210; entry for the year 1745):

> Inoue Hyōma was a samurai in the service of the shogunate in Edo. He was deeply devoted to the *Ten Phrase Kannon Sutra*, and had a printing of the sutra made to distribute to the populace. One day he fell into a swoon and descended into the realm of the dead where he encountered Emma, the Lord of Hell. "Your attempts to make the *Ten Phrase Kannon Sutra* known to your fellow men have been unsuccessful," Emma said, "because you lack sufficient spiritual virtue. At this very moment there is in your world, living in your own country, in the southern part of Suruga Province, a priest by the name of Hakuin. If this person were to propagate the sutra, he would achieve far greater success than you could ever hope for. I want you to get him to do this." The order had come directly from the mouth of Emma himself, so when Hyōma regained his senses he wasted no time. He immediately wrote a letter to Hakuin requesting his help and sent it to Shōin-ji. This is how Hakuin first began propagating the *Ten Phrase Kannon Sutra*. Later Hyōma paid a visit to Shōin-ji and told Hakuin about the vision he had seen.

A more plausible account of the events is found in a manuscript of Hakuin's work *Snake Strawberries* (HHZ 1:94; note that this passage does not appear in the published version of the work). Hakuin writes:

Ten years ago, an elderly retainer [Hyōma] in service of the shogunate stopped at my humble temple on his way through Hara. He brought with him two or three hundred sheets printed with the text of the *Ten Phrase Kannon Sutra.* "This is a sutra with extraordinary virtues," he said. "Because of certain circumstances, I was given this sutra by an august personage. I found that many marvelous things happened when I began reciting it. I decided to have some copies printed to distribute to people so the sutra would be known throughout the country. However, being a man of meager ability, no matter how much I told people about it, few of them would believe me. But if you, with your exceptional skills and influence, were to distribute the sutra to people when they assemble to hear you teach, they will recite it and experience its benefits for themselves. I myself may acquire some merit for my small part in making it known. I would like to leave the sutras with you." Unable to refuse him, I did as he requested. I have told people in the provinces of Harima, Bizen, Bingo, Kyoto, Osaka, Izu, Kai, Tōtōmi, and Suruga about the sutra. People of all kinds, even fishermen, servants, and the like have recited the sutra. I have heard that they acquired great benefit, according to the devotion with which they applied themselves to it.

Whatever the case, not long after the encounter described here, evidence begins to appear in both Hakuin's writings and letters that he was enthusiastically promoting recitation of the sutra to friends and students. In 1759, approximately fourteen years after Hyōma's visit, Hakuin published *Accounts of the Miraculous Effects of the Ten Phrase Kannon Sutra for Prolonging Life,* three thick volumes of miraculous tales similar to the one recounted in this letter, vividly narrating the experiences of people who had been miraculously saved from hell owing to virtue gained from reciting the sutra. These accounts belong to a genre of Buddhist literature known as "tales of karmic cause-and-effect" (*inga monogatari*) that has a long history in Japan. Hakuin is evidently the only Rinzai priest to publish such a collection of stories, although with a total of ten volumes of them to his credit, he more than makes up for the lack.

Although Hakuin says here that he published the collection of tales in *Miraculous Effects of the Ten Phrase Kannon Sutra for Prolonging Life* at the request of a Daimyo in western Honshu, in the work itself he states that it was compiled at the request of "a Kyushu Daimyo," probably a reference to Nabeshima Naotsune, Lord of Hizen Province. Since Hakuin had previously dedicated *Snake Strawberries*, a work that also extolls the efficacy of the *Ten Phrase Kannon Sutra*, to the Daimyo Ikeda Tsugemasa of Okayama in western Honshu, he may perhaps have confused the two works.

Spurring Students through the Zen Barrier is a collection of excerpts from Zen records and Buddhist sutras compiled by the celebrated Ming priest Yun-ch'i Chu-hung (1535–1615) that emphasize the tenacious perseverance that is necessary to achieve the goal of satori. Prior to the 1762 edition mentioned here, there were three Japanese editions, the first in 1656.

The famous story of Hakuin's chance encounter with this work is one of the classic episodes of Japanese Rinzai Zen. It occurred at the age of nineteen, in the first years of his long pilgrimage around the country. He had become deeply disillusioned with Zen training, which wasn't producing the results he had expected, and he was about to give up and turn his focus to the study of literature and painting:

> Then one day it dawned on him that even if he succeeded in becoming a writer of surpassing skill, it would not enable him to achieve peace of mind. The books in the temple library had been placed outside one of the halls for their annual airing. . . . He approached them, bowed reverently, and prayed:
> "Confucius. Buddha. Lao-tzu. Chuang Tzu. Which

one should I take as my teacher? I beg the heavenly Naga Kings that guard the Dharma to indicate the right path to me."

Closing his eyes, he reached out his hand and picked a small volume from among the piles of books. It was *Spurring Students through the Zen Barrier*. After raising it up in reverence, he opened it randomly to a section entitled "Tz'u-ming Jabs a Gimlet in His Thigh."

In a note that someone had inscribed above the text, he read, "Long ago Tz'u-ming was practicing with Master Fen-yang, devoting himself to the study of the Way with Ta-yu, Lang-yeh, and four or five other monks. When the others fled the bitter cold east of the river, Tz'u-ming continued to sit alone without sleeping through the long cold nights. To spur himself to greater effort, he told himself: 'The ancients applied themselves with arduous devotion and attained a purity and radiance that could not help but spread and prosper. Look at me. Who am I? Alive, I'm useless to my contemporaries. I'll be forgotten when I die. What use am I to the Dharma?'"

When the master read the passage, wisdom accumulated from past lives began to stir within him once again, and once again a deep and determined faith in the Buddha's Dharma arose in his heart. Casting aside all his previous views and notions, he now took as the guiding principle of his life these words of Tz'u-ming (*Hakuin's Precious Mirror Cave*, 158–59).

Details of Hakuin's later attachment to the work are found in other accounts scattered through his writings. After reading Tz'u-ming's story, Hakuin went immediately to Priest Baō and procured his own personal copy of *Spurring Students through the Zen Barrier*. On resuming his peregrinations soon after this experience, Hakuin always kept the book close at hand; when engaged in daily activities, he would roll it up and stick it inside his robe. When he found that many of the teachers in the temples he visited promoted a passive, quietist approach to Zen study, he went off by himself, "boring ever deeper into the Mu koan, ashamed that he had unwittingly allowed himself to fall in with people whose practice was diametrically opposed to the fundamental aspiration displayed by the Zen figures whose stories he had read about in *Spurring Students through the Zen Barrier*" (*Hakuin's Precious Mirror Cave*, 25).

In a colophon Tōrei contributed to the newly reprinted edition of *Spurring Students* that was presented to Hakuin, he explains why his teacher praises this particular work so extravagantly, though condemning the compiler Chu-hung throughout his other writings in the harshest terms for his advocacy of quietist, do-nothing, Nembutsu Zen (the practice of calling the name of Amida Buddha as an aid to Zen training). Tōrei begins with a general statement outlining the authentic approach to Hakuin-style Zen training:

A teacher of the past said, "To sit beneath a moonlit window illuminating your mind [by reading] the ancient teachings and to exert yourself doing zazen in the training hall are like the two wheels of a cart. Only when both are part of your practice can you measure up to the inner meaning of the patriarchal teachers." A student whose practice does not include illuminating the mind through the ancient teachings will inevitably end up with small and limited views. Heretical teachers of the Two Vehicles, people whose grasp of things has become warped and perverted, belong in this group. If a student illuminates his mind with the teachings but does not engage in zazen practice, he will sink inexorably into mere intellectual understanding. Today, priests of the Teaching and Precepts schools, Shintoists, Confucianists, as well as adherents of Patriarchal Zen, all fall into this category. This is why genuine students use authentic zazen practice to penetrate through all the roots and dusts of sensory perception, and use the ancient teachings to refine and polish their dhyana and wisdom. Of course when they have to spur themselves out of a state of unmindfulness or rouse themselves from idleness, they also follow reverently the exemples set by the Buddha-patriarchs.

Tōrei follows this with a brief sketch of Hakuin's early career up to and including the encounter with *Spurring Students through the Zen Barrier* that turned him back to Zen, after which, Tōrei says, he was constantly "illuminating his mind" with the episodes in that work. He goes on to describe Hakuin's Zen teaching:

Approaching the age of sixty, Master Hakuin began expounding and uplifting the exceptional virtues of National Master Daitō with words that caused Zen monks throughout the land to take to their heels. His great power astounded men and women of all ranks, from the emperor on down to the peasants. Did not all this become possible thanks to that small book he had constantly kept in his robe? He never ceased praising Tz'u-ming's words, and in admonishing students he was always saying, "When I was a young monk, I didn't let a day pass without repeating those words three times. Even today, as an old monk, I still do it."

He also told them, "Chu-hung wrote many works during his lifetime, but *Spurring Students through the Zen Barrier* is the only one that has made any contribution to our Zen school. One day, if some of you acquire the capacity and have the means to do it, you might want to avenge the burning grudge you feel toward me by having it republished. However, in this same work, the compiler Chu-hung tries to have students investigate their true self by engaging in recitation of the Nembutsu, a practice that has greatly sapped the spiritual energy of many outstanding Zen monks and caused them to fall into the Other-power teaching of rebirth in the Pure Land. If it were up to me, I would have all those portions deleted from the work. Why? The lion will not eat the vulture's leavings. The tiger will not touch a dead carcass. Leave the teaching of rebirth in the Pure Land to the Pure Land schools. Priests of our Zen school do not even make use the wisdom of ultimate reality, much less such provisional teachings. The only way they are able to carefully investigate the true self is by taking the ox from the farmer, by depriving the starving man of his food."

In the winter of the previous year [1761], Hakuin's student Senior Priest Ko (Gangoku Zenko, n.d.) and two or three of his comrades joined forces and resolved to fulfill the wish the master had often expressed to us for a new edition of *Spurring Students through the Zen Barrier*. The printing was made possible thanks to donations by laymen Hayashi and Watanabe and other patrons of the master. I was asked to add a few words to explain how the work came to be published. I wrote this colophon, putting down the facts as I had heard them, in hopes that this valuable work will be handed down and continue to be read by generations of students far into the future.

Tōrei Enji, Head Priest of Ryūtaku-ji, Izu Province

Several years before this, Tōrei had fulfilled the promise he had made earlier to Hakuin and allowed himself to be installed as head priest at Ryūtaku-ji. He was now, to what we can only imagine was Hakuin's infinite relief, busily training a new generation of young monks to carry on the transmission of Hakuin-style koan Zen. If Hakuin was elated at the newly printed *Spurring Students Through the Zen Barrier* that his disciples had given him, he must have been more joyful still to discover the colophon his Dharma heir had written for it, not to mention gratified to read Tōrei's clear-sighted summation of his religious career. Tōrei could speak with great authority on his teacher's life and teaching, and he could say it better than anyone else.

Glossary

(T=Taishō, an abbreviation for the standard collection of the Buddhist scriptures.)

Accounts of the Miraculous Effects of the Ten Phrase Kannon Sutra for Prolonging Life (*Emmei Jikku Kannon-gyō Reigen-ki*) ннz 6. A collection of tales of cause and effect written in 1759.

Admonitions for Buddhists (*Hsi-men ching-hsun*) T48. A Zen work of the Yuan dynasty.

Akiba Daigongen Shinto/Buddhist deity enshrined at Mount Akiba in Tōtōmi Province.

Amida Buddha The central Buddha of Pure Land Buddhism.

Ancestral Heroes Collection (*Tsu-ling chi*) Book of religious verse by the Sung priest Hsueh-t'ou Ch'ung-hsien.

Annals of Tōfuku-ji (*Tōfuku-ji shi*) by Shiraishi Kogetsu (Kyoto: Privately printed, 1930).

Attendant Kō (Daikyū Ebō, 1715–74) Recipient of Letter 5.

Biographies of Zen Priests of Modern Times (*Kinsei Zenrin Sōbōden*) ed. Nōnin Kōdō (Kyoto: Zenbunka Kenkyūsho, 2002).

Blue Cliff Record (*Pi-yen chi*) T80. The Rinzai Zen school's most important koan collection.

Bodhisattva A being who aspires to attain Buddhahood and engages in various practices to achieve that goal. Compassion is the outstanding characteristic of the bodhisattva, who postpones his or her own entry into nirvana in order to assist others.

Boku (n.d.) Hakuin attendant. Appears in Letter 3.

Book of Changes (*I Ching*) Ancient Chinese manual of divination.

Buddhist Monk Hakuin (*Shamon Hakuin*) by Akiyama Kanji (Shizuoka: Privately issued, 1983).

Ch'ang-sha Ching-ts'en (ninth century) Chinese Zen priest.

Chao-chou's Mu (koan) *Gateless Barrier*, Case 1.

Chao-chou's Mud Buddha (koan) *Blue Cliff Record*, Case 96.

Chao-chou's Seven-Pound Jacket (koan) *Blue Cliff Record*, Case 45.

Chao-chou's Two Hermits (koan) *Gateless Barrier*, Case 11.

Ch'ien-feng's Three Infirmities (koan) *Compendium of the Five Lamps*, ch. 13; see *Essential Teachings of Zen Master Hakuin*, 19–20.

Chronological Biography: Chronological Biography of Priest Hakuin Full title *Ryūtaku-kaiso Jinki Dokumyō Zenji Nempu* (*Chronological Biography of Zen Master Jinki Dokumyō, Founder of Ryūtaku-ji*), compiled by Tōrei Enji but not published until 1820. *HOZ* 1. Japanese edition, ed. Katō Shōshun (Kyoto: Shibunkaku, 1985). Translation in *Hakuin's Precious Mirror Cave*.

Chu-hung (Yun-ch'i Chu-hung, 1535–1615) Eminent Ming priest and compiler of *Spurring Students Through the Zen Barrier*.

cinnabar field (*tanden*) The "center of breath" located below the navel.

Classified Anthology of the Zen Forest (*Ch'an-lin lei-chu*) A large collection of koans classified according to subject; first published in the Yuan dynasty.

Cloth Drum (*Nuno-tsutsumi*) A collection of stories of karmic cause and effect Hakuin originally wrote in his late twenties; later published in two versions, the final, greatly enlarged edition appearing in 1753.

Cloth Drum Refitted [with a New Drumhead] (*Saiben nuno-tsutsumi*) Final version of the *Cloth Drum*, published in 1753.

Comments on the Blue Cliff Record (*Hekigan-roku hishō*) (Tokyo: Seikō-zasshi-sha, 1917). Hakuin's Zen commentary on the most important koan collection.

Compendium of the Five Lamps (*Wu-teng hui-yuan*) Zokuzō:13. Important Sung-dynasty collection of Zen records.

Complete Dharma Writings of Zen Master Hakuin (*Hakuin Zenji Hōgo Zenshū*) 15 vols., ed. Yoshizawa Katsuhiro (Kyoto: Zenbunka kenkyūsho, 2002–6).

Complete Works of Chuang Tzu trans. Burton Watson (New York: Columbia University Press, 1968) HHZ.

Complete Works of Zen Priest Hakuin (*Hakuin Oshō Zenshū*) 8 vols. (Tokyo, 1934) HOZ. Still the only comprehensive collection of Hakuin's works.

Daikyū Ebō (1715–74) Important Dharma heir of Hakuin. Recipient of Letter 5, where he is addressed as "Attendant Kō."

Daishū Zenjo (1730–78) Also Zenjo Shuso, Senior Monk Jo. Hakuin student and Dharma heir. Recipient of Letters 12–18.

A Detailed Biography of Priest Hakuin (*Hakuin Oshō Shōden*) by Rikugawa Taiun (Tokyo: Sankibō, 1965).

dharani (*dhāraṇi*) A spell or formula whose mystic power is said to protect and benefit the one who recites it.

Dharma Words of Takusui (*Takusui hōgo zuimonki*) Published 1740.

dhyana (*dhāyna*) A state of deep, concentrated meditation.

Dictionary of Zen Words and Sayings (*Zengo Jiten*) by Koga Hidehiko and Iriya Yoshitaka (Kyoto: Zenbunka Kenkyūsho, 1991).

divine death-dealing amulets (*datsumyō no shimpu*; also life-destroying charms) Originally, Taoist charms said to give the possessor life-destroying powers. Used like "claws and fangs of the Dharma cave," with which it is generally paired, in Hakuin's works.

do-nothing Zen For Hakuin, practice that does not require the student to push vigorously toward the breakthrough experience of kenshō.

Draft Biography Tōrei's original draft of *Hakuin's Chronological Biography*. A nearly complete text is found in *A Detailed Biography of Priest Hakuin*.

Dragon Staff certificate A painting of a priest's staff transforming into a dragon that Hakuin awarded in his final decades to students who attained kenshō.

Dream Words from a Land of Dreams (*Kaian-kokugo*) ed. Dōmae Sōkan (Kyoto: Zenbunka Kenkyūsho, 2003). Hakuin's Zen commentary on the *Record of Daitō*; his principal commentarial work in Chinese.

Eboku (Suiō Genro, 1716–89) Hakuin student and Dharma heir who succeeded him at Shōin-ji.

Eshō-ni (d. 1764) Zen nun; friend of Tōrei and Hakuin.

Essential Teachings of Zen Master Hakuin by Norman Waddell (Boston: Shambhala, 1994). Translation of *Talks Introductory to Lectures on the Record of Hsi-keng*, published in 1743.

Essentials of Successive Records of the Lamp (*Lien-ten hui-yao*) T79.

Extensive Records of the Buddha-patriarchs (*Fo-tsu t'ung-chi*) A history of Buddhism compiled in 1269 by the priest Chih-p'an.

Eye of Men and Gods (*Jen-t'ien yen-mu*) T48. Collection of teachings, sayings, and verse by representative teachers of the five schools of Chinese Zen.

Ferryman Monk (n.d.) A student of master Yueh-shan who taught as a ferryman at a river crossing.

Five Ranks (*go-i*) [of the Apparent and the Real] A teaching device attributed to the T'ang priest Tung-shan used in the Sōtō Zen tradition. Generally not a part of Rinzai Zen teaching, Hakuin gave it an important role in his program of post-satori training.

Four-Part Collection (*Shibu-roku*) A Japanese compilation that includes the Zen poems *Hsinhsinming* and *Chengtao-ko*, and *Ten Oxherding Pictures*.

Gateless Barrier (*Wu-men kuan*). Well-known koan collection compiled during the Sung dynasty by Rinzai priest Wu-men Hui-kai (1183–1260).

Great Cessation and Insight (*Mo-ho chih-kuan*) T65. Influential text on Buddhist meditation by the T'ien-t'ai teacher Chih-i (538–97).

Gudō Tōshoku (1579–1666) Also Gudō Kokushi, National Master Gudō. Important Rinzai priest in the Dharma lineage to which Hakuin belonged.

Gyokurinan Temple in Matsuzaki, southern Izu, built by the Yoda family.

Hakuin's Precious Mirror Cave by Norman Waddell (Berkeley: Counterpoint Press, 2009). A compilation containing translations of *The Tale of My Childhood*, *The Tale of Yūkichi of Takayama*, *Idle Talk on a Night Boat*, *Old Granny's Tea-Grinding Songs*, *An Account of the Precious Mirror Cave*, and *The Chronological Biography of Zen Master Hakuin*.

Hakuin's Zen Painting and Calligraphy (*Hakuin Zenga Bokuseki*) 3 vols., ed. Yoshizawa Katsuhiro (Tokyo: Nigensha, 2010) *HZB*. References here are all to the *kaisetsu* volume.

Hakuyū Hermit sage from whom Hakuin learned the Naikan meditation (see *Idle Talk on a Night Boat*).

Hara The village in Suruga province where Hakuin was born; the site of his temple Shōin-ji.

hard-to-pass (*nantō*) **koans** Koans Hakuin assigned students after they had attained kenshō. He gives different lists of these koans in his writings.

Hayashi Razan (1583–1657) Important Confucian teacher of the early Edo period.

Heishirō: Yamanashi Heishirō (1707–63) Recipient of Letter 7, "The Tale of Heishirō of Ihara Village."

Heroic March Sutra (*Shurangama Sutra*; Ch: *Leng-yen ching*) T26.

Horse Thistles (*Oniazami*) Hakuin work written c. 1752 as a letter to abbesses of two imperial convents in Kyoto.

Hsuan-sha Shih-pei (835–908) Chinese Zen master.

Hsueh-feng I-ts'un (822–908) Chinese Zen master.

Huang-po Hsi-yun (d. 840) Chinese Zen master.

Huang-po's Gobblers of Dregs (koan) *Blue Cliff Record*, Case 22.

Hui-neng (638–713) The Sixth Patriarch of Chinese Zen.

Ichikawa Danjūrō (1688–1757) Popular Kabuki actor in Edo.

Idle Talk on a Night Boat (*Yasenkanna*) HHZ 4. Hakuin's story of his long struggle with "Zen sickness," published 1757.

Ike Taiga (1723–76) Famous calligrapher and painter in the literati style.

Inka Certification or sanction Zen teacher gives a student to designate him as a Dharma heir.

Inoue Hyōma (n.d.) Edo samurai and votary of *Ten Phrase Kannon Sutra*.

Ishii Gentoku (1671–1751) Layman Ishii; physician and Zen student from Hina village. Recipient of Letter 3.

Itsudō Oshō (Itsudō Ekō, n.d.) Head priest of Hōfuku-ji in Bizen Province.

kalpa An incalculably long period of time; an eon.

kambun (literally "Chinese writing") Literary Chinese as written and read by Japanese.

Katayama Shunnan (n.d.) Physician of Hida Province; Hakuin student. Recipient of Letters 26–27.

kenshō "Seeing into one's own self-nature"; used more or less synonymously with *satori*, but normally limited to the initial breakthrough experience.

ki The vital "breath" or energy present in all living things; in humans, *ki* circulates through the body and is central to the preservation of health and sustenance of life.

KidaGanshō (sobriquet Kurogane-ya, n.d.) Osaka layman and Hakuin student.

Kin and Koku (n.d.) Monks and recipients of Letter 2.

Kogetsu Zenzai (1667–1751) Rinzai priest in Kyushu with whom many of Hakuin's students originally studied.

Kompira Daigongen Deity of the Kompira Shrine on the island of Shikoku.

Kuei-shan Ling-yu (771–853) Chinese Zen priest.

The Lady Burns the Hermitage (koan) *Compendium of the Five Lamps*, ch. 15.

Life-Prolonging Kannon (*Emmei jikku Kannon*) A rare form of Kannon Bodhisattva in which her image is depicted together with the inscription of the text of the *Ten Phrase Kannon Sutra for Prolonging Life*.

Lin-chi I-hsuan (d. 866) Chinese priest regarded as founder of the Lin-chi (Japanese Rinzai) line of Zen.

The Lotus Sutra trans. Burton Watson (New York: Columbia University Press, 1993). All references are to this translation.

Ma-tsu Tao-i (709–88) Chinese Zen priest.

Matsudaira Sadataka (1716–63) Oki-no-kami, Daimyo of Matsu-yama, Iyo Province. Recipient of Letter 25.

Meager (maigre) feast Vegetarian meals provided for priests, family members, and guests at Buddhist services as an act whose merit is thought to transfer to the deceased.

Medicine Peddler (*Uirō-uri*) Popular Kabuki play.

Mu koan (*Gateless Barrier*, Case 1) Famous koan traditionally assigned to beginning students: A monk asked master Chao-chou, "Does a dog have a Buddha-nature, or not?" Chao-chou answered, "Mu" [literally, "Nothing" or "Not"].

Murabayashi Koremitsu (n.d.) Lay student of Hakuin. Recipient of Letter 9.

Muryō-ji Temple in Hina village; rebuilt by Hakuin.

Naikan **meditation** ("introspective meditation") A therapeutic form of meditation Hakuin learned from the hermit Hakuyū. The story is told in *Idle Talk on a Night Boat*.

Nan-ch'uan P'u-yuan (748–835) Chinese Zen priest.

Nan-ch'uan's Death (koan) *Compendium of the Five Lamps*, ch. 4.

Nan-ch'uan's Flowering Hedge (koan) *Compendium of the Five Lamps*, ch. 4.

Nembutsu Repeating the name of the Buddha Amida in the formula "Namu Amida Butsu" (I entrust myself to Amida Buddha). The central practice in Pure Land Buddhist schools.

neo-Confucianism A form of Confucianism that developed during the Sung and Ming dynasties in China. In Edo-period Japan, it became the dominant politic philosophy of the ruling Tokugawa shogunate.

O-bon (*Urabon*) Annual observances performed for the repose of the dead held from the thirteenth to the fifteenth of the seventh month, at the end of the summer retreat.

Ogawa Gembei (n.d.) Kyoto bookseller who published a number of Hakuin's works.

Ōhashi-jo (n.d.) The daughter of a high official who was forced to sell her to a Kyoto brothel. The story of her encounter with Zen is told in *Hakuin's Precious Mirror Cave*, 217.

One Hand, the Sound of (*sekishu no onjō*) "Hear the sound of One Hand!" Famous koan for beginning students Hakuin devised in his sixties.

Oradegama. Hakuin work. *HHZ* 9. Included in *Zen Master Hakuin: Selected Writings*.

Oshō A term of respect used for temple priests; also used for priests who have completed their training.

Other-power teaching A term used to describe the Pure Land schools, in contrast to the Zen school's reliance on Self-power.

Paramitas The Sanskrit *pāramitā* means going from this shore of birth-and-death to the other shore of nirvana. This is achieved through the practice of the six paramitas: charity, commandments, patience, diligence, meditation, and wisdom.

Po-yun's Not Yet There (koan) See *Essential Teachings of Zen Master Hakuin*, 89.

Poems of Han-shan (*Han-shan shih*) A collection of poems by the eccentric Buddhist monk Han-shan first published in the Sung dynasty.

Poison Blossoms from a Thicket of Thorn (*Keisō Dokuzui*) *HOZ* 2. A ten-volume collection of Hakuin's Zen records in Chinese, probably published in 1759.

post-satori training (*gogo no shūgyō*) The practice that begins after attainment of kenshō; defined by Hakuin as carrying out the Bodhisattva's vow: working for deeper self-awakening while helping others reach liberation.

Precious Lessons of the Zen School (*Ch'an-lin pao-tsun*) A twelfth-century collection of teaching and anecdotes from the lives and sayings of Sung Zen teachers.

Precious Mirror Samadhi (*Pao-ching san-mei*) Zen poem traditionally ascribed to Tung-shan Liang-chieh.

Precious Mirror's Lingering Radiance (*Hōkan-ishō*) Hakuin work, published in 1747, extolling Gudō Tōshoku's contribution to the Zen tradition. "Precious Mirror" is Gudō's posthumous title.

Record of Daitō T81. The Zen records of Shūhō Myōchō (Daitō Kokushi), founder of Daitoku-ji.

Record of Hsi-keng (*Hsi-keng lu*) Alternate title of *Record of Hsu-t'ang*.

Record of Hsu-t'ang (*Hsu-t'ang yu-lu*) T47. Zen records of the influential Rinzai master Hsu-t'ang Chih-yu (1185–1269).

Record of Lin-chi: Zen teachings of Master Lin-chi.

Record of Sendai's Comments on the Poems of Cold Mountain (*Kanzan-shi sendai-kimon*) HOZ 4.

Records of the Lamp: Records of the Transmission of the Lamp of the Ching-te Era (*ching-te ch'uan-teng lu*) T51. The most important of the traditional collections of Zen records.

Records of the Mirror Source (*Tsung-ching lu*) T48.

Redolence from the Cold Forest (*Kanrin Ihō*) A collection of short texts from various Buddhist sources that Hakuin compiled for students.

Reigen Etō (1722–85) Hakuin disciple; instrumental in spreading Hakuin Zen to Kyoto temples.

Religious Art of Zen Master Hakuin, The by Yoshizawa Katsuhiro (Berkeley: Counterpoint Press, 2009).

ri The Japanese mile, about 4 kilometers (2.44 miles).

Rinzai I-hsuan (d. 866; Japanese, Rinzai Gigen) Chinese priest regarded as founder of an important line of Chinese Zen that was transmitted to Japan.

Rōhatsu **training session** (*rōhatsu sesshin*) The period of concentrated zazen practice held in Japanese Rinzai monasteries from the first day of the twelfth month and ending on the morning of the eighth day.

Rokuin Etsū (1685–1756) Hakuin student; priest of Ryūsen-ji. Recipient of Letter 6.

Rurikō-ji Temple in Mino Province founded by Gudō Tōshoku.

ryō A standard gold piece in use in Edo Japan weighing about 18 grams.

Ryōtan-ji Temple in Tōtōmi Province.

Ryōkoku-ji Temple in Akashi, Harima Province.

Ryūtaku-ji Temple in Mishima that Hakuin built for Tōrei.

Sakai Kantahaku (n.d.) Hakuin student. Recipient of Letters 11 and 12.

sanzen Literally, to study Zen; in Hakuin's works it normally refers to koan study and to the teacher's private interview with students.

satori Enlightenment.

Secretary Ch'en's Traveling Monks (koan) *Compendium of the Five Lamps*, ch. 4.

Senior Monk Gin (Gin Shuso, n.d.) Hakuin student; recipient of Letter 8.

Senior Priest Zenjo (Daishū Zenjo, 1720–78) Hakuin heir; recipient of Letters 13–18.

Shibata Gonzaemon (n.d.) Hakuin student and wealthy landowner of Ihara village.

Shidō Munan (1603–76) Teacher of Shōju Rōjin.

Shikyō Eryō (n.d.) Hakuin heir who taught in the Kyoto area.

Shōin-ji Hakuin's temple in Hara, Suruga Province.

Shōju Rōjin (Shōju Etan, 1642–1721) Literally, "old man of the Shōju-an hermitage [in Shinano Province]." Hakuin's teacher.

Shuso A term of respect for senior priests.

Silent illumination (*mokushō*) **Zen** A term usually associated with practices of the Sōtō school, contrasting them with Rinzai koan Zen, but Hakuin uses it for all types of Zen practice that do not make the student focus on the breakthrough to satori.

Six Paths The six ways of unenlightened existence: (1) hell, (2) the realms of hungry spirits, (3) beasts, (4) asuras, (5) human beings, and (6) devas (heavenly beings).

Snake Strawberries (*Hebiichigo*) HHZ 1. Work by Hakuin.

Sōtō Zen School founded by Dōgen Kigen in Kamakura period.

Sōyū-ji Temple in Takayama, Hida Province.

Spurring Zen Students Through the Barrier (*Ch'an-kuan ts'e-chin*) by Yun-ch'i Chu-hung. T48. See *Meditating with Koans*, trans. J. C. Cleary (Berkeley: Asian Humanities Press, 1992). A compilation of passages from Buddhist, mostly Zen texts that greatly influenced young Hakuin.

Stories from the Thicket of Thorn and Briar (*Keisō sōdan*) HOZ 1. A nineteenth-century collection of anecdotes about Hakuin and his students compiled by Myōki Sōseki. References here are to the edition titled *Hakuin monka itsuwa sen*, ed. Nōnin Kōdō (Kyoto: Zenbunka kenkyūsho, 2000).

Study of Our Shinto Shrines (*Jinja-kō*) Anti-Buddhist work by Confucian Hayashi Razan, published 1645.

Suiō Genro (1717–89) One of Hakuin's chief heirs; his successor at Shōin-ji.

Supplement (*Keisō-dokuzui Shūi*) A one-volume supplement to Hakuin's Zen records *Poison Blossoms from a Thicket of Thorn,* probably published in 1759.

Su-shan's Memorial Tower (koan) *Essentials of Successive Records of the Lamp,* ch. 22.

Sutra of the Bequeathed Teaching (*I-chueh ching*) One of the texts making up the composite work *Three Teachings of the Buddha-patriarchs.*

Ta-hui Tsung-kao (1089–1163) Important Chinese Rinzai priest of the Northern Sung dynasty.

Ta-hui's Arsenal (*Ta-hui wu-k'u*) T47. Collection of Zen stories with Ta-hui's comments.

Ta-hui's General Talks (*Ta-hui p'u-shuo*) T47. Collection of Ta-hui's discourses.

Ta-hui's Letters (*Ta-hui shu*) T47. Collection of teaching letters Ta-hui wrote to lay followers.

Takusui Chōmo (d. 1740) Rinzai priest of Daijū-ji in Edo.

Tale of My Childhood Full title *A Tale of How I Spurred Myself in My Practice* (*Sakushin osana monogatari*) HHZ 7. Translated in *Hakuin's Precious Mirror Cave.*

Tale of Yūkichi of Takayama (*Takayama Yūkichi monogatari*) HHZ 7. Translated in *Hakuin's Precious Mirror Cave.*

Talks Introductory to Lectures on the Record of Hsi-keng (*Sokkō-roku kaien-fusetsu*) HOZ 2. Translated as *Essential Teachings of Zen Master Hakuin.*

Tao-wu Yuan-chih (769–835) Chinese Zen priest.

Te-shan's Begging Bowl (koan) *Gateless Barrier*, Case 13.

Ten Ox-herding Pictures (*Jūgyū-zu*) A series of illustrations (there are various different sets) accompanied by verses showing the student's progress to final enlightenment. First published in the Sung dynasty.

Ten Phrase Kannon Sutra for Prolonging Life (*Emmei Jikku Kannon-gyō*) Brief recitation text Hakuin tried to spread among the lay community.

Tenjin Shinto deity of Kitano Tenmangu Shrine in Kyoto; the deified form of Sugawara Michizane.

Three Teachings of the Buddha-patriarchs (*Fo-tsu san-chiao*) Composite work of three texts first published in the Ming dynasty.

Tōrei Biography: Chronological Biography of Zen Priest Tōrei (*Tōrei Oshō Nempu*), ed. Nishimura Eshin (Kyoto: Shibunkaku, 1982).

Tōrei Enji (1712–92) Hakuin's chief Dharma heir; compiler of *Hakuin's Chronological Biography*. Recipient or writer of Letters 13–18.

Treatise on the Precious Storehouse (*Pao-tsang lun*) A work attributed to Seng-chao (374–414), a famous layman of early Chinese Buddhism.

Ts'ui-yen's Eyebrows (koan) *Blue Cliff Record*, Case 8.

Tung-shan's Sixty Blows (koan) *Gateless Barrier*, Case 15.

Two Vehicles The Shravaka, who achieves liberation upon listening to the Buddhist teachings, and the *Pratyeka*-buddha, who achieves liberation but does not undertake to teach others. Hakuin regarded them as inferior to the Mahayana Bodhisattva, who devotes his life to saving other beings as well.

Tz'u-ming (Shih-chuang Ch'u-yuan; 986–1039) Chinese priest whose dedication to Zen practice inspired young Hakuin.

Uematsu Suetsuna (1701–71) Wealthy friend and neighbor of Hakuin; patron of Shōin-ji.

Vimalakirti The central figure of the *Vimalakirti Sutra;* regarded in Zen as the ideal of the lay practitioner.

The Vimalakirti Sutra trans. Burton Watson (New York: Columbia University Press, 1977).

Watanabe Heizaemon (n.d.) Father of Watanabe Sukefusa.

Watanabe Sukefusa (n.d.) Childhood friend of Hakuin. Recipient of Letter 1.

Wild Ivy trans. Norman Waddell (Boston: Shambhala, 1999) *HHZ* 3. Translation of Hakuin's autobiography *Itsumadegusa.*

World-Honored One Holds Up a Flower (koan) *Gateless Barrier,* Case 6.

Wu-tsu Fa-yen (1024–1104) Chinese Zen priest.

Wu-tsu's Water Buffalo Through the Window (koan) *Gateless Barrier,* Case 38.

Yamanashi Heishirō (1707–63) Lay student of Hakuin. Recipient of Letter 7, "The Tale of Heishirō of Ihara Village."

Yanada Zeigan (1672–1757) Leading Confucian scholar; friend of Hakuin.

Yang-ch'i Fang-hui (992–1049) Chinese Zen priest.

Yen-kuan's Rhinoceros-horn Fan (koan) *Blue Cliff Record,* Case 91.

Yen-t'ou's Final Word (koan) *Praise of the Five Houses of the True School (Wu-chia Cheng-tsung-tsan).*

Yoda Takanaga (n.d.) Lay student of Hakuin from a wealthy family of southern Izu Province. Recipient of Letter 10.

Yotsugi Masayuki (n.d.) Wealthy Kyoto merchant and Zen layman; friend, patron, and student of both Tōrei and Hakuin.

Zen Dust by Isshū Miura and Ruth Sasaki (Kyoto: First Zen Institute, 1965).

Zen Master Hakuin: Selected Writings by Philip Yampolsky (New York: Columbia University Press, 1971). Translations of *Oradegama*, *Spear Grass* (*Yabu-kōji*), and *Snake Strawberries* (*Hebiichigo*).

Zen Master Hakuin's Complete Dharma Writings in Japanese (*Hakuin Zenji Hōgo Zenshū*) 14 vols., ed. Yoshizawa Katsuhiro (Kyoto: Zenbunko Kenkyūsho, 2002–6) *HHZ*. Fully annotated editions of Hakuin's Japanese writings (*kana-hōgo*).

Zen Teachings of Master Lin-ch trans. Burton Watson (Boston: Shambhala, 1993).

Zen Words for the Heart by Norman Waddell (Boston: Shambhala, 1996). Translation of *Dokugo Shingyō* (*HOZ* 2), Hakuin's Zen commentary on the *Heart Sutra*.